The Critics Bear It Away

FREDERICK CREWS

The Critics Bear It Away:

American Fiction and

the Academy

RANDOM HOUSE

NEW YORK

Grateful acknowledgment is made to the following for permission to reprint
previously published material:

CAMBRIDGE UNIVERSITY PRESS: Excerpts from *Ideology and Classic American Literature*
by Sacvan Bercovitch and Myra Jehlen (1986). Reprinted by permission of
Cambridge University Press.

FARRAR, STRAUS & GIROUX, INC.: Excerpts from *The Habit of Being* by Flannery
O'Connor. Copyright © 1979 by Regina O'Connor. Reprinted by permission of
Farrar, Straus & Giroux, Inc.

ALFRED A. KNOPF, INC.: Excerpt from *Roger's Version* by John Updike. Copyright
© 1986 by John Updike; excerpts from *Midpoint* by John Updike. Copyright
© 1969 by John Updike. Reprinted by permission of Alfred A. Knopf, Inc.

KENNETH S. LYNN: Excerpts from *Hemingway* by Kenneth S. Lynn. Reprinted by
permission of Kenneth S. Lynn.

THE UNIVERSITY OF CHICAGO PRESS: Excerpts from *Dark Twins: Imposture and Identity
in Mark Twain's America* by Susan Gillman. Reprinted by permission of
The University of Chicago Press.

UNIVERSITY OF TEXAS PRESS: Excerpts from *Faulkner's Marginal Couple: Invisible,
Outlaw, and Unspeakable Communities* by John N. Duvall. Copyright © 1990. Reprinted by permission of the University of Texas Press.

Library of Congress Cataloging-in-Publication Data

Crews, Frederick C.
The critics bear it away : American fiction and the academy /
Frederick Crews
p. cm.
ISBN 0-679-40413-9
1. American fiction—History and criticism—Theory, etc.
2. Criticism—United States—History—20th century. 3. Canon
(Literature) I. Title.
PS371.C75 1992
810.9'0001—dc20   91-51029

Manufactured in the United States of America

24689753

First Edition

Book design by Mia Vander Els

For Robert Silvers

Acknowledgments

Two editors, occupying very different roles, head my thank-you list for indispensable services to this book. One is my dedicatee, Robert Silvers, who has provided me with inspiration, tolerance, keen criticism, and an ideal forum in *The New York Review of Books*. The other, as always, is Elizabeth Crews, the most exacting of readers and best of friends.

For encouragement, challenge, and advice, I am grateful to the following people among others: Paul J. Alpers, Robert Alter, Julia Bader, Nina Baym, Jackson J. Benson, Richard Bridgman, Louis J. Budd, Peter Carafiol, Ruby Crews, Sherwood Cummings, Annie Dillard, Victor A. Doyno, Amy Edelman, Everett Emerson, Jason Epstein, Jacob Fuchs, Alan Gribben, T. Walter Herbert, E. D. Hirsch, Jr., Robert H. Hirst, Lawrence Howe, Kenneth T. Jowitt, Justin Kaplan, Steven M. Knapp, Frank Lentricchia, Robert Lescher, David Leverenz, Richard L. Levin, James B. Longenbach, Kenneth S. Lynn, Anne L. Middleton, Jack Miles, Maryam Mohit, Gary Saul Morson, Hershel Parker, Ralph W. Rader, Robert D. Richardson, Jr., John Searle, George A. Starr, Eric J. Sundquist, and Cecelia Tichi. Much as I would like to, I cannot blame any of the above for errors and follies in the text.

For a conference invitation that led to Chapter Four, I thank Darryl Baskin and the Center for Mark Twain Studies at Quarry Farm, Elmira, New York. Chapters Two, Three, Five, Six, Seven, and Eight appeared originally, with minor differences, in *The New York Review of Books* and are reprinted here with permission. I also thank James Clark and the University of California Press for permission to reuse my afterword to the 1989 reprint of my book *The Sins of the Fathers: Hawthorne's Psychological Themes*, which appears as Chapter One here.

Contents

Acknowledgments   ix

Introduction   xiii

ONE   The Sins of the Fathers *Revisited*   3

TWO   *Whose American Renaissance?*   16

THREE   *The Parting of the Twains*   47

FOUR   *A Yankee in the Court of Criticism*   73

FIVE   *Pressure under Grace*   89

SIX   *Faulkner Methodized*   113

SEVEN   *The Critics Bear It Away*   143

EIGHT   *Mr. Updike's Planet*   168

Notes   187

Index   207

Introduction

THE ESSAYS AND ESSAY-REVIEWS that make up the greater part of this book date from the later 1980s and early 1990s, a period when their connecting theme—the way American novelists are being apprehended and misapprehended in the academy—has become involved in a larger and quite acrimonious debate. I mean, of course, the furor over "political correctness" and the alleged betrayal of our cultural heritage by professor-theorists bent upon egalitarian leveling. Inevitably, some of my conclusions here will be read as corollaries of a more general stand against the politicizing of literary study—a phenomenon I am on record as deploring. But though my book is indeed meant in part as a report to nonacademic readers about shifts of opinion in the English departments, it is driven by no conscious agenda other than a concern for understanding American fiction with as few illusions as possible. And the particular illusions I will be examining originate in conservative as well as radical impulses—in, for example, New Critical formalism, orthodox intentionalism, Christian or Agrarian moralism, and outright hero worship of the sort that transforms an Ernest Hemingway or a John Updike from a spiteful, ethically confused, yet often compelling writer into an icon of pure masculinity or matchless sophistication.

This interest in pinpointing the limitations as well as the peculiar strengths of famous American novelists sets me at cross-purposes with the contemporary academy's most implacable adversaries. I am thinking of such cultural nostalgics as William Bennett, Allan Bloom, Lynne Cheney, and Roger Kimball—people who conceive of the ideal university as a pantheon for the preservation of great works and great ideas.[1] All of those commentators implicitly subscribe to a "transfusion" model of education, whereby the stored-up wisdom of the classics is considered a kind of plasma that will drip beneficially into our veins if we only stay sufficiently passive in its presence. My own notion of learning is entirely different. I want keen debate, not reverence for great books; historical consciousness and self-reflection, not supposedly timeless values; and continual expansion of our national canon to match a necessarily unsettled sense of who "we" are and what we ultimately care about. Literary culture, I believe, ought to be an instrument not of fearful elitism but of democracy—and this means that a certain amount of turmoil surrounding the canon should be taken in stride. In my view there can be no such thing as a sacrosanct text, an innately civilizing idea, or an altogether disinterested literary critic.

I emphasize these disagreements with the cultural nostalgics because a casual reader might otherwise perceive this book as a contribution to their cause. The truth is that we have in common just one attitude, an opposition to what I have elsewhere called Left Eclecticism, or the idea that educational diversity is best served by filling literature departments and their course offerings with representatives of each currently popular radical doctrine.[2] And even here my reasoning diverges from that of the conservatives. For Roger Kimball, left-wing convictions are inherently anti-academic, and there can be no excuse for allowing "tenured radicals" to woo students away from "Western civilization" and "literature." In contrast, I see political belief of one kind or another as part of the motive force behind most intellectual and cultural interests. The problem with Left Eclecticism, in my opinion, is not that it allows "subversives" access to the academy but that it makes for a closed shop in which scholarly questions tend to be answered aprioristically and in which only a small band of opinion is considered tolerable. This divergence of outlook from the defenders of great books may appear slight, but it is really fundamental; whereas they want the literary academy to be set apart as a temple for initiation into high culture, I want it to remain a pluralistic arena.

Above all, I reject the rightists' apocalyptic account of the current state of criticism, whose complexities altogether escape them. To hear them tell it, something comparable in gravity and finality to the 1949 "loss of China" is occurring before our eyes. Already, they say, a guerrilla band of Marxists, feminists, homosexuals, and professional ethnics, armed with lewd concerns and self-evidently preposterous but destructive theories, has seized control of the scholarly societies, the university presses, and the leading departments of literature, leaving those who care about intellectual and aesthetic standards utterly disenfranchised. Although this image provides a certain Spenglerian thrill, it grossly misrepresents the contemporary literary academy's balance of interests and movements—a balance that has indeed been shifting to the left, but much less decisively and irreversibly than the conservatives would have us believe.

It is an old story, really: academics who sense that their hour has passed, or malcontents who have failed to find or keep the academic careers they once dreamed of, have always identified their outmoded school of thought with the lost cause of civilization itself. When my own career began in the 1950s, for example, the forebears of today's conservative Jeremiahs—the old-boy "humanists" who favored impressionistic immersion in the ennobling beauties of Chaucer, Shakespeare, Spenser, Milton, Keats, and Browning—regarded the ascendant New Critics as barbarians who would reduce the universities to factories for the production of soullessly mechanical "readings." Later, when the Gallic "theorists" and their disciples arrived on the scene, it was the New Critics' turn to cry doom. But no faction ever took over completely, and none is likely to now.

Instead, we can be fairly sure that the most prestigious emergent schools will undergo jealous scrutiny, be obliged to modify some of their more vulnerable premises, and be further diluted through the practice of uncommitted critics who have been attracted—but warily—to fresh intellectual possibilities. What outsiders like Kimball can't perceive is that the real story of "what they are doing to literature" is chiefly this work of negotiation, whereby advanced methodological trends are subtly but inexorably drawn back toward the empirical center. Moreover, the most vigorous and telling critiques of ostensibly left doctrines usually come from segments of the left itself that continually deflate fashionable theories for their failures of social inclusiveness, concreteness, and practical utility. To treat all academic radicals as partaking of a single conspiracy against literary art is therefore to miss the point disastrously.

This holds doubly true because the left, unlike the right, has made some indisputably fertile contributions to the recent evolution of literary study. It is radicals who brought about today's general realization that criticism must become more self-aware about the ideological coordinates of the positions it takes. Again, it was their insistence on *historicizing*—that is, on tracing the contingent sociopolitical interests served by given beliefs and practices—that broke the hold of a timidly moralizing, unity-minded formalism that had long outlived its usefulness. And of course we have the left to thank for launching a fundamental debate about the canon and for bringing minority concerns into the foreground—developments that are especially striking and revivifying in my own field of American literature.

The New Americanists, as I have called the now dominant faction in my field, all take their bearings from a rejection of the "liberal consensus" about American literature that prevailed in academic criticism from the forties through the mid-sixties.[3] The liberals had rallied around a small core of classics by (on the whole) well-connected white males, using those texts to celebrate moral earnestness, dense aesthetic texture, and a genially democratic idea of the American dream and its gradual fulfillment in history. In the eyes of New Americanists, that consensus reflected not an objective apprehension of our nation and its literature but a passing ideological moment—a snuffing out of Depression era social consciousness and a projection of postwar America's hegemony and self-regard onto the literary-historical screen. Who, the New Americanists have been asking, was excluded from the liberals' patriotic literary feast, and to whose advantage? What struggles and oppressive deeds became invisible when America and democracy were treated as virtual synonyms? And how did formalism and national chauvinism reach their strange entente—whereby, for example, the anti-abolitionist politics of Nathaniel Hawthorne could be overlooked while his aesthetic greatness was located in New Critical ironies and paradoxes beyond the reach of a mere "propagandist" like Harriet Beecher Stowe? These are essential questions, and their effect on academic discussion of American literature and on most of us who deal professionally with American literature has been far-reaching.

At the same time, however, a growing restlessness within New Americanist ranks portends a much sharper break with tradition. The founding members of the group, writing in the late seventies and early eighties and struggling to make a break from their liberal mentors, were so successful that they gave rise to a second cohort of zealous followers who, lacking even an ambivalent recollection of the former dispensation, now accept a new conventional wisdom based on emancipatory values and a dismissal of "artistic" issues as inherently retrograde. These young academics launch their arguments from a base of egalitarian pieties about race, class, and gender as routinely as the cold war liberals started from formalist aesthetics, the Founding Fathers, and the canon according to F. O. Matthiessen. Predictably, then, the latest New Americanists are now beginning to turn against their mentors for continuing to dwell ambivalently on the old canon and the forgettable academic giants of the forties and fifties.

Although no one—not even the editors of the quintessentially New Americanist *Heath Anthology of American Literature*—

has as yet proposed that classic authors be banned outright, the most militant young academics are increasingly inclined to demand primary allegiance to the ethnic- and gender-based anticanon.[4] In doing so, they strangely resemble their opposite numbers on the cultural right. Both parties prefer to keep politically noxious books out of students' hands so as to allow the beneficial works to inculcate correct ideas without distraction. Both are overwhelmingly preoccupied with social order— on one side with maintaining it, on the other with inverting it. And both are convinced that the ideals and textual operations of literature professors greatly matter to the structure and future direction of society at large.

On this last point, however, they are surely mistaken. Whether on the left or right, literary indoctrination today stops absolutely at the university's gate. Its field of operation is simply the curriculum and the faculty's makeup—areas of importance, surely, for students' sense of cultural inclusion or exclusion, but still Lilliputian terrain compared to the realms of business and popular culture to which those students remain continuously oriented. Except for the tiny minority who themselves seek careers in "English," undergraduates of the nineties are proving indifferent to their professors' blandishments, which detain them only insofar as they signal what tone it would be prudent to take in papers and exams. Even when they distrust the society's promises, their reaction is not to spurn the bureaucratic-technological-capitalist order but to redouble their efforts to find employment and security in a time of reduced expectations.

But a still more disappointing irony lies embedded in the literary-critical evangelizing undertaken by many New Americanists. It has to do with their habitual recourse to the dense vocabulary and esoteric postulates of *poststructuralism,* a body of thought and method that lies beyond the comprehension of the students they hope to wean from bourgeois errors. If those students *could* catch the true poststructuralist spirit, furthermore, they wouldn't necessarily be led toward revolutionary consciousness. Taking its cues from such thoroughgoing enemies of democracy as Nietzsche and Heidegger, poststructuralism projects a deep negativity about the possibilities of both knowledge and social progress—a negativity so unrelenting that it decomposes the individual human "subject" into a helpless vector of forces that typically cannot even be located, much less stemmed. Obviously, you can't be a very effective spokesman for freedom when your philosophy tells you that it doesn't exist.

As John Patrick Diggins has recently argued, it is not coincidental that poststructuralism took hold in Western universities immediately after the theatrical student revolutionism of 1968 came crashing down.[5] Poststructuralist fatalism toward established power served a consoling function, assuring the disillusioned survivors of the New Left that the collapse of their emancipatory dreams was built into the nature of things. At the same time, its private jargon, its token allegiance to all things "marginalized" by the capitalistic West, and its vision of interpretation without ground or end fostered a clannish leftism-of-the-library that promised immunity from further rude surprises.

Methodologically, the key feature of poststructuralist criticism is its downgrading of what Michel Foucault belittled as "the author function." Once writers have been discounted as the primary shapers of their works, critics are free to "liberate signifiers from the signified"—that is, to make a text mean anything or nothing according to whim. From Roland Barthes through Jacques Derrida to Foucault himself, poststructuralism has conflated such quasi-libidinal linguistic play with political liberty, as if a carnival of unconstrained textuality could somehow serve as a proxy for the actual release of oppressed social groups from neglect and exploitation. As many observers have noted, however, the Foucauldian model of social action—now the leading paradigm for New Americanists among other theorists on the academic left—is rigidly deterministic. If even major authors are to be regarded as altogether "socially constructed" from the "discourses of power" surrounding them, what hope can the rest of us entertain for taking some control over our lives?

Not all New Americanists, it should be emphasized, have ensnared themselves in these debilitating contradictions. Those who have personally experienced marginalization—feminists, lesbians and gays, members of ethnic minorities—tend on the whole to be wary of doctrines that conceive of society as a seamless fabric of undifferentiated and mystified oppression. Classical Marxists, too, often fault poststructuralism for its neglect of "uneven development" among different underclasses at any given historical moment. As the social ineffectuality of Foucault's world view becomes more generally apparent, New Americanism will surely evolve toward a less quixotic critical style.

The main weakness in New Americanist criticism today, however, is not poststructuralism but intellectual opportunism—the ad hoc adjusting of investigative premises to forestall politically unwelcome implications. New Americanists tend, for example, to treat the authors of slave narratives, sentimental novels, and other approved works as fully conscious, socially engaged agents whose writings indict the whole scheme of dominant values; elements of conventionality and conformism in such works are simply put under the rug. But the same critics often refuse to grant any real autonomy to mainstream authors, brushing aside overt themes and cutting straight through to the racism, sexism, and class rule that they regard as the liberal order's secret essence. Or, conversely, a New Americanist may decide to rescue a seemingly offensive work from shame by ascribing to the text itself a Spartacus-like unconscious that is said to resist the oppressive manifest content. Some intrepid critics are even ready if necessary to undertake a *total theme transplant,* whereby, for example, Flannery O'Connor's Catholic theology is allegorically replaced by a more pleasingly modern and disruptive viewpoint, such as Lacanian psychoanalysis.

In the long run, it seems unlikely that New Americanists will induce many readers to believe that literary value coincides with the presence of politically acceptable notions in a text. Will we really want, say, a William Faulkner who has been purged of his saturnine resentment of women or his deep ambivalence toward blacks? For now, increasing numbers of critics seem to be answering *yes,* even if that means rating *Requiem for a Nun* above *The Sound and the Fury.* Common readers, however, unless they have been academically retrained to distrust their pleasures, sense the difference between calculatedly progressive pap and art that flows from a vision, albeit a feverish one. I prefer to honor that distinction, even while exploring the challenge to criticism posed by a major writer's blatant prejudices.

I mentioned earlier that no critic can ever claim with justice to be politically disinterested, and I hardly constitute an exception to the rule. By situating my book as far as possible from great-thoughts conservatism on one side and death-of-the-author theory on the other, I am expressing my unshaken allegiance to liberalism in the broadest meaning of that term. I do not mean simply that I favor secular skepticism, ample social sympathies, and expanded civil liberties; a "discourse radical" could go along with me that far. I also mean that I value singular departures from established belief and practice, even when those efforts produce clouded results. The best American novelists have themselves been liberal in this sense, courting isolation and incoherence in the hope of making something new. I believe that critics, without abandoning their sense of history, should be ready for a parallel if lesser effort, putting preconceptions in abeyance and following the writer's individual path wherever it may lead. My discussions of American novelists and their professor-critics will show that even within the theory-saturated academy, truly liberal criticism still exists—and that it is all the more praiseworthy for being rare.

The Critics Bear It Away

ONE

The Sins of the Fathers *Revisited*

FOR REASONS that I have explained in fuller detail else-where, I now number *myself* among the critics of American literature who have "borne it away" through an excess of methodological zeal. The most influential of my critical studies, *The Sins of the Fathers: Hawthorne's Psychological Themes* (1966),[1] helped to establish a vogue for Freudian criticism not just of Hawthorne but of American writers generally. My enthusiasm for psychoanalysis, however, began to wane at the end of the 1960s, and by 1988, when the University of California Press approached me with a proposal to reprint the book, I had long been a vocal apostate from the Freudian faith. Still—and some-what to my surprise—I found some continuing merit in my Hawthorne study. Since there would be no opportunity to revise it, I told the press that I would agree to its reprinting only if I could add a clarifying afterword, as follows.

REGARDLESS of the stir it may cause for a decade or two, virtually every literary-critical study eventually finds its way to the remainder shelf and thence to oblivion. The only question in a given case is whether the process will begin promptly after publication or be delayed for a decorous inter-val. If a piece of criticism could beseech posterity for mercy, I suppose it would pray to become merely obsolete—that is, to make enough of an impact to be judged after a while as *no longer* very useful or appropriate or politically enlightened. Such a

work, like Auden's departed Yeats, would still survive tempo-
rarily in the guts of others—at first in polite or huffy references
and later anonymously, as having helped to form one generation's conventional wisdom.

The Sins of the Fathers was remaindered long ago, and I am not
naïve enough to think that its resuscitation by the University of
California Press will allow it to make a fresh dent in critical
consciousness. I would not even want it to—not at least in its
original spirit, as unmodified by this retrospect. The book's
reappearance in 1989, almost a quarter-century after its debut,
will allow it to find some new readers, but most of them will
greet it in a historicizing and patronizing mood, not as a guide
to Hawthorne's real themes but as a representative product of
its era. So *this,* they will say, is how people saw Hawthorne back
then, before deconstruction, feminism, social constructionism,
New Historicism, ethnic consciousness, Lacanian psychoanalysis, and Marxist cultural materialism had made their mark!

Anticipating that response, I immediately want to say two
things in behalf of my doddering brainchild. First, the book
really did represent a sharp break with existing Hawthorne
studies, which in their combination of moralism and formalism
had reached exactly the intellectual dead end that I so sarcasti-
cally described in the opening pages. *The Sins of the Fathers* was
not the first book on Hawthorne to adopt a psychological point
of view, but it was the first to cry "Enough!" to the churchly
symbol-mongering that had plagued the literary academy for
the previous decade or so.

And second, my book did have an effect not only on the
critical tone but also on the premises of subsequent Hawthorne
criticism. When Jane Tompkins, for example, tells us in *Sensational Designs* that "*The Scarlet Letter* is a great novel in 1850, in
1876, in 1904, and in 1966, but each time it is great for different
reasons,"[2] she is thinking specifically of my book as having
defined a Hawthorne for the sixties and beyond. In a later
chapter, recalling that Hershel Parker in the 1979 Norton an-

thology treated Hawthorne's tales as (in her words) "somber Freudian texts,"[3] she makes the point explicit:

> We may feel that the Norton editor is right, and that Hawthorne really was the "master of psychological insight" he is represented as here. But that is because our sense of Hawthorne's art, like Parker's, has been influenced by books such as Frederick Crews' *The Sins of the Fathers.* . . . Crews' reading of Hawthorne . . . helped to determine *which* of Hawthorne's tales would be read by hundreds of thousands of Norton readers, and also *the way* those tales would be interpreted. The critical strategy that guides Crews' reading in effect constructs a new Hawthorne, who becomes for a time *the* Hawthorne—the only one that many students will ever know.[4]

Needless to say, Tompkins is not aiming at flattery here. She is advancing the epistemologically radical notion that, effectively, the "real" Hawthorne to be revealed by criticism does not exist; we can never encounter an author or text other than those constructed by ruling critical paradigms. For her, then, the alteration in critical judgment wrought by *The Sins of the Fathers* constitutes not a nearer approximation to the truth about Hawthorne but simply a cultural episode akin to every other.

Understandably, I find myself inclined to resist such cognitive pessimism. I believe that Hawthorne's fiction enduringly contains some paradigm-independent traits that would be "really there" even if no critic ever called attention to them.[5] And I further believe that *Sins* uncovered some of those traits. It showed, for example, how rigorous and unconventional Hawthorne's irony is—how little of his rendered fictional world is encapsulated in the "morals" of his works.

But whether *Sins* presented an adequately balanced account of Hawthorne's work is, unhappily, another matter. Since I myself no longer subscribe to all the theoretical tenets under-girding my book, I have long been aware that my Hawthorne was a composite figure, drawn partly from life but partly as well from the arbitrary template of a dogma. Indeed, when, with the prospective reprint in mind, I recently sat down to peruse *Sins* for the first time since the sixties, I was not sure I would find anything in it that still seemed valid. My reaction, I feared, would be like Hawthorne's upon reopening his *Mosses:* "I am a good deal changed since those times; and to tell you the truth, my past self is not very much to my taste, as I see myself in this book."

To my relief, however, I found that by 1966 my own "past self" had not yet become so sure of the Freudian revelation as to apply it to literature with unhesitating deductiveness. In every chapter, though with gradually diminishing effect, hom-age is paid to empiricial scruples. The author of *Sins* does not declare that he will submit Hawthorne to routine psychoana-lytic treatment; he tells us that Hawthorne's texts display ambi-guities that previous critics in their search for didactic content have been unwilling to tolerate. To take full account of those ambiguities, he argues, we need a method of analysis that is especially adapted to making sense of mixed intentions. And even after settling down to the exercise of Freudian principles, *Sins* keeps pausing to address possible objections and to admit that some of its conclusions are speculative.

If much of *Sins* still feels right to me today, that is because Hawthorne-as-problem, not Freud-as-solution, usually remains in view. Here I have in mind what I would still defend as accurate insights into peculiarities that Hawthorne's moralizing critics had minimized: his fear of passion; his tendency to re-duce historical issues to a psychomachia between impulse and inhibition; his antiradicalism, combined, however, with a radi-cal's distrust of authority and institutions; his misogynistic streak; his self-reproach as a voyeuristic bystander, and his association of art with that guilty role; his clinical coldness, which works at cross-purposes with his endorsements of affection and community; his yearning toward a Phoebe- or Hilda-like blandness to swallow up his morbidity; and, as a result of all this, his profound loneliness and premature world-weariness.

In this portrait there was nothing that intrinsically demanded to be accounted for in Freudian terms. Yet Hawthorne himself, I had observed with growing excitement, adopts a proto-psychoanalytic stance toward his characters' obsessions. It is Hawthorne who says that Reuben Bourne's motives operate "unconsciously to himself," and whose Reverend Hooper sermonizes about mysteries we "would fain conceal from our own consciousness," and who declares in his own voice that our dreams often undo an "unconscious self-deception" that we practice when awake. Hawthorne and Freud, I saw, were two of a kind—introspective and prying Romantics who distrusted appearances, brooded over the poisonous effects of long-held secrets, and harbored a tragic sense of the psychic price that must be paid to civilize an unruly species. And most strikingly of all, both of them—one systematically, the other in scattered thematic hints—linked sexual inhibition and other deformations of personality to the mixed appeal and horror of incest.

If, in the early sixties, psychoanalysis had been less current in intellectual circles than it was, I would probably not have allowed myself to take the next, and decisive, step—namely, to conclude that Hawthorne's fiction *corroborates* the central propositions of Freud, which in their turn can be "rigorously" invoked to explain what really troubled both Hawthorne and his heroes. Alternative avenues, I later realized, were open to me. To acknowledge, as I did, that Freud and Hawthorne were both Romantic thinkers offered me a chance to shift the issue of their kinship away from the realm of scientific truth and into that of cultural history. And when I remarked that Hawthorne's ancestral legacy and childhood situation gave him ample grounds for brooding about incest, here again I faced—but passed up—an opportunity to pursue determinate biographical considerations as opposed to dogmatizing about the universal Oedipus complex.[6] Instead, I set about to show, in the words I chose for the dust jacket, that "to a remarkable extent [Hawthorne's] characterizations anticipate the findings of psychoanalysis, and the innermost concerns of his art are invariably those to which Freud attributed prime importance."

That statement deserved a skeptical reading which I will now belatedly supply. To say that fictional *characterizations* anticipate a psychological theorist's *findings* is surely a category error, a confounding of behavioral phenomena (the actions of Hawthorne's personages) with one set of possible explanations for those phenomena. If other explanations are thinkable, then "characterizations" alone prove nothing about the merits of any given psychology. And in declaring that Hawthorne's "innermost concerns" are "invariably" those highlighted by psychoanalysis, I was egregiously begging the question. Who is to say which of an author's themes are "innermost"? What this meant, I am afraid, is that my love affair with psychoanalysis had reached the point where a given theme would be considered preeminent in Hawthorne's mental economy precisely by virtue of its correspondence to Freudian theory.

This circular logic would have had fewer damaging effects if Freudian metapsychology were the universally valid theory of mind that it purports to be. As I painfully came to realize in the decade following *Sins*, however, psychoanalysis amounts to a classic pseudoscience—that is, an allegedly scientific doctrine that fends off counterexamples, and thus shields its postulates from falsification, in indefensible ways. In its normal practice, psychoanalysis gratuitously proliferates constructs and hypotheses; it seizes upon "deep" causal factors without first weighing simpler ones; it turns its back on the scientific requirement that a given explanatory framework be tested against others instead of just being employed and elaborated; it relies on anecdotal and self-servingly edited instantiations; it uses tainted data (any-thing-but-"free" associations) as supporting evidence; it en-courages extraordinary hermeneutic liberties that allow the interpreter to see confirmations of his hunches everywhere; it wildly overstates its therapeutic successes and then cites them as demonstrations of the theory; and it declares that the only people qualified to criticize that theory are those who have been indoctrinated in the lengthy regimen of thought reform accompanying it. These are telltale signs of a cultlike indiffer-ence to the risks of error.

At the time I wrote *Sins,* I was already dimly aware of these liabilities, but they struck me as the institutional and behavioral lapses of epigones who had fallen away from Freud's scientific rigor. It gradually sank in on me, however, that Freud had initiated every psychoanalytic malpractice, from chronically lying about his cures to accusing his critics of mental illness to plugging leaks in the theory with such improvisations as "the constitutional factor," the repetition compulsion, the death instinct, and Lamarckian memory traces of a primal crime. When I could finally bring myself to ask what objective grounds he had produced to warrant acceptance of his system, all I could find was a cloudy tale about a heroic self-analysis; a series of artfully composed case histories about patients who, one could make out, had been browbeaten by the therapist without experiencing lasting relief from their symptoms; and many suave assurances about imminently forthcoming or pre-viously supplied proofs that are nowhere to be found in the record. It is logically possible, of course, that a theorist could commit all these offenses against the empirical ethos and still be justified in his substantive claims. But someone would be ill-advised, I finally saw, to take the prospect very seriously.

When seized by the mood of Freudian exclusiveness, a critic cannot help but underrate any number of other dimensions to his subject's work. The author of *Sins* tells us that American history interests Hawthorne *"only* as it is metaphorical of individual mental strife," that *The House of the Seven Gables* is "about" the risks of seizure by unconscious wishes, that incest fear is *the* reason why the late romances could not be finished, and that intrapsychic conflict encompasses *all* of "the biographical implications of Hawthorne's art." Whereas *Sins* at its prudent best complements a number of other approaches to Hawthorne, its "intercourse with the world" gets nullified at precisely those points where it most insists on its Freudianism.

More seriously, some of the raw textual facts cited in *Sins* turn out, on a closer look, to have been contaminated by the theory they purportedly corroborate. Take, for example, my claim that Hawthorne's reduction of witches to mothers and of devils to fathers in "Young Goodman Brown" is "confirmed in psychoanalysis." Since a non-Freudian reader would not perceive these symbolic equations in the first place, the assertion is vacuous. Again, when "the strictest Freudian expectations are fulfilled" by Clifford Pyncheon's sense of oppression by his "father" Jaffrey, that is because the psychoanalytic critic has already taken the liberty of promoting a cousin to the role of symbolic father. Such tampering, whereby the text is gratuitously awarded certain Freudian properties which then prove triumphantly pliable to Freudian analysis, vitiates the central justification that I offered for pursuing a psychoanalytic Hawthorne: "one method is better than another if it can incorporate more evidence and follow the logic of plot structure more closely."

A sad but useful irony suggests itself here. In the opening chapter of *Sins,* I proclaim that the time has come to rescue Hawthorne from allegorically inclined critics by doing full justice at last to "the emotional texture of [his] imagination." In some measure, I think, that is what the book manages to accomplish. But wherever Hawthorne's singular mind gets assimilated to Freudian generalities, the flavor of his consciousness is lost; an off-the-shelf model of the psychic apparatus and of its shaping traumas predetermines the "real meanings" around which everything else in Hawthorne's mental and artistic world supposedly revolves. At such junctures *Sins* itself becomes yet another instance of allegorical criticism.

If I were to rewrite *The Sins of the Fathers* today, I would still insist on Hawthorne's diffidence, slyness, and suggestiveness, but I would not presume to explain his inhibitions by reference to a core of "the repressed." Nor, obviously, would I consult Freudian theory in order to decide just which, if any, of his themes were too psychically threatening to become fully conscious. Since my book first appeared, students of antebellum culture have emphasized that Hawthorne was an avid reader of sensational fiction and journalism and that many of his contemporaries were less constrained by prudery than was once supposed.[7] In a revised *Sins*, I would give less attention to the author's putative struggle with his unconscious and correspondingly more to his deliberate toying with his readers' expectations. After all, if we are to be truly faithful to Hawthorne's psychology, we should not be in a rush to explain away its surface features, including the extraordinary self-control with which he simultaneously manipulated literary conventions and ironically distanced himself from them.

Which is not to say that I would now discount the role of anxiety in the writer's life and art. When Hawthorne teases his readers with the unfathomability of his "inmost me," he is not just being coy but attempting to steel himself to a sense of alienation that will never cease to nag at him. Rather than supply a pat Freudian content for that unease, I would hope to take it more seriously as a primary fact. Hawthorne's strongest fear, I suspect, was not that he would succumb to oedipal fantasies but that, like so many of his curiously evanescent characters, he lacked a stable self—that *he* would not know how to go about locating an "inmost me." There is evidence to indicate that he saw something of himself in those compulsive protagonists of his who, mysteriously excluded from the pleasures of mundane life, can only be galvanized into action by surrendering to some absurdly pretentious project which then marks them as outcasts and thus redoubles their isolation.

To be sure, this quintessentially Hawthornian plight is identified as such in *Sins*. Yet it deserves more attention for its own sake than my Freudian agenda allowed me to give it, and its social context needs to be more fully spelled out. On a second try, I would want to correlate Hawthorne's psychological isolation more fully with his circumstances as a shabby-genteel heir to colonial magistrates and with his consequent feeling of inborn superiority to both the plebeians and the nouveaux riches. His prose resounds with "belatedness"—with a sense of his having been born into a practical century that could never abide either the social or the artistic pretensions that he found himself unable to forgo. Hence his sardonic but never altogether sincere self-denigration, his poison-dipped satirical humor, and a certain impenetrable ceremoniousness that hints at aristocratic disdain for the coarse Jacksonian world. Hawthorne may have suffered less from secret guilt, after all, than from distaste at having to hawk his Romantic wares to a bumptious and impatient public.

A full accounting of "Hawthorne's psychological themes," then, would not confine itself to the intrapsychic realm from which psychoanalysis so rarely ventures forth. An author's psychology takes coloration from every element in his background, genetic endowment, upbringing, and milieu, and it leaves its signature not just on plots and images but on everything he does. If I could rewrite my book today, I would follow the lead of certain critics who, mindful of my own early probings but going well beyond them, have been revealing the subtle interconnectedness between Hawthorne's precarious social status, his politics of antifanaticism, his conduct as a husband and father, and the anxieties about manhood that do indeed peep through his prose.[8] It is as an episode in the education of such critics, I would say, that *The Sins of the Fathers* now chiefly survives.

If I can contribute nothing further to a resolution of Hawthorne's "case," however, there is another that remains to be laid to rest: my own. My drastically changed relation to *Sins* and to psychoanalysis has itself, I realize, become a topic of academic notice, provoking responses ranging from puzzlement to titillation to dismay. Such a recantation would seem to have few precedents outside the sphere of political and religious deconversion. How, it has been asked, could someone exercise sustained Freudian ingenuity in a critical study, go on to proselytize for applied analysis, and then, not long thereafter, vigorously denounce the whole psychoanalytic tradition and many of his own critical conclusions?

True to form, Freudian commentators, including some I have never met, have not been slow to offer depth-psychological reflections on this curiosity. Even some non-Freudians have speculated about an apparent inability on my part to find a middle ground. I know for myself, however, that my disillusionment with psychoanalysis occurred in minute stages over many years—in retrospect, too many! The appearance of suddenness arose from my eventual realization that the opposing arguments I had been deflecting with increasingly feeble rationalizations were unanswerable.

Most literary academics feel that we should be wary of Freudian dogmatism but grateful for a small body of "indispensable Freudian insights"; this is the perspective from which my anti-Freudianism looks as extremist as my early faith. In my experience, however, such observers always turn out to be ignorant of the actual history of psychiatric thought. Thus, for example, they credit Freud with having discovered "the unconscious" and its attendant compulsions, obsessions, and perversions. In fact, however, virtually all the syndromes that Freud tried to explain had been amply described by others. The defenders of "Freudian insights" confuse a behavioral domain with one overreaching theorization of that domain.[9] It cannot be too emphatically stated that in rejecting psychoanalysis root and branch, I am not declaring the mind to be a simple thing; I am saying that its intricacies confute the attempt of Freudians to insist on a handful of universally explanatory factors.

The main reason that my public reversal has struck many academics as eccentric, I believe, is that it put me out of phase with the Zeitgeist. Thanks to the ascendancy of structuralism and then poststructuralism in various forms, "advanced" criticism since 1966 has become much more, not less, Freudian in a high-flying, deductive, and often explicitly anti-empirical way. Moreover, as the loftier reaches of the academy have become at once more partisan and more entrepreneurial, the idea that a critic might want to renounce his influential theory and release his followers has come to seem incomprehensible; it smacks of self-destructive mania. Why choose to dissolve a personal fiefdom, when by now a consensus has developed that criticism, like literature itself, is essentially a means of exercising power?

My reply can be brief: I don't consider myself a party to any such consensus. Nor, I think, do most scholars who continue to concentrate on single authors like Hawthorne as opposed to grand ideological agendas. Those scholars are rarely heard from when breakthroughs of theory are announced and new movements are born. Yet they still make up a majority of the literary professoriate, and a description of their normal practice would constitute a good working account of the empirical attitude. This may help to explain why, in renouncing a sectarian brand of criticism that binds its practitioners in defensive solidarity, I feel that I have gained many more friends than I have lost.

The split in our currently polarized academy, I believe, falls not between "theorists" and "antitheorists" but between apriorists of various kinds and what I would insist on calling empiricists. For apriorists, a theory is worth exercising if it yields results that gratify the critic's moral or ideological passions; no further demands need be placed on it. To an empiricist, however, the justification for a theory must reside in its combination of logical coherence, epistemic scrupulousness, and capacity to explain relatively undisputed facts at once more parsimoniously and more comprehensively than its rivals do.[10] The partisans of these opposed attitudes toward knowledge occupy the same corridors and go through the same institutional motions, but in a profound sense they live in different worlds.

The Sins of the Fathers was written by a still-young critic caught between those worlds before their incommensurability became as apparent as it soon did. For me, I thought at the time, Freudian theory would serve not as an alternative to the empirical attitude but as its instrument— an efficient route to depths that I would expound without tendentiousness, since my only goal was accurate knowledge about Hawthorne. Some readers—those who believe that ideological considerations should and always do come first—will feel that it was my expectations for impartial knowledge, not my expectations for psychoanalysis, that proved naïve. I remain convinced, however, that if *Sins* amounts to something more than a mere exercise in dogmatism, the credit belongs to its search for a "real Hawthorne" beyond the reach of any fixed method or political cause.

Whose American Renaissance?

F. O. MATTHIESSEN, *American Renaissance: Art and Expression in the Age of Emerson and Whitman* (New York: Oxford UP, 1941; rpt. 1968).

WALTER BENN MICHAELS and DONALD E. PEASE, eds., *The American Renaissance Reconsidered: Selected Papers from the English Institute, 1982–83* (Baltimore: Johns Hopkins, 1985).

RUSSELL J. REISING, *The Unusable Past: Theory and the Study of American Literature* (London: Methuen, 1986).

SACVAN BERCOVITCH and MYRA JEHLEN, eds., *Ideology and Classic American Literature* (New York: Cambridge UP, 1986).

DONALD E. PEASE, *Visionary Compacts: American Renaissance Writings in Cultural Context* (Madison: Wisconsin UP, 1987).

JANE TOMPKINS, *Sensational Designs: The Cultural Work of American Fiction, 1790–1860* (New York: Oxford UP, 1985).

DAVID S. REYNOLDS, *Beneath the American Renaissance: The Subversive Imagination in the Age of Emerson and Melville* (New York: Knopf, 1988).

PHILIP FISHER, *Hard Facts: Setting and Form in the American Novel* (New York: Oxford UP, 1985).

I

EVERY FEW DECADES, in any given field of literary study, we can expect the publication of a multivolume collaborative history that will become known as the standard reference work. Typically, its chapters are parceled out to eminences who have long ruled the acknowledged fiefdoms of that scholarly realm and who, to the amusement of reviewers, appear to contradict one another wherever they touch on the same topics. These "picaresque adventures in pseudo-causality," as Geoffrey Hartman once called them, these "handbooks with footnotes which claim to sing of the whole but load every rift with glue,"[1] are tolerated precisely so long as they are perceived to be patchwork creations. A time comes, however, when another generation begins to see what is really standard about the standard guide—namely, the unwitting conformity of all of its contributors to deep-seated assumptions that are now considered pernicious. A sharply divergent major effort is sure to follow soon thereafter.

One case in point is the often consulted, sometimes politely cited, but increasingly vilified *Literary History of the United States (LHUS)*, edited by Robert Spiller and others, which entered the scene in 1948. For a generation, Americanists indulgently savored the contrast between Spiller's harmlessly eccentric theory of "cycles" in the national literature and the indifference of his collaborators to that same theory. But as the cultural revolution that began in the 1960s has consolidated itself in the academy, *LHUS* has ceased to amuse. Now it is perceived by many as the supreme expression of something called, without affection, "the liberal consensus"—and that means that its days on the conscientious young professor's shelf are numbered.

There is more than one effort afoot to supplant *LHUS*,[2] but the most ambitious and closely watched project is a five-volume *Cambridge History of American Literature*, originally scheduled for publication in 1989 but now overdue. Thanks to early procedural and methodological revelations by its general editor, Sacvan Bercovitch, Americanists have already had a chance to glimpse the lineaments of this work.[3] They know that it will be very different from *LHUS*, beginning with the way its team has been assembled. Instead of the usual assortment of aging dignitaries, Bercovitch's contributors will all be, as he says, "Americanists trained in the sixties and early seventies," making up "twenty-one spokespersons for dissensus." They will dissent, that is, from the leading liberal myths about American history and the application of those myths to criticism of our alleged classics. No one will have to wait twenty years to discern the figure in this carpet.

Predictably, the Bercovitch project is already being greeted in some quarters with resentment and anxiety. It isn't that anyone believes *LHUS* to have stated the final word about American literature, but that relative youth and radicalism are thought to be dubious criteria for participation in an undertaking of this kind. Shouldn't Bercovitch have tried to enlist the most knowledgeable rather than the most likeminded team of writers? A good many Americanists with no conscious investment in the Spiller world view believe that *CHAL* will strike a blow against disinterestedness and for the ideologizing of scholarship.

To this charge, however, Bercovitch and his colleagues have a carefully pondered two-part answer. In the first place, they say, the study of American literature has never lacked a ruling ideological mood. When the academic field was created some seventy years ago, it was patently a gentleman's club—one whose exclusive social pretensions were mirrored in its reverence for the Fireside Poets and in its conception of art as a fragile kingdom lying somewhere beyond the vulgar material world. That dispensation was overthrown by the nativist and progressivist approach championed by Vernon L. Parrington, with its chauvinistic celebration of such sturdy-looking realists and democrats as Walt Whitman, Mark Twain, Theodore Dreiser, and Sinclair Lewis. And then came the New Critical or modernist era, elevating such masters of indirection as Thoreau, the later James, Eliot, and Faulkner while placing a premium on irony, obscurity, symbolism, and withdrawal from public commitment—in short, the badges of post–World War II quietism. The backers of all these paradigms believed they were taking their guidance directly from "literary values," but in each case those values functioned as ideology—that is, as seeming universals that disguised and facilitated historically discrete interests.

Hence the second and bolder part of the dissensus critics' reply to their detractors. The New Americanists, as I will call them, claim to belong to the first scholarly cohort that does *not* consist of ideologues. According to Bercovitch's definition, ideology is "the system of interlinked ideas, symbols, and beliefs by which a culture . . . seeks to justify and perpetuate itself; the web of rhetoric, ritual, and assumption through which society coerces, persuades, and coheres."[4] Ideology, then, resides in the "absolute values" that a social system projects before its own gaze. Its function is inevitably a conservative one: to keep power relations out of focus and thus safe from fundamental criticism. And if so, the investigators and critics of ideology, even if they subscribe to a definite radical politics of their own, are not to be thought of as ideologues but as unmaskers.

For readers only passingly acquainted with the professional study of American literature, the most familiar issue on the New Americanist agenda will be that of the canon. We have all heard a good deal lately about the need to "uphold tradition," to "honor aesthetic standards," and to expose our students to time-tested "great thoughts." But to New Americanists (and to many others), this is all sheer ideology, false consciousness that calls for the exposure of its historical determinants. Which branches of literary effort, the dissensus critics ask, have been demoted to insignificance by "the tradition," and to whose benefit? Where do "aesthetic standards" come from if not from the cliques whose dominance is no longer to be acquiesced in without debate? And what factions have used the "great thoughts" to improve their circumstances—and again, at whose expense? Once set in motion, the secularizing impulse will not allow any of these constraining pieties to go unanalyzed.

This questioning of absolutes is now being conducted in all branches of literary study; it reflects an irresistible trend in the academy toward the spurning of unified schemes and hierarchies of every kind. What gives the New Americanist critique a special emotional force, however, is its connection both to our historic national shames—slavery, "Indian removal," aggressive expansion, imperialism, and so forth—and to current struggles for equal social opportunity. When a New Americanist shows, for example, that a canonical work such as *Huckleberry Finn* indulges in the stereotypical "objectifying" of African Americans, Native Americans, women, or others, a double effect results. First, the canon begins to look less sacrosanct and is thus readied for expansion to include works by long-dead representatives of those same groups; and second, their contemporary descendants are offered a reason for entering into an academic dialogue that had previously slighted them. In short, the New Americanist program aims at altering the literary departments' social makeup as well as their dominant style of criticism.

It ought to be clear, then, that we have here something more definite and consequential than the latest permutation of "theory" as we knew it in the sixties and seventies. To be sure, the New Americanists are broadly poststructuralist in sympathy; they refuse to draw categorical distinctions between literature and history, foreground and background, art and advocacy, and they distrust all "foundational" claims, whether they be for fixed aesthetic quality, authorial autonomy, a specifically literary kind of discourse, or scholarly detachment. But they scorn the daisy chain of indeterminacies with which the once dandyish but now crestfallen Yale deconstructionists used to caper. For a New Americanist, social struggle must always be kept in view, and any concepts obscuring it—concepts, for example, of the "American character," of the representative masterpiece, of the impish freeplay of signifiers—are to be not just rejected but exposed as ideology.

For the immediate future, the New Americanists' rapidly

growing sway is virtually guaranteed by the academy's mood of social pluralism, iconoclasm, and antinationalism—a mood deriving ultimately from revulsion against America's role in the Vietnam era. It is not surprising that the dissensus critics have made their strongest impression thus far through their critique of the "liberal consensus" of the forties and fifties. Growing up a decade later, they were schooled by activists to distrust not only the shibboleths of patriotism and the melting pot but also such honorific terms as "art," "unity," and "complexity"— concepts that figured centrally in their liberal predecessors' lexicon.

II

As Russell J. Reising discloses in a useful if somewhat pedestrian study, *The Unusable Past: Theory and the Study of American Literature,* the New Americanists would like us to think of the liberal consensus as extending from the 1940s straight through to the present. Thus conceived, it would embrace many styles of scholarly work, including the "Puritan origins" literary history practiced by Perry Miller and the early, preradical Sacvan Bercovitch; "cultural" criticism à la Richard Chase, Lionel Trilling, R.W.B. Lewis, Leslie Fiedler, and Leo Marx; and "self-reflexive" criticism from Charles Feidelson, Jr., to Richard Poirier and such very recent figures as John T. Irwin and Kenneth Dauber. As a sympathizer with the dissensus movement, Reising neglects to ask whether this herding of several generations into one corral may not be something of a rhetorical stunt, a means of making everyone but the New Americanists themselves appear hopelessly outdated. Instead, Reising joins in insisting that all these schools and figures have subscribed to one or another version of "Americanness"—the idea that this nation, despite the crassness of its commercial life, possesses a special, and admirable, character of spirit that is epitomized in certain works of imagination.

Wherever the near boundary of the liberal consensus ought

to be drawn, there can be no doubt that the postwar liberal critics, for all their rejection of progressivist sentimentalities about "the people," acquiesced in a literary nationalism that went largely unchallenged until the New Americanists began their assault on it. As Henry Seidel Canby's "Address to the Reader" introducing *LHUS* put it in 1948, our literature has been

> profoundly influenced by ideals and by practices developed in democratic living. It has been intensely conscious of the needs of the common man, and equally conscious of the aspirations of the individual. . . . It has been humanitarian. It has been, on the whole, an optimistic literature, made virile by criticism of the actual in comparison with the ideal.[5]

That is the voice of the original liberal consensus speaking with unselfconscious complacency.

The most nuanced expression of that consensus is to be found in the "cultural" authorities who helped to forge it during the period surrounding World War II. Those former or chastened leftists arrived at the postwar era at once alarmed by the exposure of Stalinist barbarity and exhilarated by America's new preeminence and guardianship of democratic values. They were still politically minded enough to resist the sheer formalism of the New Critics—hence their now familiar designation as cultural critics—yet their retreat from proletarian consciousness into an "anti-ideological" equipoise also allowed them to drift remarkably near to formalism and mythic, timeless universalism. The idea that literary art follows its own rigorous imperatives, apart from everyday language and the demands of material interests, held a special appeal for them. And they were eager to celebrate a body of national classics—works that could be called quintessentially American by virtue of their unconventionality, their unboundedness, and their affirmation of innocence and democracy.

Perhaps the key shaper of "Americanness" criticism was the Lionel Trilling of *The Liberal Imagination* (1950), who helped to replace Parrington's sociological conception of American literature with an explicitly cultural one. For Parrington, American history was a record of successive emancipations from aristocratic and sectarian European roots, and American literature in all its variety reflected that record of linear democratic progress. It followed, for Parrington, that we should cultivate all those elements of our heterogeneous literary tradition that manifest that record. But a culture, Trilling wrote in rebuke of Parrington,

> is not a flow . . . ; the form of its existence is struggle . . . it is nothing if not a dialectic. And in any culture there are likely to be certain artists who contain a large part of the dialectic within themselves, their meaning and power lying in their contradictions; they contain within themselves, it may be said, the very essence of the culture.[6]

The real America is to be sought, then, in those relatively few books produced by "dialectically" capacious minds.

As Nina Baym has pointed out in a justly celebrated article, all the writers who satisfied Trilling's criterion proved to be white middle-class males from nonimmigrant northeastern families.[7] Born into the mainstream but modestly alienated from it by their literary vocation, they "contained" just the right "contradictions" to produce what Trilling called "the most suggestive testimony to what America was and is."[8] As for women writers, their association with domestic life cast them as personifications not of the treasured dialectic but of the blandness which true (critical) culture must heroically oppose. The likelihood that Trilling and his followers would find the right stuff in a female author was scarcely greater than that of seeing Miss Watson board up her house and light out for the Territory.

In recent years, however, it has not been Trilling but F. O. Matthiessen who has come to personify the liberal consensus in the minds of its antagonists. The case is worth dwelling on, for it was Matthiessen, in his monumental *American Renaissance: Art and Expression in the Age of Emerson and Whitman* (1941), who coined the name of our putative golden age and decisively shaped the way it has been apprehended until now. *American Renaissance* was not only a tour de force of personal sensibility; it was the first book both to claim international stature for the alleged giants of the mid-nineteenth century—Emerson, Thoreau, Hawthorne, Melville, and Whitman—and to demonstrate their responsiveness to the New Critical techniques of analysis that were helping to illuminate another recently secured canon, that of modernism. But both modernism and New Criticism now stand accused of ideological lackeyism—and Matthiessen's influence, it is felt almost forty years after his death, still inhibits a truly egalitarian grasp of our literature.

Two critiques of Matthiessen and his magnum opus have been especially important in shaping the now ascendant paradigm. These English Institute papers of 1982–83, which can be found in Walter Benn Michaels and Donald Pease's collection, *The American Renaissance Reconsidered,* were written by Jonathan Arac and by Pease himself. They allege that by ingeniously intertwining two strands of practice, nationalism and formalism, Matthiessen devised a kind of cold war criticism before the fact. Inflating certain books to superpower status and then concentrating almost exclusively on their formal properties, he is said to have deflected potentially embarrassing questions about the state of American democracy in the mid-nineteenth and mid-twentieth centuries alike.

Many liberal readers would regard this as a curiously grudging account of *American Renaissance*. In honoring his five classic authors, after all, Matthiessen reasonably assumed that he was favoring anticonventionalists and champions of the ordinary citizen against the patrician blandness of Irving, Longfellow,

Lowell, and Holmes. Matthiessen himself was an active socialist who seconded the presidential nomination of Henry Wallace, and the explicit theme of *American Renaissance* was the uses of literature for enhancing and broadening democracy. Its preface quoted with approval Louis Sullivan's challenge: "Are you using such gifts as you possess for or against the people?" (Matthiessen, xvi).

But a growing number of Americanists who were educated in the sixties and after have not been mollified by this record. In practice, they ask, was Matthiessen's idea of "the people" truly inclusive? Were his great authors as democratic in spirit as he maintained? Did they actually *do* much of anything about the social evils of their day? And had Matthiessen's newly solidified canon really been determined, as he maintained, by "successive generations of common readers,"[9] or did it rather express the avant-garde bias of Wastelanders who fetishized inconsecutiveness, irony, self-division, privatistic revolt, and detachment from the vulgar mob?

American Renaissance is indeed an ambivalent book, poised between communitarian longings and an admiration for eccentric isolatoes who had cast their conflicts into ambiguous symbolism. Emerson in particular exasperated Matthiessen with his watery ideality and his gilding of Jacksonian greed, yet the critic also maintained that because "all souls were equal" for Emerson, his "value can hardly be exaggerated for those who believe now in the dynamic extension of democracy on economic as well as political levels."[10] Matthiessen's efforts to live with such contradictions have struck many readers, especially those who knew him personally, as a mark of heroic integrity. But for critics who acquired their political loyalties in the Vietnam era and have never experienced the disillusionment that befell Matthiessen's own generation of leftists, his waverings look like a surrender to the interests he nominally opposed.

In his own eyes, Matthiessen had stuck to his socialist ideals by, for example, deploring Captain Ahab's demented individualism—a dark variant on the Emersonian program of assimilating the "not-me" to the "me"—while highlighting the humane and democratic flexibility of an Ishmael. In Ahab, Matthiessen argued, Melville had issued a prophetic warning against "the empire builders of the post–Civil War world."[11] But Arac, Pease, and their colleagues point out that such a formulation preempts close scrutiny of the *pre*war world, the one from which most of Matthiessen's literary giants themselves half-averted their gaze. Were not the railroad barons already consolidating their monopolies in the 1850s, meanwhile quoting Emerson on hitching one's wagon to a star? And what about the Civil War itself, which gets casually mentioned in *American Renaissance* but earns no entry in the index? What, above all, about slavery? As Arac puts it,

> Matthiessen demonstrated that his object of study, the literary, functioned for writers as an evasion, though not a complete disengagement, from a political life of which they did not wholeheartedly approve. . . . But his interpretations of this compromise failed to reckon with the affirmative support that compromise still gave to dubious policies. It is both more understandable and less commendable than Matthiessen suggested that Hawthorne, despite his skeptical conservatism, supported the party of Jackson. For the Democratic party's commitment to slavery made "the Democracy" include much less than "all the people." Rather than facing up to divisions within the renaissance, Matthiessen divided the renaissance from the war and segregated qualities "before" and "after." His wish for wholeness led to disconnection.[12]

Unlike some commentators who simply identify Matthiessen with a smugly hegemonic liberalism, Arac brings out the pathos lurking in *American Renaissance*. Matthiessen thought he was forwarding the Popular Front program of international cultural pluralism, but his postwar successors found that they could turn his book to nationalistic ends with no difficulty at all. Again, Matthiessen's Christian principles reinforced his vision of universal brotherhood, yet they also led him to highlight the politically conservative concept of sin and thus, as Arac says, to overdramatize "the evil individuals who obstruct the common good of an otherwise united American People."[13] And as a closet homosexual in an age when his career would have been shattered by disclosure, Matthiessen was helpless to reveal his fervent, erotically based kinship with the one authentic egalitarian in his "Renaissance," Whitman. Indeed, he explicitly disavowed it, alluding aversively to "a quality *vaguely pathological and homosexual*" marring a stanza from *Leaves of Grass*.[14]

Arac shows that *American Renaissance* is really two books in dialogue, or, more accurately, one book vainly petitioning the other for rebuttal time. Behind the impersonal Eliotic order and the canon-forming monumentality, one can detect a muffled cry for recognition of the transient moment, the wayward impulse, the denigrated outcast and rebel. In this sense, the critics who now seek to do justice to the full ethnic, sexual, and class diversity of the literary 1850s—the age that Matthiessen ironically helped to reduce to the work of a few male Anglo-Saxon masters—regard themselves as forwarding his real agenda in more propitious circumstances than his own.

Whether Matthiessen's New Americanist interpreters have fully grasped those circumstances, however, is another question. For Pease, who treats the paranoid cold war mentality without reference to the Soviet Union and its policies, one sign of post-1945 American irrationality is the fact that Matthiessen was "designated a 'fellow traveler' "[15] shortly before the suicide that capped his martyrdom to that same cold war. The quotation marks are eloquent; it is clear that for Pease there was no such thing in the real world as a fellow traveler. Other accounts, however, reveal that from the thirties onward Matthiessen was precisely a fellow traveler—that is, someone who abstained from Party membership while generally hewing to positions set forth by the Kremlin. And insofar as his suicide registered political as well as personal despair, the disillusioning shock of Soviet realpolitik in eastern Europe had as much to do with it as McCarthyism. Pease's failure to recognize these well-established facts would seem to constitute a textbook illustration of partisan myopia, and more generally to cast some doubt on the New Americanists' belief that they have put ideology behind them.

III

IN ANY EVENT, the project of fulfilling Matthiessen's "real agenda" requires the dissensus critics to take up a very different stance from his own toward the relations between ideology, history, and literary merit. As Myra Jehlen has observed in her introduction to a provocative collection of essays that she and Sacvan Bercovitch have edited, *Ideology and Classic American Literature,* in the glory days of the liberal consensus

> the common critical wisdom was that in literature, ideology was a trace of incomplete combustion in the transformation of the material of history into the spirit of literature. To call a writer "ideological" was to mean that he or she was less accomplished; an "ideological" work was by that definition less literary.[16]

That was precisely Matthiessen's understanding; his "Renaissance" masters had transcended the politics of their age. But this "sidelining of history,"[17] as Jehlen calls it, this pretense that great art must be decoupled from the struggle for social dominance, makes no sense to the New Americanists. Or rather, it makes sense to them only as a repressive strategy, a means of keeping the lid on divisive differences of interest such as those between slave masters and slaves, land clearers and those whose territory was thereby seized, and more recently between the purveyors of "Americanness" criticism and the groups that find their traditions frozen out by that criticism.

To see why the dissensus critics regard such neglect of the marginalized as inexcusable, one could consult two formidably learned and unrelenting books by a contributor to the *Ideology* volume, Richard Slotkin: *Regeneration through Violence* and *The Fatal Environment.*[18] Rendering the "frontier experience" from the vantage of the decimated natives and the ravaged landscape, Slotkin's work constitutes a macabre correction of the late Henry Nash Smith's classic (and classically liberal) *Virgin Land: The American West as Symbol and Myth* (1950). In one of Smith's last, characteristically magnanimous, essays, included in the Bercovitch-Jehlen collection as a kind of trophy, he acceded to Slotkin's implied critique of his work, confessing that he had been blind to the way such catchwords as "free land" and "frontier initiative" had served to rationalize atrocities. There could be no more affecting testimony to the power of ideological analysis, in conjunction with thorough research, to put liberal illusions to rout.

As Bercovitch conceives it, a New Americanist's goal in studying American "classics" is to solve a problem that the liberal critics never perceived, since they took at face value the "No, in thunder!" posture of those mildly alienated books. What, Bercovitch asks, is the *real* role of dissent in a nation that was founded on a massive defiance of authority? Is not the rhetoric of dissent a safety valve for the system, a means of reaffirming the Revolution without triggering another and less welcome one? If so, our standard authors were not the idealists and mavericks that they supposed but ideological jesters in the court of a tyrant, laissez-faire capitalism. While they thought they were urging their countrymen to resist the tyranny of the majority, they were actually doing the bidding of a socioeconomic regime that had learned how, in Bercovitch's words, "to circumscribe the bounds of perception, thought, and desire."[19]

Here we see something akin to Herbert Marcuse's once modish notion of repressive tolerance being retrofitted to the antebellum world. That notion automatically posits a state or Machiavellian elite that orchestrates dissent from behind the scenes. But these are severely impoverished premises for understanding the Jacksonian period, in which a stable ruling class worthy of the name could scarcely be said to have existed. Not a fine-tuned repressiveness but a raw dynamism, working toward ends that few paused to imagine, characterized the society as a whole. And thus it may be a quixotic gain for critics to brush aside the "deceptive" appearance of moral independence in, say, Emerson or Thoreau in order to reveal a puppet of the system.[20] If the "safety valve" argument has any verisimilitude at all, it might be more plausibly applied to the New Americanists' own recent dissent, which is proving to be quite compatible with the normal pursuit of academic self-interest.

In the best sixties spirit, both Bercovitch and Jehlen are committed to regarding the democratic American dream mainly as an instrument of social control. Yet they also remain liberal enough to concede that the application of this idea to literary texts causes them some misgivings, on two counts. In the first place, the goal of stripping liberal fudge from classic texts can turn the critic, in Jehlen's words, into "a sort of adversary of the work she or he analyzes."[21] Wary of being taken in by an establishment author's rhetorical charm, a New Americanist will maintain a clinically humorless attitude toward, say, the extravagant experimentalism of a Melville or the whimsical irony of Hawthorne or Thoreau. The resultant discourse, to judge from some of the *Ideology* chapters, can get bogged down in its own methodological complexities, meanwhile resisting on principle the sophistication of the text itself.

Concomitantly, there is the problem of reductionism, which Jehlen names as such. As she says with confessed uneasiness, for a New Americanist, "The work that presents its conception of the world as natural through the apparent spontaneity of character and story conceals that way 'its real ideological determinants,' which it is the critic's task to reveal. The ideal and apparently absolute world orbits an ideological star in a contingent universe."[22] This striking image is meant to imply that the critic will be paying scant attention to the verbal texture and manifest structure of a given work, but it has a further connotation as well: the choice of a "star" at such remote range can be an arbitrary deductive matter. What New Americanists discover in a standard work is usually a defect of consciousness that they had posited from the outset—most often some form of compliance with Jacksonian selfishness, racism, sexism, homophobia, or environmental rapacity. The conclusion can prove disappointingly commonplace after the dazzling theoretical moves that have led up to it.

To see such adversarial reductiveness at closer range, consider one of the essays in the Bercovitch-Jehlen book, "The Politics of *The Scarlet Letter*," written by the same Jonathan Arac who gave us the subtle and balanced assessment of Matthiessen's struggles. For Arac, *The Scarlet Letter* can be best understood as a fictional counterpart of Hawthorne's sycophantic *Life of Franklin Pierce*, an indirect brief for a "progressive conservative" quietism ultimately directed against abolition. Hester Prynne's failure to make a lasting choice for "passion" over "principle" leaves her, so far as Arac is concerned, "a double of the Puritan establishment"—a standpatter in her time as Hawthorne was in his. And the novel as a whole, by positing an act of personal sin as the cause of Hester's misery, retracts its tentative hints of feminism and substitutes the political soothing syrup of "trust in the future."[23]

"Students," writes Arac, "judge *The Scarlet Letter* an intransitive 'work of art,' unlike, say, *Uncle Tom's Cabin*, which is 'propaganda' rather than 'art,' for it aims to change your life. If recent revaluation has shown that *Uncle Tom's Cabin* is also art, may it not be equally important to show that *The Scarlet Letter* is also propaganda—*not* to change your life?"[24] In other words, Hawthorne's real message is that we needn't get agitated over slavery and the oppression of women. The fact that slavery is not actually mentioned in *The Scarlet Letter* cannot faze the critic, since his method points an accusing finger at precisely what the text has "repressed."

Indeed, that method allows Arac to sermonize about any peripheral topic that crosses his mind:

> *The Scarlet Letter* ends with the death of Hester, and its writing began with the death of Hawthorne's own mother. The difference is that Mrs. Hawthorne committed no crime in marrying a mariner who then happened to die in Surinam of yellow fever. Hawthorne's novel transforms his life situation by adding accountable guilt. A complex social fact—involving American trade relations in the Caribbean, the inadequacy of mosquito control, the conditions of medical knowledge—is turned into a crime. Something that might require political action—as it did to empower public health undertaking in the nineteenth century—becomes a matter for ethical judgment and psychological reflection.[25]

Caught up in this righteous diatribe, a reader could almost forget that the fictional "transformation" of the elder Hawthorne's death, when the romancer-to-be was just four years old, into Hester Prynne's adultery is a pure invention of Arac's, unconnected to a single cited line of *The Scarlet Letter*.

Arac does realize that his wrath is taking him ever farther from the romance that Hawthorne actually wrote, and he tries to introduce qualifications to the argument. But they come to nothing, for in Arac's mind the real scarlet letter belongs to Hawthorne for having cobbled together the *Life of Franklin Pierce*. And we can appreciate his dilemma. How is a New Americanist to remain true to his democratic principles without despising a sacred-cow author who not only temporized over slavery but tied his fortunes to those of an anti-abolitionist president?

One potential solution does beckon. As Bercovitch points out, ideological analysis can be either negative or positive, stripping humanist absolutes of their universal pretensions or, alternatively, locating in those same absolutes "a utopian criticism of the status quo, a vision of human possibilities that provides the ground for reconstituting the moral and material norms of society."[26] The liberal critics had practiced only the latter, positive-ideological, kind of analysis, praising literary visionaries such as Whitman and Thoreau for upholding an antimaterialistic conception of the American dream. But when a New Americanist prefers to spare certain authors from destructive treatment, he can apply this same approach in a less "spiritual" variant. Such is the tack adopted by Donald Pease, the other chief Matthiessen revisionist, not only in his *Ideology* chapter on Melville but also in his recent book, *Visionary Compacts: American Renaissance Writings in Cultural Context.*

Pease, we recall, had earlier charged the liberal-consensus critics with having misread the American Renaissance according to a cold war bias—that is, as a morality play between good (democratic, artistic) individualism and bad (conformist, popular) regimentation. But as Pease now emphasizes, the great threat in the 1850s was not conformism but secession, and the dominant myths of self-realization and material progress offered no hope of preventing the approaching cataclysm. In this setting, according to Pease, our great writers perceived "the need for a recuperated public will,"[27] and so they proposed "visionary compacts" that could renegotiate the American Revolution in humane and collective terms. It seems, then, that the authors whom Matthiessen had praised for their superiority to mass politics, and whom Arac distrusts for much the same reason, were actually practical thinkers, would-be midwives to a national rebirth that could have obviated the Civil War if only they had been heeded.

In one sense or another Pease considers Emerson, Whitman,

Hawthorne, Melville, and even Poe to have shared in this search for forms of collective responsibility contrary to the "Revolutionary mythos" of sheer self-development and laissez-faire. Oddly enough, his hero among these figures is Arac's villain, Hawthorne, whose "disgust with the corruption of partisan politics"[28] led him, in *The Scarlet Letter,* to offer a contrary model whereby Jacksonian anarchy is checked by the Puritan covenant.[29] "Hester and Arthur," he notes approvingly, eventually learn to "put their most intimate needs into the service of the community's."[30] Here Arac's thematic opposites, passion and principle, get their valences reversed; it is presumably by having opted for the public good that both Hawthorne and his protagonists are now said to be surmounting fictive cheap thrills and showing us how to avert a war or, what seems even worse from Pease's standpoint, personal isolation.

In contrast to Arac, then, who grasps Hawthorne's penchant for equivocation and disapproves of it, Pease treats *The Scarlet Letter* as a virtual tract, a hymn to the Puritan polis whose members "care for each other, precisely because their relations are grounded in a collective memory."[31] Yet one point on which Hawthorne does not equivocate is his harsh judgment of that very community, "the most intolerant brood that ever lived."[32] In order to cling to the only thesis that can allow him to respect *The Scarlet Letter,* Pease substantially rewrites Hawthorne's romance.

Pease fares no better in trying to credit other "Renaissance" figures with having urged visionary compacts upon their contemporaries. Poe, as he observes, supplies only a negative example, a registering of extreme dispossession and cultural vertigo. Thoreau, who gets mentioned in this study as seldom as possible, "elevates disconnection into a national ideological value," and so in his way does Emerson, whose doctrine of self-reliance, Pease remarks, "enjoined all Americans to share Emerson's contempt for the masses."[33] Presumably, this is not what a visionary compact is supposed to accomplish.

For some reason, however, Pease remains undeterred by these rebuffs. As a culminating instance of the visionary compact at work, he addresses *Moby-Dick,* which, in the "cold war" reading, allegedly pits Ahab's totalitarianism against Ishmael's democratic pluralism. Such an apprehension of Ishmael, Pease claims, turns the individualistic "negative freedom" of Melville's age and ours into a saving virtue, whereas Melville actually took pains to show that the irresponsibly "transcendentalizing" Ishmael *needs* the imperiously resolute Ahab as a palliative for his chronic depression and boredom. "If the Cold War consensus would turn *Moby-Dick* into a figure through which it could read the free world's survival in the future struggle with totalitarianism, Melville, as it were, speaks back through the same figure, asking us if we can survive the free world Ishmael has handed down to us."[34] Here, in the guise of rescuing *Moby-Dick* from one anachronistic reading, Pease subjects it to another one; if Melville isn't proleptically endorsing the cold war, then he must be warning us against it.

What chiefly marks Pease as a New Americanist, despite his indulgence toward the Matthiessen canon, is his eagerness for moral certainties about the relation between the books and the politics that he admires. He cannot rest until he has thinned out *Moby-Dick* to a sermon that a liberated eighties congregation could approve while passing the plate for the nuclear freeze. No room is left for the improvisational and morbid sarcasm that make the actual experience of reading *Moby-Dick* such a rollercoaster ride. Pease, it appears, cannot imagine that a great writer could have at once depicted and shared a deadly incapacity either to believe in anything or to rest content with his lurking nihilism. But Melville, as his rapid descent into the maelstrom of *Pierre* suggests, hearkened to inner voices that had nothing at all to say about visionary compacts with his countrymen.

IV

PEASE'S AND ARAC'S HANDICAPS in dealing with canonical books could be said to come down to the perennial problem of whether, and how, to honor the principle of authorial intentionality. Pease feels compelled to invent new, politically upbeat intentions for nineteenth-century works so as to purge them of their distasteful irresoluteness and irony. Arac, as a "negative-ideological" seeker of hidden complicities, sees the injunction to honor conscious intentions as a reactionary trap; he wants to interrogate Hawthorne with a brighter bulb than that master of twilight effects would have found comfortable. And other New Americanists, expressing poststructuralist convictions, deny on epistemological grounds that authorially determined meaning can be reliably ascertained at all; "intentions" are just artifacts produced by interpretations.[35]

Such scruples must be put aside, however, when New Americanists turn from analyzing the canon to proposing additions to it. The only way to resuscitate a disprized tradition—literature written by evangelical women, escaped slaves, regionalists, and members of the working class—is to reconstruct what its exponents were trying to accomplish and lend one's respect to that effort. At such a time, it is hard to tell the difference between a New Americanist and, say, a traditional historical scholar who allowed the New Criticism to come and go without being at all dismayed by "the intentional fallacy." Sooner or later, though, an abrupt shift of theoretical posture will remind us that this objectivity toward selected movements has a polemical, establishment-baiting motive. Whenever a New Americanist offers to bind interpretation to original intentions, it is understood that no canonical authors need apply.

Take, for example, Jane Tompkins's *Sensational Designs: The Cultural Work of American Fiction, 1790–1860.* This book is already widely considered the strongest defense of the sentimental novel, and thus the most damaging assault on the Matthiessen canon, yet devised. And predictably, it advocates a strict intentionalist approach to the works it tries to rescue from disfavor, not just *Uncle Tom's Cabin* and Susan Warner's *The Wide, Wide World* but also lightly regarded novels by Charles Brockden Brown and James Fenimore Cooper. All of them, says Tompkins, produce redundant and implausible effects not through ineptitude but through didactic intent. They are—indeed, literary texts in general are—best understood "not as works of art embodying enduring themes in complex forms, but as attempts to redefine the social order."[36]

This austere definition is aimed against critics who disregard differences of genre and try to rank all works by "eternal" standards of judgment—in reality, modernist ones. And Tompkins's argument succeeds brilliantly in persuading us to give Cooper and the others a second look. As she urges,

> The endlessly repeated rescue scenes in *Arthur Mervyn* and *The Last of the Mohicans,* the separation of families in *Uncle Tom,* and the Job-like trials of faith in *The Wide, Wide World,* while violating what seem to be self-evident norms of probability and formal economy, serve as a means of stating and proposing solutions for social and political predicaments. The benevolent rescuers of *Arthur Mervyn* and the sacrificial mothers of *Uncle Tom's Cabin* act out scenarios that teach readers what kinds of behavior to emulate or shun. . . ."[37]

We must grant these purposes from the outset, says Tompkins in the voice of an orthodox intentionalist, or stigmatize ourselves as prisoners of a single time-bound aesthetic.

But when Tompkins turns to her bête noire, Hawthorne, and contemplates his status as the critics' darling, she reverses her premises entirely. Now she denies that we will ever be able to establish what Hawthorne meant those works to say, since all we can ever see in them is *our own* evolving intentions. For

Tompkins the cognitive skeptic, "the 'true nature' of a literary work is a function of the critical perspective that is brought to bear upon it."[38] Critics, then, don't "overlook" and then "discover" certain features inhering in the work; they quite literally *create* an essentially new text in the act of declaring it to contain those features. This theory has the desired effect of minimizing the credit that Hawthorne deserves for his fame. Unfortunately, however, it boomerangs on all the rest of *Sensational Designs*. If there is no ongoing Hawthorne to be understood by the light of his intentions, then there is no Warner or Stowe, either, and Tompkins's efforts to demonstrate the enduring merits of *Uncle Tom's Cabin* and *The Wide, Wide World* become pointless.

On a closer look, moreover, Tompkins appears less committed to intentionality even for the outsider texts than she lets on. In particular, she feels no reluctance to ascribe her own radical feminist inclinations to the sentimental authors whom she champions against male chauvinist detractors. According to her reading, *Uncle Tom's Cabin*—which *was* written by a feminist, though a moderate and domestic one—has less to do with abolishing slavery than with curbing male power. At the heart of the book, Tompkins asserts, lies Stowe's yearning for a "new matriarchy" featuring "the removal of the male from the center to the periphery of the human sphere."[39] But this antagonistic conception is false to the spirit of a novel whose hero is a man, whose most repulsive figure after Simon Legree is a woman, Marie St. Clare, and whose every page cries out for charity and reconciliation, not sex war.

As for the touching but monotonously homiletic *Wide, Wide World*, Tompkins does what she can to compensate for the fact that its heroine, Ellen Montgomery, receives much of her moral guidance from a sanctimonious young preacher who, with Warner's enthusiastic approval, teaches her to abase herself before another authoritative male, Christ. Ellen and other sentimental heroines, Tompkins wishfully asserts, were made to perfect themselves in Christian submission only because it "gave them a place from which to launch a counter-strategy against their worldly masters that would finally give them the upper hand."[40] The lifelong evangelical Warner would have been mortified by the drawing of such a lesson from her pious apologue.[41] Tompkins's distortions of both Warner and Stowe appear to betray a worry on her part that such spiritualizing authors may need cosmetic improvement before they can find acceptance among secularist contemporary champions of women's rights.

It is easy for Tompkins to show, however, that writers like Warner were discriminated against from the outset by the kingmakers of literary culture. Perhaps the liveliest pages in *Sensational Designs* are those comparing Hawthorne's personal connections with Warner's disadvantages. "Unlike Hawthorne," Tompkins writes, "Warner had not lived in Concord, did not know Emerson and his circle, was not published by Fields, had not known Longfellow at college, had not roomed with a former [*sic*] President of the United States whose campaign biography she would write and who would get her a consulship when she needed money."[42] The idea is that this old-boy network, extended down through succeeding generations, is mainly responsible for Hawthorne's canonical status.

The building of literary reputations *is* a political matter, just as Tompkins says; powerful cliques select "classics" that will flatter their own values, interests, and claims to special discernment. Yet not even Tompkins can finally convince herself that Hawthorne, in contrast to the luckless Warner, made it all the way from the 1830s until now on the strength of his connections alone. There is, she grudgingly says, "something there" that has allowed *The Scarlet Letter* to serve as the culture's Rorschach blot. "That very description of *The Scarlet Letter* as a text that invited constant redefinition," she admits, "might be put forward, finally, as the one true basis on which to found its claim to immortality."[43]

What could that "something" be that has underwritten the remarkable staying power of *The Scarlet Letter*? Surely it must have to do with the book's famous ambiguity—not just its surface coyness, which can become tiresome, but its capacity to sustain any number of plausible general interpretations without losing its power as a story. That ambiguity, we recall, strikes some New Americanists as nothing more than the expression of a contemptible political cowardice—a cowardice, I should add, of which Hawthorne may well have been guilty. But until now at least, "posterity" doesn't seem to have cared. Even if, as Tompkins insists, posterity is only an unending chain of interest groups, the net effect of all that diversity has been to give at least some advantage to authors who can lend imaginative sympathy to rival characters and points of view.

All the liabilities of the New Americanist enterprise that I have touched upon—its self-righteousness, its tendency to conceive of American history only as a highlight film of outrages, its impatience with artistic purposes other than "redefining the social order," and its choice of critical principles according to the partisan cause at hand—suggest that there may yet be a role for other styles of reading American literature. It ought to be possible for critics who are politically unembarrassed by ambiguity and irony to leave "cold war" rationalizations behind, branch out from the canon, yet continue to affirm what radicals sometimes forget, that there is no simple correlation between political correctness and artistic power.

That is precisely the aim of an ambitious and at least partially successful new book that professes cultural pluralism while departing sharply from New Americanist premises: David S. Reynolds's *Beneath the American Renaissance: The Subversive Imagination in the Age of Emerson and Melville.* Drawing on prodigious research in obscure sources, Reynolds introduces us to a great many little-known and forgotten popular writings in the antebellum era—works that abound not only in the prudish moralism we have been led to expect but also, more surprisingly, in atheism, nihilism, licentious sensationalism, and working-class anarchism. That fact in itself should give pause to theorists like Bercovitch who claim to know how the Jacksonian order "circumscribed the bounds of perception, thought, and desire."

Reynolds, however, has no wish to adopt nineteenth-century iconoclastic writers as political heroes. The "subversive imagination," for him, is not a standard of virtue to which we should hold our classic authors accountable; it is rather something those authors found ready at hand in their culture—raw material that they needed to bring under control before they could write works of permanent interest.

In making this point, Reynolds is disputing the high-culture emphasis of Matthiessen's *American Renaissance,* which linked its literary giants to Shakespeare, to Coleridge, to T. S. Eliot, and to one another but not to the everyday world they actually inhabited. On the other hand, Reynolds accepts without question Matthiessen's canon, modestly and uncontroversially expanded to include Dickinson and Poe. Indeed, he dares to specify a quality, "literariness"—a dense, archetypally concentrated suggestiveness deriving from the fusing and decontextualizing of many rhetorical strategies—that allegedly distinguishes all the classic works of the period from their thematically similar but "shapelessly skeptical" counterparts in the penny press.[44]

Reynolds shows in convincing detail that every one of the "Renaissance" heavyweights was significantly affected by popular culture but managed to replace its sensationalism and its crude contradictions with an inclusive vision. Thus Poe began his career in the world of journalism, borrowing its lurid themes, but he purged them of gore, sensuality, and rant. His fiction shifts attention from the grisly deed to the mind that is driven to it. Analytic power, humor, even moral judgment—a trait that many critics, ignorant of the quasi-pornographic fiction and reportage that Poe subtilized, have failed to detect in him—lend his fiction a crucial detachment and control.

As for *The Scarlet Letter,* Reynolds shows that none of the ingredients of its plot could have surprised Hawthorne's contemporaries. The sinning preacher and his fallen parishioner who must wear a dishonoring letter on her dress, the female reformer, the wronged and vindictive husband, the hypocritical

Puritans, even the child who impishly botches her catechism were all anticipated in widely read works. In those books, however, moralism and prurience coexisted without reconciliation; one was merely an excuse for the other. By contrast, *The Scarlet Letter* is unrelievedly *about* morally purgative efforts that only make matters worse. As in Poe's case, but with more sustained ethical intensity, the focus has shifted from shocking acts to boundary-testing minds that weigh the consequences of those acts. And in Hester Prynne Hawthorne merged the antithetical stereotypes of the sinner and the social angel, thus salvaging complexity and tragedy from the unpromising stuff of melodrama.

One further example, that of Whitman, can epitomize Reynolds's approach—and also begin to suggest its limitations. Here again the critic denies that "subversiveness" arises spontaneously in the alienated author without a prior grounding in the culture. As against the common assumption that Whitman "had begun as a conventional hack writer of moralistic fiction and poetry and then experienced some dramatic change that made him a literary iconoclast,"[45] Reynolds traces the iconoclasm to popular sources. In his journalistic years, Reynolds argues, Whitman "let reformist vitriol flow from his pen for the sheer subversive delight of it, without much attention to programs for change."[46] His early, best-selling temperance novel *Franklin Evans* is a fairly standard exemplar of "dark" or "immoral" reform literature, whose centerpiece is the nominally condemned depravity in which it wallows.

Whitman's fiction and journalism of that period, Reynolds says, dealt with sordid materials—drunkenness and delirium tremens, crushing poverty, depraved lust, infanticide—that were still considered too indecorous for inclusion in a serious poem. To become the Walt Whitman whom we know, he needed only to alter his vantage on those materials, moving from sensation mongering into moral paradox and self-dramatization as the man who turns his back on nothing. Reynolds

notes this change occurring in Whitman's earliest known jot-
tings in free verse, in his notebook of 1847:

> *I am the poet of slaves, and of the masters of*
> *slaves. . . .*
> *I am the poet of sin,*
> *For I do not believe in sin.*

Here, says Reynolds, "we find Whitman starting his flight
beyond slavery or antislavery, beyond sin or reform of sin to
broader moral regions. . . . The intensity of dark-reform rhetoric has carried him beyond conventional moral categories altogether. . . . *The poeticization of sin has led toward literariness.*"[47]
   What does it mean, however, to say that "the intensity of
dark-reform rhetoric" itself was responsible for creating Whitman's new, all-encompassing persona? Nothing comparable
occurred to other practitioners of such rhetoric. If Whitman in
1847 is already heading toward "broader moral regions" than
those envisioned in his sources, something besides those sources
must be taking him there.
   Consider, for example, Whitman's awareness of his homosexuality, a fact whose importance Matthiessen gauged but was
cowed into minimizing. To disbelieve in sin was for Whitman
a liberating achievement, a deflection of potential self-blame
into a defiantly healthy public stance. But Reynolds, amazingly
in view of the biographical tradition since Roger Asselineau's
The Evolution of Walt Whitman in 1960, refuses to acknowledge
the poet's erotic bent at all. It was merely Whitman's disapproval of tacky romance fiction, says Reynolds, that led him "to
emphasize adhesive love, or affection between men," as a literary theme; he was just employing a "means of avoiding the love
plot."[48]
   Unfortunately, *Beneath the American Renaissance* repeatedly falls
into such mechanical insistence on its taxonomies. Reynolds's
efforts to find "frontier humor" and "macabre newspaper

imagery" in Emerson and Hawthorne are sometimes far-fetched.[49] *Walden* strikes him as aiming chiefly not at articulating a transcendental, nature-based individualism but merely at "reinvigorating" a range of imagery borrowed from labor, temperance, antitobacco, antilicentiousness, and antislavery movements.[50] And he further maintains that in calling *Moby-Dick* a wicked book, Melville meant only that it exposed certain "visionary and Oriental devices" from popular literature as "mere fantasy and wish fulfillment"[51]—an apprehension even more remote from the living Melville than Donald Pease's "anti–cold war" reading. It is hard to remain impressed by Reynolds's insistence on "literariness" when he keeps subordinating it to such influence hunting and pigeonholing.[52]

Of much greater concern for our purpose here, however, is Reynolds's deductive approach to literary value. Take, for instance, his telling declaration that *Uncle Tom's Cabin*, though praiseworthy in several respects, "misses literary status because its warring elements do not *fuse* to create metaphysical ambiguity or multilayered symbols."[53] It is something of a shock, so late in the game, to see these Brooks-and-Warren New Critical criteria taken as defining the boundary between real and ersatz literature. *Beneath the American Renaissance*, blithely subtracting aesthetic points from books that advocate a cause and make their meaning plain, will strike critics like Bercovitch and Jehlen as a perfect instance of what they mean by ideology—as an attempt, that is, to bind us to "standards" that look eternally valid but merely reflect the liberal reluctance to embrace a nonhierarchical idea of culture.

The broader qualities that Reynolds upholds—moral inclusiveness, resonance, psychological complexity, irony, wit—do form a sound rationale for the canon that has prevailed since Matthiessen's day. But this is hardly surprising, since the choosing of "classics" and the naming of indispensable virtues that a classic must exhibit are really a single act. It does not occur to Reynolds that there are arguably major works of American literary art—*Sister Carrie* is one, and *Uncle Tom's Cabin* is surely another—that wield enormous cultural and emotional power without showing much distinction at the sentence level. A critic should be prepared to set aside his checklist of authentically literary traits and ask how this can be so.

In *Hard Facts: Setting and Form in the American Novel,* for example, Philip Fisher maintains that it is not Stowe's artistic deficiency but our own immersion in modernist conventions that accounts for the trouble twentieth-century readers have experienced in coming to terms with *Uncle Tom's Cabin.* According to Fisher, our contemporary expectations for a great novel have been conditioned by ironic post-Flaubertian fiction that bristles with alertness against clichés and unearned feelings. But in the history of the Anglo-American novel from Richardson onward, the central tradition has been a quite opposite one—precisely that of sentimentalism. At the heart of the sentimental novel, Fisher says, lies "the experimental extension of . . . normal states of primary feeling to people from whom they have been previously withheld. . . . Sentimentality is . . . anti-ironic in exactly the degree that the modern ironic form is antisentimental."[54] As Fisher demonstrates, when *Uncle Tom's Cabin* is reread as an expression of this expansive impulse, it appears as a richly complex and self-integrated epic—subtle, various, and legitimately moving.

Yet we needn't have waited for Fisher or for Tompkins to come to Stowe's defense. Already in 1962, Edmund Wilson found *Uncle Tom's Cabin* "a much more impressive work than one has ever been allowed to suspect."[55] "We feel," wrote Wilson, "that the dams of discretion . . . have been burst by a passionate force that, compressed, has been mounting behind them, and which, liberated, has taken the form of a flock of lamenting and ranting, prattling and preaching characters, in a drama that demands to be played to the end." Stowe outdid herself in this one novel, according to Wilson, by virtue of the nobility and urgency of her theme: the mortal peril that slavery was posing to an entire nation's soul. Her vision of a truly Christian Union not only fired her imagination, it also spared her from the sectionalism and scapegoating that had marred most abolitionist literature.[56]

F. O. Matthiessen's precariously balanced aesthetic-political vision, at once poignant and impossible, has by now split into two styles of thought that tend to correct each other's prejudices. Jane Tompkins and David Reynolds could be said to epitomize that standoff. The radical Tompkins grasps the relativity of literary values and fruitfully defies the elitism of taste that the "aesthetic" Matthiessen tradition has never overcome, but she and other New Americanists have trouble establishing methodological ground rules to cover both the works they promote and the works they resent. Reynolds, unconstrained by left politics, can freely acknowledge, as Matthiessen did, that the political elusiveness of already canonical "Renaissance" texts is intimately connected with their durability, but he turns that elusiveness into a universally valid test for entry to the pantheon, a nonnegotiable demand that would freeze the canon where it is.

The canon will change nonetheless, for a simple reason that Tompkins and her sociologically minded colleagues are best prepared to grasp. While we have all been debating which nineteenth-century works "have lasting appeal," most of us have forgotten to ask: *appeal to whom?* As the academy has come to dominate what is published and taught about premodern literature, the whole notion of making a diffuse "educated public" into an arbiter has become ever more implausible. The truth is that for any works written before the last seventy years or so, the most influential academics get to decide who's in and who's out. And the New Americanists themselves seem destined to become the next establishment in their field. They will be right about the most important books and the most fruitful ways of studying them because, as they always knew in their leaner days, those who hold power are right by definition.

THREE

The Parting of the Twains

SUSAN GILLMAN, *Dark Twins: Imposture and Identity in Mark Twain's America* (Chicago: U of Chicago P, 1989).

SHERWOOD CUMMINGS, *Mark Twain and Science: Adventures of a Mind* (Baton Rouge: Louisiana State UP, 1988).

> *"How empty is theory in presence of fact!"*
> —Hank Morgan in *A Connecticut Yankee*

I

ONE NEED GET no further into Susan Gillman's *Dark Twins* than the back cover to become aware that this will be a landmark book—one establishing a previously untested, if also an inevitable, vantage on America's best-known writer. In Gillman's study, says the publisher's description, Mark Twain "stands forth finally as a representative man, not only a child of his culture, but also as one implicated in a continuing American anxiety about freedom, race, and identity." And then follows a seal of methodological approval from Frank Lentricchia of Duke, now arguably the most influential of academic critic-theorists. Gillman's "superb book," Lentricchia says, "comes out on the side of those who find too much recent theory as [*sic*] needlessly abstract, formalistic, ahistorical; on the side of those, that is, who call for a materially dense, historically engaged practice."

We see at once, then, that in the academic theory wars Susan Gillman has joined the currently ascendant army, which eschews the "formalistic" and the "ahistorical" (alias Yale-style deconstruction) in favor of a vaguely Marxizing ("materially dense, historically engaged") spirit. And we get a forecast of the predictable result: here Mark Twain, that testy and rambunctious would-be individualist, will be exposed as merely "representative" after all, "implicated" in furtive anxieties that he shared with other men of the Gilded Age.

If this sounds a bit lugubrious, it is: *Dark Twins* turns out to be a grimly humorless work which all but overlooks Twain's own humor. It does so, however, not through ineptitude but by design. Humor, in Twain's assessment, is "the natural enemy of royalties, nobilities, privileges and all kindred swindles"— which is to say that the humorist is a born democrat who knows hypocrisy when he sees it. But in asserting that Mark Twain was "a deeply historicized writer,"[1] Gillman means to erase any such analytic distance between Twain and the objects of his satire. In the righteous outlook that Gillman, Lentricchia, and the academic-critical vanguard in general now share, to "historicize" an author is precisely to set forth the ways in which, lacking full autonomy as a reflective consciousness, he fell in with the self-protective mental strategies of his day.

This sort of analysis is known in the profession as social constructionism, as in "the social construction of reality." Social constructionists, that is, take as their starting point a belief—plausible enough in itself—that no values, ideas, or even selves are or have ever been primary units that resist further reduction. Instead, all aspects of culture, including the standards by which we might be tempted to judge the meaning or importance of a literary work, are thought to have emerged from power struggles, and the real object of critical attention ought to be the aftermath of such struggle—namely, the ideology devised by the winning party. The function of ideology is to justify the new structure of domination as something ordained by God or nature or history; and the proper function of criticism is to undo that mystification.

In theory at least, social constructionism looks like a promising if somewhat inconsistent agenda. (Inconsistent because, of course, social constructionists will not brook seeing their own values, ideas, and selves submitted to reductive analysis.) After all, culturally sanctioned "reality" in any given era is indisputably an artifact that serves the interests of ruling groups while suppressing or at least failing to tap the greater part of human potentiality. So long as social constructionists confine themselves to studying the common denominators of a majority belief system—its tacit consensus, say, about medical wisdom, political virtue, sanity and insanity, foreigners and outcasts, licit sexual practices, gender roles, race relations, or the supernatural—they can produce eye-opening results.

It is already evident, however, that this still-young style of discourse risks becoming a bore and even something of a sham. In the first place, the social constructionists' exclusive claim to a skeptical apprehension of history is simply false; their sense of mission in purporting to strip the mask from a vanished society's guilty face is made possible by a willful obliviousness to other people's scholarship. Where they really part company with traditionalists is in their puritanical concern to maintain a politically correct position—one that will be guiltless of sexism, racism, economic individualism, and other distortions of a presumed state of nature. In practice, this spirit of post-sixties conformism translates into a perpetually scandalized relation to the past—a phobic manner that is the very reverse of historiographic sophistication.

When social constructionism turns its focus from mass phenomena to the work of major artists, moreover, another crippling limitation comes to light. Most serious readers value classic writings not for their typicality but for whatever seems unique and irreplaceable about them. But the social constructionists' campaign against hierarchy and transcendence leaves them unwilling to dwell on anything that might appear to exempt an author from the collective unconscious of his age. The result is a sharp disjuncture between our experience of the writer's work and the critic's leveling account of it. As this movement increases its sway, "implicating" more and more authors in its indictment of the past for falling short of egalitarian rectitude, we can begin to feel like viewers of *Invasion of the Body Snatchers,* wondering which literary figure will be the next to be replaced by a hollow automaton. And now we know: it is Mark Twain.

From the opening pages of *Dark Twins,* Gillman gives fair warning that she will be doing her best to submerge Twain in the ideological climate surrounding him. Her goal, she says, is to pass beyond "Mark Twain's own unstable personal identity" and "to (re)create the dialogue between Twain's language of identity and the cultural vocabularies available to him." Such "literary analysis of cultural history" will allow her to show "how Twain's most apparently unique and idiosyncratic representations of problematic identity engage with late-nineteenth-century efforts to classify human behavior within biological, sexual, racial, and psychological parameters." "At the same time," she adds, "Mark Twain's America is also representative in its denials and silences, in what he, like his culture, dismissed as trivial, disguised, or concealed, or simply did not acknowledge." Correlating Twain's personal repressions with those of his milieu, Gillman will allow "otherwise apparently incoherent, vestigial, and even rather silly texts to begin to articulate themselves."[2]

Articulation, however, is not a concept with which social constructionists can feel altogether comfortable. It smacks to them of those tidy unities of theme and form that the long-vanished New Critics were all too eager to celebrate. Criticism, they insist, must now become centrifugal or "dialogic," welcoming the warring voices and mixed effects that result from a thorough interpenetration of literature, culture, and material conditions. It is these innumerable correlations that Gillman intends to develop, remaining careful to avoid the fallacy of "privileging" any single factor over the others. As a consequence, her language remains deliberately opaque, relying on such all-purpose couplings as "speaks to," "engages with," "becomes entangled with," "situates at the intersection of," "perceived in terms that replicate," and "thoroughly saturated in the context of." The real point of *Dark Twins* would seem to be less an explicit thesis than the weaving of these loops, thereby thwarting at every turn the "idealizing" reader's urge to consider a given work a willed creation or to situate Mark Twain himself somewhere outside the sphere of generally shared ideology.

It is nonetheless possible to discern in *Dark Twins* a more particular biographical argument—even if it rarely stays in focus for long. Gillman takes as her starting point the familiar observation that Mark Twain, who was always fascinated by the idea of twinship or doubling, eventually developed a full-scale theory of dual personality and unconscious creativity. "I argue," she declares in a characteristically soft-edged passage,

> that Twain's early reliance on literal, literary conventions of external, consciously divided identity becomes entangled with a social conception that treats identity as culturally controlled and then gives way to an imposture that is increasingly internal, unconscious, and therefore uncontrollable: a psychological as opposed to a social condition. Finally, though, even these distinctions—external/internal, conscious/unconscious, waking/dreaming—collapse into an undifferentiated darkness, as Mark Twain, during the much-debated dark period of "pessimism" and artistic "failure," confronted the impossibility of his arriving at any foundation of self and other. . . .[3]

According to this scheme, Twain began as a deft exploiter of conventions involving paired characters who bore a private meaning for his divided mind; later, influenced by current psychological and parapsychological theory, he transmuted those conventions into laws of mental functioning; and finally, wracked by a despair for which Gillman will provide her own psychopolitical explanation, he found himself unable to ascertain which was the impostor, his dream self or his waking self.

As it happens, this distinctly melodramatic account of Twain's decline contravenes the judgment of some recent scholars—most notably Louis J. Budd and Everett Emerson— who have found that the author in his last decades was neither so consistently morbid nor so befuddled as was once believed.[4] One wants to know, therefore, what new evidence of a collapse into "undifferentiated darkness" Gillman has turned up and how she feels entitled to discount the contrary findings of others. But to pose this challenge is to ask for a kind of scholarly give and take that social constructionists consider backward and servile. In their own view, they are diving for deeper psychological treasure than that which the traditionalists' allegedly positivistic assumptions will allow them to perceive. Thus Gillman already knows on a priori Freudian grounds that even in the years when everything was going right for Mark Twain, under his seeming resilience seethed a cauldron of terror, guilt, and incipient disintegration. No particular evidence, then, needs to be brought forward in confirmation of his later collapse.

The hermeticism of Gillman's method stands out clearly in the way she treats Mark Twain's notion of his own creativity. In various testimonials to what he called his "amanuensis" or subliminal helper, the author counted himself fortunate to possess a benign and reliable muselike power. The following famous recollection about the interrupted composing of *Tom Sawyer* is typical:

> I made the great discovery that when the tank runs dry you've only to leave it alone and it will fill up again in time, while you are . . . quite unaware that this unconscious and

profitable cerebration is going on. There was plenty of material now, and the book went on and finished itself without any trouble.[5]

This, surely, is a straightforward and confident statement that requires no gloss. To Gillman, however, the very term *unconscious* conjures up "unacceptable or forbidden knowledge" that must have "jeopardized" Twain's fragile peace of mind. "Unlike some literary men," she remarks, "Twain experienced creativity not through the model of the pen-penis disseminating its writings on the virgin page, but rather as illegitimately sexualized, a threateningly uncontrollable power."[6] Playing by these hermeneutic rules, the critic would have no trouble detecting a cry of pain in a greeting card.

One might think that even Gillman, in her effort to reduce Mark Twain to a "representative man," would be unable to discount the fact that he was a critic of his age and a habitual partisan of the excluded. Indeed, she hastily concedes as much. Yet on a deeper level, she finds, he proved to be something less admirable—indeed, something not quite forgivable: a Caucasian man living in a time of "segregation for blacks and medicolegal regulation of women's lives." "For a white male in particular," she explains, "what blackness and femaleness have in common is that they afford a psychic means of staking out an identity and of individuating the self by dint of difference and separation."[7] Which is to say that Twain's very selfhood, or rather his galling pretension to selfhood, was a form of segregation and patriarchal appropriation. Never pausing to ask herself why the "individuation" of white males alone and not, say, of oppressed black females as well should be considered pathological, Gillman sets out to show that the social forces Twain allegedly tried to exclude from consciousness enacted a proper revenge on his psyche.

To make this case, the critic must first establish that Twain felt a susceptibility to all things black and female. And here, for once, supporting material lies everywhere at hand. With regard to race, for example, it is clear that Twain harbored a special, lifelong fondness for the slaves who had befriended him in his boyhood and who were never far from his thoughts. Furthermore, as Gillman emphasizes, in his equatorial travels in the mid-nineties he was aesthetically smitten by black bodies and the bright clothing that adorned them—by what he called "that incomparable dissolving-view of harmonious tints, and lithe half-covered forms, and beautiful brown faces . . . and movements, free, unstudied, barren of stiffness and restraint."[8] Such language is chiefly striking, however, for its rhapsodic openness—its notable *lack* of the prurience we might be inclined to associate with "the repressed." What is missing from Gillman's argument about Mark Twain and race, then, is not raw evidence of a taboo-crossing sympathy but an acknowledgment of its place in Twain's conscious mental economy.

As for gender envy, here again we have Twain's own word that he experienced it. He railed, for example, against the drabness of Victorian male attire, voiced nostalgia for the vanished age of gaudy male costumes, eventually donned a theatrical white suit as his year-round uniform, and confided to his first biographer that "I should like to dress in a loose and flowing costume made all of silks and velvets resplendent with stunning dyes, and so would every man I have ever known; but none of us dares to venture it."[9] And as Gillman adds with a diagnostically knowing air, he kept reverting to cross-dressing themes in his fiction, briefly putting even Huck Finn in drag and writing a whole book about a woman, Joan of Arc, who compulsively garbed herself as a soldier.

In *Dark Twins,* all of these facts are made to appear self-incriminating, but the charge itself is never specified. Was Mark Twain a transvestite? A closet homosexual? Did he fear that he, like many another Southerner, would not be considered certifiably white if all his ancestors were known? Gillman doesn't say, and it seems unlikely that she has thought these questions through. All that matters for her purpose is that we acknowledge in Twain's psyche the same guilty divisions that characterized post-Reconstruction America at large. These will then become the fault lines along which his final "collapse" can be regarded as occurring.

"Mark Twain's views of sexuality," Gillman writes,

> were never formulated as consciously or self-consciously as they were on the (for him) closely allied subject of race. . . . But when sex was wedded to race, as in antebellum legal regulation of miscegenation and in turn-of-the-century popular fiction justifying Negrophobia on the grounds of uncontrollable black sexuality, the pair was obsessively returned to, in a kind of cultural return of the repressed. In this context, Mark Twain was very much a representative man.[10]

Which is to say that the critic will feel entitled to treat even Twain's *disapproval* of racial and sexual myths as a sign of his unconscious complicity in them.

Unquestionably, Mark Twain did chafe against Victorian gender roles even while subscribing to the moral proprieties that safeguarded them. Unquestionably, too, he felt a powerful identification with the blacks whom he nevertheless kept as servants, and whose aunts and uncles could have been his own father's occasionally abused slaves. We will never unravel all the complexities that such tensions caused in him. Yet a less prosecutorial critic than Gillman might well see strength rather than weakness in Twain's ability to extend his empathy freely across racial and sexual lines and to brave ridicule and gossip by finally dressing as he pleased. Gillman's own evidence, minus the raised-eyebrow rhetoric that accompanies it, suggests not that Twain's manhood was precarious but that he felt no anxious need to put up walls of machismo around his sensuous and inquisitive imagination.

Here I must emphasize that it is methodological necessity, not obtuseness, that causes Gillman to get Twain wrong. Once the critic has plugged in her Freudian interpretative machine, with its automatic sorting of everything sexual, self-aggrandizing, and cynical into "the repressed," she has no choice but to subtract those same qualities from Twain's conscious mind. The author who allegedly trembled before the black/female Other must be cast as a model Victorian gentleman—one, for example, whose "deep attraction to authorial power" had to remain wholly submerged.[11] Twain, however, was perfectly cognizant of that attraction on his part; he wrote about it at length and without apology. No less obviously, he made sex and egoism and cynicism, discreetly managed, into the tools of his daily trade as a humorist. And his comic wit derived crucially from his insistence on exempting no one, least of all himself, from his low opinion of humankind as foolish, selfish, and habitually dishonest. In order to restrict her attention to a "socially constructed" Twain, Gillman must leave out of account most of what *really* "individuates" him.

Nevertheless, Gillman's Mark Twain did eventually distinguish himself from his contemporaries on one salient point. It is, she implies, the lone respect in which he came to his post-Cartesian, antibourgeois senses. In his miserable final period—brought on in large measure, we are told, by the intolerable burden of trying to repress the black/female Other—he was allegedly compelled to realize that he had been foolish to rely on the white/masculine domains of science and law to stave off mental chaos.

In Twain's time, Gillman asserts, "neither the law, which permitted and enforced the farce of 'separate but equal,' nor science, which shored up racism with theories of 'natural' degeneration, would hold out any promise of addressing America's most pressing social problem." Nor, she hints, should we ourselves ever trust "the ostensibly neutral, value-free variables of sciences and the syllogistic structure of logical reasoning," since "increasingly complex systems of knowledge that divide and quantify experience" are nothing but vain attempts to "compensate for a lack of control over experience." Twain, she notes with satisfaction, had to learn this lesson the hard way, repenting of his delusive faith in science and recognizing the law at last for what it was, "an effort to determine individual identity and responsibility in a world where identity was unknowable."[12]

"The process that once outlawed slavery in the late 1860s legalized segregation in the 1870s and 1880s," writes Gillman, as if she had here caught out "the law," an indivisible entity, in a shameful self-contradiction. A person of good character, one gathers, should give a wide berth to such an untrustworthy institution. But as Gillman's historical examples suggest, the enemy will pop up wherever vigilance is relaxed for even a moment. She remarks fastidiously that turn-of-the-century newspapers showed themselves incapable of protesting the outcome of a trial without also "granting [the law's] premises, assuming its modes of inference," and she finds it noteworthy that Mark Twain, while contracting a healthy distrust of the judicial system, nevertheless failed to purge his vocabulary of such legalisms as "I judge" and "proves him a fool."[13] Odd as it must seem to outsiders, such alarm over everyday social practice is common among those critics who now most strenuously insist on the need to "historicize" and "contextualize."

The real trouble with Gillman's argument, however, is that Twain's deepening pessimism about human affairs did not include the rejection of science and law that she alleges. As we will presently see, in his middle and later years he became progressively *more* committed to a scientific (Darwinian) outlook that fed directly into his cosmic pessimism and his deflation of human moral pretensions. This friend of Thomas Edison's, who claimed with pride that he was the first novelist to use the telephone, the fountain pen, the typewriter, and the dictating machine, always assumed that the technological fruits of science were integral to the extension and consolidation of American democracy. As for the law, he remained capable, as Gillman is not, of distinguishing between its constructive and reactionary uses and therefore of pressing for its reform.

Gillman, one would think, could hardly avoid conceding this latter fact, since she devotes her final chapter to the last of Twain's lobbying visits to Congress, in 1906, in behalf of that most "individuating" of legal causes, copyright reform. For her, though, his performance "subverted itself, making its actual legal goals appear irrelevant." (To whom, one wonders?) On that very day, she points out, he first wore his flashy white suit, thus distracting attention from copyright to "male identity" and "gender roles."[14] But Congress apparently proved less susceptible to such distraction than Gillman is. The copyright code did get liberalized in 1909, as it had previously been in 1891, and there is good reason to think that Twain's agitation contributed to both outcomes.

Gillman's reluctance to concede these facts inevitably leads her into drastic misreadings of Mark Twain's fiction. Take, for example, *Pudd'nhead Wilson* (1894), whose penultimate twist of melodrama comes when the lawyer and amateur scientist David Wilson, hitherto considered a dunce by the self-regarding citizens of Dawson's Landing, proves through the newly developed technique of fingerprinting that a light-skinned slave must have been exchanged in infancy with the patrician child who was to become *his* slave. In the process, Wilson also solves a murder to the satisfaction of all concerned, especially Mark Twain himself, who was relieved to have found such a riveting and up-to-date way of extricating himself from a rather jumbled plot. For Gillman, however, "what is on trial in the courtroom conclusion is Wilson's method of deducing identity, his 'scientifics,' the fingerprinting system." And her verdict is guilty: "When the novel ends, its various scientific and legal bodies of knowledge—definitive means of identification and differentiation—result in no certainty at all." "Not even in the world of his own making," Gillman declares, "could [Twain] imagine liberation under the law or discover a secure basis for knowledge of self and other."[15]

To see how the critic could possibly arrive at such an inference, we need to recall the final twist of plotting in *Pudd'nhead Wilson*. The murderer, it turns out, cannot be sentenced; if he was really a slave when he committed the crime, then he was mere property and not a responsible agent. And so, in a bitter and callous flourish of comic justice on Twain's part, the former slavemaster is sold down the river and the novel abruptly ends. This final surprise conveys the author's loathing for the arbitrary and dehumanizing fictions that had kept the slave system in place. What it assuredly does not do, however, is to discredit science, technology, or law. On the contrary, as most readers have readily perceived, the technology of fingerprinting, combined with David Wilson's brilliant use of forensic logic, is precisely what *reintroduces* certainty and a measure of justice into the deceitful, fantasy-warped world of Dawson's Landing.

Gillman denigrates fingerprint analysis in part by stressing that its inventor, Francis Galton, expected it to reveal racial as well as individual traits, thus corroborating what was widely presumed to be the advanced evolutionary standing of whites. Here, then, is one of those sinister conjunctions between science and oppression that social constructionists love to bring to light. Galton, however, was obliged to admit that he had been wrong; in his own words, his "great expectations" about finding objectively discernible racial characteristics in fingerprints had been "falsified." Though Gillman quotes this statement, she fails to see its plain implication. Fingerprinting proved to be a *blow against* theories of innate racial superiority, and that blow could be struck precisely because Galton and his empirically minded readers, including the enthusiastic Mark Twain, felt beholden to impersonal standards of verification. Gillman's animus against such standards at once secures her vanguard academic credentials and renders her incapable of empathizing with Twain's mental universe.

A final sign of this failing can be found in Gillman's treatment, or rather her neglect, of *Huckleberry Finn*—of all Twain's books the one that most memorably pits the claims of experience against the dehumanizing forces of prejudice and the herd instinct. Precisely because *Huckleberry Finn* demands to be read as a work of conscious irony about race and caste, Gillman has little to say about it; she feels more at home with what she twice calls Twain's "ostentatiously incomplete" late fragments, which serve up morbid fantasies without the nuisance of ethical or aesthetic shaping. What she does remark in passing about *Huckleberry Finn*, however, is revealing enough in its way. For her, not just the troubling conclusion but the entire novel amounts to an attempted cop-out; it illustrates Twain's supposedly typical quixotic attempt to flee from history. "This evasion," Gillman says, "is especially potent in *Huckleberry Finn*, a book which gives vent to the writer's will to turn his back on civilization and light out for the territory, but always by circling back to and through the Mississippi River valley."[16] In this formulation, any elements in Twain's novel that complicate adolescent escapism are credited not to his moral intentions but to the unconscious pull of historical circumstance.

But we need only consider *Huckleberry Finn* in the light of its predecessor novel, *Tom Sawyer*, to realize that the primary impulse behind the later work cannot possibly have been escapist. In *Tom Sawyer* Twain had already tried his hand at creating an antebellum childhood idyll—albeit one that is haunted by violence, fear, guilt, sadism, and suggestions of universal egotism and cowardice. The condescending and self-satisfied narrative voice in that novel lulls us into blurred perception, allowing us both to distance ourselves from our nostalgic impulses and to indulge them anyway.[17] *Huckleberry Finn*, by contrast, abolishes such comfort with one bold stroke—the elevation of an escaped slave to a major role. However disturbing are the consequences of this metamorphosis of sleepy St. Petersburg for both the author and his readers, we can hardly deny that in *Huckleberry Finn* Twain went out of his way to render the central shame of American democracy. Thus the most telling, but in another sense the most understandable, deficiency of Gillman's *Dark Twins* is that it proposes to deal centrally with Mark Twain and race but cannot come to grips with the most pertinent and suggestive document in the record.

If, unlike Gillman, we wish to meet Mark Twain and his flawed masterpiece on terms that register what is distinctive about them, we must set aside deterministic schemes and attend to all the evidence we can find of authorial will. Which is not to say that we must rule out any interpretations that swerve from the author's conscious apprehension of his work. If Twain happened to be torn between incompatible goals—as he surely was in writing both *Huckleberry Finn* and *Puddn'head Wilson*—nothing prevents us from laying out the confusion in all its detail. Indeed, to discover just where he was being expedient or forgetful is more enlightening in the long run than to merge him with the supposed collective unconscious of his age.[18]

II

As if to illustrate these points, and more specifically to refute Susan Gillman on Mark Twain's apprehension of science and race, a very different book demands our attention here: Sherwood Cummings's *Mark Twain and Science: Adventures of a Mind*. In contrast to the social constructionist Gillman, Cummings is a committed intentionalist who sets out to depict Twain's philosophical development in all its intricacy and then to show how that knowledge affects an understanding of the fiction—including and especially *Huckleberry Finn*. While Cummings, too, is not without his blind spots, he is able, as Gillman conspicuously is not, to convey a sense of why readers care about Mark Twain and *Huckleberry Finn* in the first place. Looking at Twain through Cummings's analysis, we can appreciate the crucial difference that is made by granting an author a fully active mind, capable of reasoning its way into new positions that fundamentally affected his art.

The Twain who takes shape in Cummings's pages is no less

troubled a figure than Gillman's. Cummings understands, however, that the author's conflicts issued not in Gillman's "undifferentiated darkness" but in a remarkably energetic struggle to make sense of a world that had come unhinged from traditionally given meanings. Thus Cummings can treat Twain's eventually full-blown pessimism and determinism—most adamantly expounded in *What Is Man?*—not as a clinical phenomenon but as the bold and at times exuberant development that it was. And this may mark a long-overdue shift of emphasis in Twain studies. Not that Cummings is a lone pioneer; he acknowledges his debts to Louis J. Budd, Howard G. Baetzhold, and Alan Gribben among others.[19] With Cummings, those scholars have begun to correct the long-standing impression that Twain was an anti-intellectual who never bothered to think through the implications of his ad hoc ideas.

It remains true, however, that most critics continue to shrink from Twain's late vision of God as a morbid prankster, of man as a defectively programmed robot, of life as a meaningless chain of predators and prey, of civilization as a disease, and of death—preferably prior to emergence from the womb—as the only worthwhile gift. But as Cummings shows, Twain was responding creatively to a crisis that involved much more than his own feelings. He was exploring the metaphysical void that had been opened by scientific reductionism, whose implications he seized upon more tenaciously and dramatized more radically than any of his contemporaries.[20]

Mark Twain and Science is substantially concerned with tracing Twain's long preparation for that voyage. The story begins, of course, with the intimidating Calvinism and biblical literalism to which he was exposed in boyhood. It continues through his absorption in the deism of Thomas Paine's *Age of Reason,* the mechanistic philosophy of Oliver Wendell Holmes's *Autocrat of the Breakfast-Table,* the moral utilitarianism explained (though not advocated) in W.E.H. Lecky's *History of European Morals,* the inductivism of Hippolyte Taine's *Ancient Regime,* and, finally, the evolutionism of Darwin's *Descent of Man.* We have known for some time now that all of those books bore extraordinary significance for the autodidact Twain; Cummings now shows us precisely how and why.

Twain's readings, as Cummings says, "laid down incompatible strata" in his mind.[21] But Paine and Darwin in succession—the first actively welcomed, the second resisted for decades and then embraced with a kind of bitter zeal—sufficed to doom his faith in anthropocentrism of any kind. From Paine he learned to regard the creation as strictly obedient to divine laws—the only exception being man himself, a free agent who could live according to the findings of his reason. And Darwin then taught him, appallingly, that the exception was false: man was just another species, subject to the same indifferent forces governing all the others. No higher purpose whatsoever, then, could be discerned behind the eons of nightmarish prehistory in which our ancestors and their predecessor species scrabbled for survival. The universe must be starkly absurd, and humankind nothing more than an assemblage of stardust that has somehow evolved unique forms of cruelty and a bottomless appetite for self-delusion and self-regard.

Thanks to Cummings, we can now appreciate why the sciences that Twain originally preferred were astronomy and the classifying branches of biology: they seemed to validate the deistic harmonies celebrated by Tom Paine. By contrast, Twain sensed from the first that archaeology, paleontology, anthropology, and Darwinian biology harbored threats to his culturally given idea of a special and benign creation, and he made uneasy fun of those disciplines for as long as he could. Geology, too, was a danger area—yet Twain himself in his silver mining days had been an amateur geologist and had noted such disturbing signs as a layer of oyster shells in mountain rock, thousands of feet above sea level. Throughout his middle years, including the brief period when he tried to conform to his wife's Congregationalism, his religious feelings warred against his devotion to fact for its own sake. But he had read and annotated *The Descent of Man* with pungent intensity soon after it was published in 1871, and two decades later he gave up the struggle against Darwin's apparently unanswerable logic.

For philosophically minded American writers like Howells, Dreiser, Crane, and Norris, Darwin was the scientist who had proved that absolutes or ideals are only a hindrance to the proper understanding of nature, which he had represented not as a piece of handiwork or an illustrated sermon but merely as a locus of interlocking processes. Howells's realism, Dreiser's determinism, Crane's satire on puny man, and Norris's retreat into secular mysticism have all been plausibly associated with the impact of that revolution. Mark Twain, however, has been largely exempted from the account, thanks to both his critics' weakness for Freudian explanations and his own unsystematic practice as a novelist. Yet Cummings shows that Twain learned the Darwinian lesson more thoroughly than his friend Howells, who was given to vestigial idealizing about an underlying truth to which appearances supposedly attested. And whereas sardonic nihilism came effortlessly to the fin-de-siècle cynic Crane, it was Twain whose surviving theism was subjected to a real collision with evolutionary theory.

Twain himself, Cummings reminds us, was keenly aware that the Calvinist God could never be completely dislodged from his mind. "The religious folly you are born in you will die in," he wrote in middle age, "no matter what apparently reasonabler religious folly may seem to have taken its place meanwhile and abolished and obliterated it."[22] Thus we see in him, not surprisingly, a budding atheist who nevertheless continued to quarrel with—even to tremble before—the personal God he had deemed superfluous.

From his deistic phase onward, Twain in his more sanguine moments privately enjoyed portraying the Almighty as a doddering blusterer who lacked an adequate education in science. In the margin of Paine's *Age of Reason,* for example, he wrote: "The God of the Bible did not know that the mountains & the everlasting rocks are built on the bones of his dead creatures";

and in 1908, annotating an obsolete geology text that had proclaimed, "The far-seeing Planner of the universe stored the carboniferous fuel in the repositories where it could never perish, and where it could await the uses of the coming race of man," he added, "And man was on earth 200,000 years before God remembered whom it was He built the coal for."[23]

But Cummings reminds us that such Voltairean condescension couldn't suffice to free Twain altogether from his childhood notion of a divine tyrant and persecutor. "Nature's attitude toward all life," he wrote in 1895, as if "nature" were an immanent deity, "is profoundly vicious, treacherous, and malignant." And when his daughter Susy died of meningitis while he was off recuperating from his debt-paying world tour in the following year, he bitterly observed to Howells "how exactly and precisely it was planned; and how remorselessly every detail of the dispensation was carried out." These are not the comments of someone whose whole spirit is permeated with Darwinism. No wonder Twain could still remark of hell, quite late in his life, "I don't believe in it, but I am afraid of it."[24]

As Cummings acknowledges, however—here following the important lead of Howard Baetzhold—the chief conflict in Twain's mature mind was not between belief and unbelief but between the two moral philosophies that W.E.H. Lecky had dubbed intuitive and utilitarian. An intuitionist holds that people can naturally discern the difference between right and wrong and will generally feel obliged to choose the right, whereas a utilitarian considers all moral notions to be products of training and thus socially relative. Temperamentally, by upbringing, and by midlife exposure to the culture of Hartford and Boston, Twain was inclined to be an intuitionist. Intellectually, however, he found his intuitionism thwarted by one overwhelming phenomenon that continually gnawed at him: caste prejudice, whose most extreme form was the slaveholding system in which he himself had been comfortably and unselfconsciously raised.

Cummings's Mark Twain, then, is very far from being that

manikin of simplistic "influences" scholarship, the figure who is passively tossed from one provider of "background" to the next. Rather, he is a man possessed by an anguishing moral paradox. How could his own extended family—how could the whole American South—have professed Christian ideals while deliberately brutalizing a class of fellow human beings whom they chose to regard merely as property? It is only a small exaggeration to say that Twain's career as a serious writer was an extended meditation on that question and its historical corollaries. If he ended by embracing an extremely mechanistic form of utilitarianism, it was not necessarily because he had plunged into despair over his personal tragedies but at least partly because he needed a radical explanation for the human record as he had witnessed it.

Once we have grasped the thematic core of Twain's thought, Cummings shows, we can sense the emotional urgency that underlay his adventures in reading. It was more than the Zeitgeist, for example, that drew him to Taine's causative doctrine of "race, surroundings, and epoch" and to Holmes's declaration that "the more we observe and study, the wider we find the range of the automatic and instinctive principles in body, mind, and morals." Those sources offered him an absolving theoretical perspective on the caste intolerance practiced not just in prerevolutionary France and the cotton belt but in his own boyhood family and at the very fountainhead of his pastoralism, his uncle John Quarles's farm. The same need to locate an impersonal necessity behind oppression left him susceptible to social Darwinism, which taught him, as he put it in 1904, that "man has not a single right which is the product of anything but might."[25] And his cardinal idea from the 1880s onward, that conscience is shaped entirely by social pressures and thus can be enlisted in even the grossest evils, was at once a direct borrowing from *The Descent of Man* and a further means of putting slavery beyond the realm of personal moral responsibility.[26]

Twain persisted in being a residual intuitionist through it all, never ceasing to hope that his readers could be jarred by his bitter prose and their own dormant humanity into awakening to the wickedness of racism and its overseas extension, imperialism. Once he had become a Social Darwinist in the nineties, however, his impatience and disgust with mob psychology tended to muffle his sympathies. The icy analytic detachment of the hero in *Pudd'nhead Wilson* turned out to be a portent for the rest of his creator's career. As Cummings fully appreciates, if we want to see Mark Twain's mind and heart, his utilitarianism and intuitionism, fully at work together—not in concert but at the highest pitch of intensity—we must return to *Huckleberry Finn*.

In Cummings's analytic approach, the classic issue of divided purpose in *Huckleberry Finn* comes down to the question of whether that novel was written primarily in a sentimental (intuitionist) or a deterministic (utilitarian) spirit. On one interpretation—the most popular one among critics since the 1950s—the core of *Huckleberry Finn* resides in Huck's stirring but transitory resolution to "go to hell" if necessary for Jim's sake. Personal moral revolution, then, *is* possible even when every social pressure conspires against it; in Twain's own language, a "sound heart" can trump a "deformed conscience." Yet if this is so, how can we account for the coarse and trivial concluding chapters, in which Huck unprotestingly obeys the conformist Tom Sawyer, for whom Jim is a pawn and slavery an unexamined given?

The opposite reading says that institutions *must* win out over untutored feelings, as indeed they do here; Twain had no choice but to re-infantalize his characters at the end, diverting our attention to proposed high jinks in the Territory rather than coming to terms with the unaltered facts of the slave system. Critics who take this line enjoy an advantage over those who think of the early Huck as a personification of antisocial freedom. They can show, first, that Twain's hero has never, not even in his grandest hour of defiance, been free from the weight of prevailing opinion about the correctness of slavery; second, that for an alleged outlaw he is remarkably amenable to socialization by the Widow Douglas, the Grangerfords, the Wilkses, and Aunt Sally; and third, that he is quite capable of putting Jim out of mind whenever a prolonged distraction beckons. Still, we cannot purge our own minds of the great scenes of bonding and reconciliation on the raft. Why did Twain bother to create those scenes if he intended to reduce Huck to a satellite and Jim to a minstrel darky, agog over forty dollars?

Cummings's way of addressing this problem, like that of such prior critics as Bernard DeVoto, Henry Nash Smith, and Walter Blair, is to study the emergence of *Huckleberry Finn* from Twain's notes and drafts and to ask whether his mood may have shifted at some point. As is well known, the case for such an approach to the novel is especially compelling because of the notable hiatuses in its composition.[27] In 1876, in the period just following the publication of *Tom Sawyer*, Twain wrote about one-third of *Huckleberry Finn* but then put the manuscript aside, apparently stymied for a plot development that could keep an escaped slave heading down the Mississippi, along banks that Twain was determined to write about because he knew them well, instead of mounting the unfamiliar Ohio toward freedom. In 1879–80, most critics have assumed, Twain composed chapters seventeen and eighteen, covering the Grangerford-Shepherdson feud, but the "downriver" problem remained unsolved. When he took up his pen again in 1882, however, he had found his key device: the comico-sinister King and Duke, who virtually capture Huck and Jim and thus shut off the novel's pastoral phase.

What Cummings adds to this picture is both a proposed revision of Walter Blair's compositional scheme and an argument that something graver than the quest for a neat conclusion troubled the later chapters of *Huckleberry Finn*. I will not recapitulate Cummings's carefully reasoned and, in my view, convincing argument. Suffice it to say that he plausibly contends that part of chapter seventeen and all of chapter eighteen acquired their final shape and tone not in 1879–80 but after Twain's trip down the Mississippi from St. Louis to New Orleans in 1882—a trip that definitely predated the writing of nearly all the subsequent chapters. Cummings's general view of *Huckleberry Finn* does not stand or fall on this speculation, but he does succeed in showing that the feud chapters mark a watershed in theme as well as in time of composition.

It is in chapter eighteen, when the Grangerford family suddenly appears in an aristocratic light and when Buck Grangerford catechizes Huck about the propriety of feuding, that Twain first broaches the training-is-everything lesson that was to become his hobbyhorse. The Grangerfords are there transformed into exemplars of the "Walter Scottism," or Southern pseudo-medievalism, that Twain had come to regard, in Tainean fashion, as the main cause of the Civil War; and the Grangerford-Shepherdson feud, which happens to be situated precisely on what was to become the Union/Confederate border, serves as an allegory of that fratricidal bloodbath.

Cummings sees two significantly different Mark Twains at work before and after the 1882 foray into the Deep South. The author of (roughly) the first sixteen and a half chapters was a northernized Southerner who felt that he had a vital message for people who hadn't grown up among blacks as he had: the intuitionist revelation that feelings can be shared across racial lines. Twain knew it from his memories of "Uncle Dan'l," a slave on the Quarles farm who had befriended him, and who became the prime model for Jim; and he was stirred by more recent experiences, especially his hearing the life story of Rachel Cord, an ex-slave and now his servant, who had been separated from her son Henry on the auction block and dramatically reunited with him toward the end of the war.

In "A True Story Repeated Word for Word as I Heard It," Twain had recounted not just Rachel Cord's moving tale but her awakening of a "Mr. C." to her full humanity—and by implication to his own. A small masterpiece in the sentimental vein, "A True Story" fed directly into Twain's fictional project of humanizing Jim in Huck's eyes and our own. As Cummings puts it,

> From "A True Story," Mark Twain took both the main plot and theme for the first part of *Huckleberry Finn*. Henry's determination to escape from slavery and earn money to buy his mother's freedom is similar to Jim's plan to run away to a free state, there to work and save money to buy his wife and two children out of slavery. As for theme, what Mr. C. learns in a flash about the equal humanity of blacks is akin to Huck's growing love for Jim; and the sense of ritual and commitment with which "A True Story" ends is perhaps echoed at the end of Chapter 15, where Huck "could almost kissed" Jim's foot before humbling himself to him.[28]

Up until 1882, the Twain who had fled from the Civil War and had never embraced abolitionism did everything he could to convince himself that the race issue in America had been all but settled; in due time the victory of the North would inevitably lead to tolerance and opportunity. Traveling down the Mississippi and meeting in New Orleans with the acerbic civil rights activist George Washington Cable, however, he saw a very different picture: a resurgent Southern racism that was as bent as ever on caste oppression and dehumanization. Twenty-one years of absence from the Deep South, he realized, had kept him from grasping that its old blend of vileness and aristocratic pretense was still intact.

The result was, on the philosophical plane, a surrender to social determinism; and artistically, a recognition that it would be a historical travesty to grant Jim authentic freedom as an adult. It was in the light of that knowledge, according to Cummings, that Twain wrote the horrific scenes of Buck Grangerford's death, of the redneck animality of Bricksville, of Colonel

Sherburn's murder of Boggs, and of Sherburn's scornful address to the lynch mob indicting its herd mentality. Here emerged the Mark Twain who could eventually identify himself with Satan, anaesthetized against the incurable failings of a contemptible species.

Cummings thus sides with the increasing number of Twain critics who find yet another mini-allegory in *Huckleberry Finn:* the final episode of Jim's artificially prolonged imprisonment alludes to the post-Reconstruction fate of the ex-slaves, freed in name but subjected to depersonalization and physical terror. Yet Cummings also recognizes that, just as the relatively cozy Wilks chapters resist the antisentimental tide of Twain's post-1882 mood, so the Jim Crow allegory fails to account for all the details of the "evasion" episode. *Huckleberry Finn* remains open to "currents and countercurrents" of feeling that are ultimately traceable to what Cummings calls Mark Twain's "moral loneliness," produced by his combination of affection for the black race, mortification over his early failure to embrace abolitionism, and emotional loyalty to family members who had never doubted that slavery was God's will.[29]

Penetrating though it is, this approach to the contradictions in *Huckleberry Finn* must still be called incomplete. Cummings, it may be, suffers from an amiable but besetting weakness among traditionalist Twain critics: a need to supply altruistic-looking alternatives to nakedly commercial motives. As other commentators have stressed, *Huckleberry Finn* began as a "boy's book," and Twain as a best-selling author felt obliged to finish on the same note. At the end, he may have been not so much struggling to keep Huck's new moral grandeur intact as trying to prevent the still-scandalous theme of interracial brotherhood from alienating his least enlightened readers. After all, there is no sign that he felt the least remorse about "cheapening" his great novel with a juvenile finale. On the contrary, it is reasonably clear that in wrapping up this "sequel" to *Tom Sawyer,* he was doing his best to whet appetites for the next sequel, the unproblematically shallow (but never completed) *Huck Finn and Tom Sawyer among the Indians.*

Cummings's idea of Twain's "moral loneliness," however, is not invalidated but merely complicated by this tangle of motives. In addition to his mercurial relation to the past, we must make allowance for an ongoing struggle in Twain's personality between democratic impulses and an irrepressible opportunism and theatricality—a struggle not very different in the end from Huck Finn's own. As in Huck's case, the outcome is not a fixed position but a kaleidoscopic succession of initiatives to extend sympathy, to denounce injustice, to avoid needless trouble, and to advance his interests by telling people what they want to hear.

To take due account of Twain's calculating side, finally, is by no means to hand him back to the systematically ungenerous social constructionists—to those, that is, who would merely assimilate him to the crassness and prejudice of his age. As we saw in exploring the limitations of Gillman's *Dark Twins,* Twain's self-division is not reducible to a standard contest between noble protestations on the one hand and "the repressed" on the other. It is precisely because he was *consciously* both guilt-stricken and grandiosely ambitious, both sentimental and cynical, that we can never be quite sure we have got Mark Twain right. Only a flexibly biographical criticism—one that is ready, without ideological tendentiousness, to entertain every manifestation of a conflicted authorial will—can explain why sensitive readers feel frustrated and even betrayed by Twain's greatest book, yet also feel compelled to keep returning to it and testing its hopes and compunctions against their own.

FOUR

A Yankee in the Court of Criticism

WHEN *A Connecticut Yankee in King Arthur's Court* was first
published in 1889, few readers entertained doubts as to either
its mood—namely, good-humored satirical fun—or its thematic import, which Mark Twain himself anonymously formu-
lated in the *Hartford Courant* on the eve of publication. "The
character of the book," he wrote, "is an arraignment of all
shades and kinds of monarchy and aristocracy as shams and
swindles, ridiculous and played-out anachronisms, silly and
criminal survivals of ancient savagery."[1] As he put it in one of
the unused prefaces to the novel, anyone inclined "to rail at our
present civilization ought to sometimes contrast it with what
went before and take comfort and hope, too."[2] Twain's contemporaries, beginning with William Dean Howells in a generous *Harper's Magazine* review, fell right in with that reading, as
did nearly all literary critics until the past three decades.

But something strange has befallen this would-be commercial for the bustling, hygienic, democratic nineteenth century.
By today, the *Yankee* rates as Twain's most critically trouble-
some work, outranking even *Pudd'nhead Wilson* in that respect.
Its sadistic closing episode—the "battle of the Sand Belt," in
which Hank Morgan electrocutes twenty-five thousand English
troops while dooming his entire corps of faithful republican
"boys" to slaughter—is now widely seen as constituting what
Henry Nash Smith called "one of the most distressing passages
in American literature."[3] Taking their cue from that scene,

recent observers have increasingly perceived the whole of *A Connecticut Yankee* as compromised by ambivalence on Twain's part not only toward Hank Morgan's imperialistic drive to "boss" Arthurian England but also toward the very ideas of democracy and technological efficiency.

Ideological wavering aside, Twain's characteristic attempt to make his book do too many things at once left the *Yankee* and its hero not just ambiguous but verging on outright incoherence. Since he expected this novel to be his last, he felt that he could use it to vent his political philosophy without hindrance; yet still wishing to please the mass audience he had acquired through semiclownish works like *The Innocents Abroad* and *Roughing It*, he also felt obliged to sabotage the decorum of the narrative with farcical episodes and "signature" sarcasms. That clash of purposes plays havoc with consistency of representation throughout *A Connecticut Yankee*.

Take, for instance, the disconcerting fact that Hank must battle the assembled knighthood of Britain shortly after being rescued from hanging by a squadron of those same knights mounted on bicycles. The two episodes serve rival aims—one to provide lighthearted burlesque and the other to dramatize the tenacity of custom and superstition. Considered together, they are senseless; but we would be taking more trouble than Twain himself did if we tried to make the contradiction meaningful. Similarly, the progressive and enlightened Hank's illiberal penchant for ordering the summary execution of those who annoy him can be set down to mere comic opportunism on Twain's part. At such moments Hank is not even playing his own role; he is simply a stand-in for the facetious lecturer Mark Twain who, for example, used to profess regret that Jane Austen had been allowed to die a natural death.[4]

The problem of unclear motivation is not resolved in those scenes where Hank does behave as a fully "characterized" personage. Depending on which chapter or even which paragraph we focus on, we can make him out to be a boor and an ignoramus or a deeply informed and humanitarian student of history. On one page he is devoid of sentiment, but on another he is neck-deep in it. Shunning mayhem in some incidents, he cheerfully courts it elsewhere. And what, at bottom, *are* his political convictions? Does he yearn to enlighten the confused masses, or would he prefer to keep them mystified while he humiliates the self-satisfied and the mighty, leaving himself as the sole figure left standing tall? Does he despise all rank, or is he a closet monarchist who believes that at least a few kings, such as his good friend Arthur, are inherently dignified and worthy of reverence?

Beyond such inconsistencies lies the broader question of whether, as increasing numbers of critics allege, Mark Twain intended us to judge his hero harshly. If so, why is Hank allowed to evolve into a sentimentalized Victorian pater-familias—one who is betrayed by ingrates and scoundrels while attending to a family crisis, and who is finally undone not by any vice of his own but by a generous and merciful impulse? To be sure, Twain also depicts Hank as brash, vulgar, and better suited to sheer bustling innovation than to governance. But those were precisely the traits that Twain's antagonist pro tempore Matthew Arnold had ascribed to the whole American civilization that he haughtily condemned. In fashioning an upstart Yankee Doodle protagonist and having him expose the grotesqueness of an established church and an aristocratic state, Twain "grants the English their argument," as Roger B. Salomon puts it, ". . . and then tries to show that vulgarity is better than inhumanity."[5]

For a story purportedly showing how the application of modern notions could have obviated the horrors of the Dark Ages, however, *A Connecticut Yankee* is curiously unforthcoming with examples. Thus the freeing of slaves, anticipated as a major plot development, never materializes on more than a local scale, well within the bounds of feudalism. The liberal institutions that Hank imposes on sixth-century Britain are scarcely allowed to make an appearance, and when they do, it is mostly in a parodic form that renders them dismissible. We are left to wonder, for example, just what benefit newspapers are supposed to confer on a still illiterate population, or why we should be enthusiastic about advertisements for products that don't yet exist. Why, furthermore, is Hank's revolution, such as it is, allowed to collapse so suddenly behind his back, without any dramatic representation of the process?

A Connecticut Yankee, it seems, merely goes through the motions of developing an on-the-scene alternative to feudalism, reserving its main energy for diatribes against human cravenness in every age. Indeed, by drawing so many horror stories from the relatively recent prerevolutionary era in France, from American slavery, and even from the parliamentary British state of his own time, Twain undermined his hero's Whig account of steady progress through the centuries.[6] As the initially good-natured burlesque of Malory is increasingly supplanted first by propaganda for democracy and technology and later by harangues and scenes of oppressive terror, until Hank himself becomes a terror in the Sand Belt, we cannot escape the suspicion that Mark Twain is being gripped by moral exasperation or by some other source of profound unease—no doubt the same feeling that prompted him to complain to Charles L. Webster in August of 1887 that his novel, whose very title "requires fun," was being overtaken by a "funereal seriousness."[7]

In short, then, the *Yankee*'s "remainder" of thematically recalcitrant material is so imposing that it threatens to negate Twain's manifest emphasis. Yet this state of affairs differs only in degree from what we encounter in many another significant work—the classic example, of course, being *Paradise Lost,* whose piety is challenged by its own portraits of a priggish, illogical, unjustifiably vindictive God, a Satan who is goaded beyond reason, and an Adam and Eve who never stand a chance of avoiding punishment for the frailty that has been programmed into them. *A Connecticut Yankee* is hardly a work of Miltonic stature, but in this one respect—its radical ambiguity—it puts

Paradise Lost in the shade. For while Milton evidently felt torn between his worship of divine power and his sympathy for hapless human victims of that power, in Twain's case *the ideology itself* appears to waver.

The way a critic responds to such a work will, I believe, depend less on unmistakable signals within the text than on his or her general tolerance for indeterminacy. But how much tolerance is appropriate? To schematize the issue, let me isolate four approaches that cover a spectrum from the most "disciplinary" to the most chaos-welcoming posture:

1. First, there is *intentionalism,* by which I mean something more rule-bound than a mere belief that everything in the *Yankee* must have originated in Mark Twain's mind. An intentionalist will acknowledge the *Yankee*'s "contrary" signals only on condition that they be quarantined as falling outside the *one* global meaning that, in his view, the whole work was devised to exemplify.

2. Second, there is *ironic incorporation* of the work's subversive elements. Ironizing critics, like intentionalists, allege a single purpose for the text, but they read that purpose as the undermining of shallow manifest assertions. Thus every aspect of the work is assigned a meaningful function, whether as "bait" or as the secret truth to which we should tumble.

3. Third, a believer in what I will call *empiricism* is inclined to accept the *Yankee*'s contradictions without attempting to sublimate them into a higher unity, and then to investigate their origin in an irresolute or conflicted authorial mind. Such a critic demands order not from the text per se but from congruence between textual and biographical evidence.

4. Finally, there is *deconstruction,* seemingly the most agnostic of critical schools, which holds a degree of self-unraveling to be the normal fate of all attempts at verbal communication. According to deconstruction, in one critic's summary,

> words do not refer to things in the real world but only signify other words; authors do not create the meaning of their texts by composing them, but instead readers, by

reading them; texts do not have a particular meaning that can be investigated but are limitless in their meaning because of the free play of signs; a careful reading does not give knowledge of a text, because all readings are misreadings; whatever the obvious meaning of a literary text is taken to be, one must stand that meaning on its head.[8]

Let me begin with the last of these options, since the skeptical principles of deconstruction look ideally suited to *A Connecticut Yankee*'s retreat from its own apparent message. One might expect Twain's novel, then, to be on prominent display in the Derridean trophy room. Oddly, however, I have been unable to locate a single deconstructive study of the *Yankee*. And on reflection, I think we can understand why not. In order to go through its predictable paces, deconstruction requires a seeming stability of "naïve" meaning that can then be subjected to displacement; but not even the staunchest intentionalists perceive *A Connecticut Yankee* in that light. Precisely because its inconsistencies are already patent to ordinary readers, Twain's novel preempts the deconstructionist's script. Those inconsistencies clearly take their origin not from anything so vast as "Western logocentrism," and still less from a slippage inherent in all linguistic utterance, but rather from the impetuous, mercurial, yet haunted mind of Mark Twain, which demands to be understood in its historical embeddedness.

At the opposite end of the critical spectrum we meet the intentionalism of E. D. Hirsch, Jr.—a school which flourished in the seventies and early eighties largely because it looked to many of us like a rational bastion against deconstruction.[9] For me among others, the key point in Hirsch's favor was not his insistence on a single intention per text; it was the idea of historical constraints on interpretation. By maintaining that a finished work must have emanated from an intending mind whose relevant access to cultural issues necessarily ceased at the moment the work was completed, Hirsch attempted not only to thwart critical anachronism but also to fix a criterion by which better and worse interpretations could be judged; those that highlight what Hirsch called "symptomatic" (thematically contrary) features without first acknowledging the work's unitary "verbal meaning" had to be considered wild.[10]

As it happens, the most frequently cited piece of *Yankee* criticism, Everett Carter's 1978 article "The Meaning of *A Connecticut Yankee*," is a classic Hirschean exercise that provides a revealing test of the intentionalist approach.[11] In seeking to uncover the *Yankee*'s meaning, Carter says, he will follow Hirsch's distinction between "meaning" and "significance"— that is, between what the author intended by the novel and what we may be inclined to make of it for our own ends. Like Hirsch, he takes the ascertaining of that one global meaning to be a paramount imperative. "What," he asks, "in all probability, and on the basis of all the internal and external evidence, did Mark Twain mean by the total fiction *A Connecticut Yankee in King Arthur's Court?*"[12]

In Carter's eyes, recent criticism celebrating the antimodern side of the *Yankee* flies in the face of Twain's clear intention to satirize aristocracy, custom, and superstition. That intention, he maintains, is conveyed by "six direct, unambiguous [authorial] statements" outside the novel and by any number of scenes and comments within it.[13] If we insist on being appalled by Hank Morgan's violence, says Carter, we are simply overlooking the conventions of frontier humor. And if we think that the closing scenes subverted Twain's plan, we are defying ineluctable biographical facts, since the Battle of the Sand Belt and Hank's defeat were envisioned from the novel's conception.

To be sure, even Carter acknowledges that *A Connecticut Yankee* suffers from inconsistencies of tone, and he speculates that the "general metaphysical framework" upholding Twain's belief in "reason, common sense, and applied science" had "begun to show signs of stress" by 1889. By the end of the book, Carter admits, Twain appeared to be struggling with his "latent ambivalence towards the common man and towards the doctrine of his natural goodness." But the Hirschean directive to honor *one* overarching intention admits no impediment. For Carter, then, "the meaning of *A Connecticut Yankee* is, as the author repeatedly said it was, that the American nineteenth century, devoted to political and religious liberalism and technology, was better than the traditional past."[14] And that is all that need be said. "No one is going to convince the modern readers who see the book as a reinforcement of their dread of technological progress that it is anything other," Carter declares. "I shall not try."[15] The implication is that only peaceniks and tree huggers, not real scholars, will care about pursuing the *Yankee*'s significance for a generation later than Twain's own.

But Carter's argument runs into difficulties that turn out to be characteristic of his school. Observe, for example, that he uses what Twain "repeatedly said" *about* his work as tiebreaking evidence of what Twain must have meant *within* that work. That is standard intentionalist practice, developed in reaction against the New Critics' emphasis on unforeseeable meanings arising autonomously from the internal play of signifiers. Yet every time a critic claims to establish intention through extratextual authorial statements, a crucial question is being begged. Even supposing that the author harbored just one intention during several years of composing and that his memory of that intention is infallible—and both assumptions are surely open to challenge—it seems naïve to accept his word about it as definitive. The writer, after all, is never merely transcribing his intention when he comments about it; he is either predicting what he *hopes* to convey in his work or commenting about *what he would like people to think* about his finished achievement. If we have reasons for doubting the presence of a unifying vision within the text, why should we assume that the writer's self-interested attempts to do away with such doubts bear a special authority?

Some of Twain's definitive-sounding comments about *A Connecticut Yankee* offer a case in point, for they appear on close inspection to be little more than feats of propaganda. As author, publisher, and publicity manager combined, Twain took extraordinary pains not only to highlight his forthcoming novel's most widely agreeable features but also to suppress those that might limit its sales. We know, for example, that he cunningly steered public attention away from the *Yankee*'s anti-protectionist economic preaching and its virulent anti-Catholicism, instead playing up the anti-aristocratic angle that virtually all American readers would find congenial. We know, too, that in attempting to deflect attention from a justified charge of having stolen his time-travel premise from a certain Max Adeler, he labored to convince the public that a more innocent and metaphorical form of "plagiarism" was afoot: Hank Morgan's republican proclamation, he declared, had found an uncanny echo in that of insurgent Brazilian nationalists who were capturing American headlines on the eve of the *Yankee*'s publication. So eager was Twain, in fact, to cash in on the revolutionary sentiment of the hour that he misstated the outcome of the *Yankee*'s final battle, allowing readers of the *Hartford Courant* to infer that Hank's fledgling republic actually puts feudalism out of commission.[16] Evidently Twain had more compunction about his novel's climactic episode than Everett Carter does; that is why he went to such lengths to misrepresent it in the press.

Even so, if the *Yankee* possesses a single general intention, Carter has probably got it right. But consider how much of the novel gets left out of this "meaning." Above all, there is the bullying and megalomaniac side of Hank Morgan's character, which other critics have studied in illuminating detail.[17] They are hardly mistaken in insisting, for example, that Hank is treated more and more unsympathetically once he has acquired authority and that his failure to spread the benefits of democracy to very many people invites correlation with his lust for individual glory.[18] When Carter has had his say, we are still left with Hank's need to depersonalize and "annihilate" others,

his adolescent yet ominous affinity for detonators that will reduce towers to rubble and flesh to hamburger, and his consum-
ing enviousness, which tends to make his opposition to
aristocracy look more venal and driven than disinterested. If
the intentionalist approach can cope with this side of the novel
only by ruling it out of bounds, we ought to abandon intentionalism as a bad bargain.

To do so, however, is by no means to deny that literary texts
eventuate from intentions. In some way or other, every one of
a work's features must correspond to a contemporaneous dispo-
sitional state on the writer's part. But the only way to establish
what those myriad states were would be to infer them from the
text. Moreover, they must have been shaped not just by plan-
ning but also by the immediate exigencies of composition. And
since meaning must arise from an interplay of finely revised and
reconciled effects, it can never be entirely a matter of prior
intention, whether one or many. To say that a piece of literature is an intentional product, then, is a truism without any
practical implications.[19] Only when we posit a single gross
meaning for what Carter calls "the total fiction" does intentionalism acquire consequences—chiefly the fostering of a specious
assurance about what should and shouldn't be taken seriously
in the text.

In recoil from that unyieldingness, we may find ourselves
drawn toward the critical alternative I have called ironic incorporation, whereby the novel's conflicting thematic strands get
resolved within an overarching "complex ironic vision." That
strategem, familiar since the heyday of New Criticism, continues to appeal to critics who, unlike Everett Carter, want to
assign a function to this novel's subterranean currents. They do
so by treating the text's disparities as having resulted not from
haste or muddle on Mark Twain's part but from cunning
manipulation of our expectations. By initially enticing us to
share Hank Morgan's contempt for the backwardness of Camelot, the ironizing critics assert, Twain sets a trap for the morally

shallow reader, who will enjoy the jingoistic fun but miss seeing Hank as what he really is—an imperialist antihero who mistakes his own grasping ambition and ruthlessness for benevolence.[20]

Whether or not we can credit Twain with this degree of forethought, the ironic reading looks consonant with the *Yankee*'s eventual effect on its most acute modern readers. As Twain's initial optimism slipped away, he did admit into his text an implicit critique of imperialism, mechanized war, and the forced modernization of "underdeveloped" societies. Haltingly at first, but eventually with memorably morbid power, the *Yankee* suggests a certain necessity behind Hank's turn toward implacable, unfeeling violence. The vulnerable Western castaway, Twain seems to say, if he is to survive "the primitive" at all, must choose either to assimilate or to dominate, and the choice to dominate will automatically cause him to dehumanize the indigenous populace and steel his mind for possible genocide. In this light, several of Hank Morgan's anomalous-looking traits—his satisfaction in designing Cortés-like spectacles that cow the credulous masses, his strangely vindictive outbursts toward English allies who momentarily vex him, his swerving between wanting to improve and annihilate the human "muck" of Camelot—take on a canny profundity.[21]

It is a short step from this recognition to the idea that Mark Twain must have been aiming at such effects all along. In Clark Griffith's reading, for example, the *Yankee* acquires the stature of a Dostoevskyan masterpiece, a portrait of a tormented soul who, precisely because his social conscience has been awakened, "can no longer bear to look upon the 'grisly' and the 'terrible' without in some way—ultimately in any way!—trying to banish them from sight."[22] And Judith Fetterley, pointing to Hank's inability to feel personal guilt for the crimes he witnesses, posits psychic defenses that must be prompting him on the one hand to generalize about the lowly human race and on the other to "aggress against the aggressors and kill the killers."[23] She even finds profound authorial insight in Hank's penchant for choosing exaggeratedly evil enemies and in his recourse to a tension-discharging farcicality immediately after gruesome scenes of woe.[24]

But here two intractable problems loom. First, if Twain planned from the outset to undercut his hero, it is strange that no hint of that design can be found in the extratextual record. The evidence is overwhelming that Twain expected us—*all* of us—to like Hank and to take patriotic satisfaction from his outwitting of Camelot's assorted fools and villains. And second, close ironic reading becomes misreading when it gratuitously treats the objective events of a plot as psychological projections on one character's part. It is not Hank Morgan, as Griffith would have it, but Mark Twain who "banishes 'the terrible' from sight" by inserting frivolous material wherever he feels that the tone is becoming too grim. And again, since Hank obviously doesn't choose the adversaries who keep trying to kill him, we cannot join Fetterley in blaming him for being pitted against straw-man slave drivers and a satanic church. As Everett Carter rightly insists, that melodramatic matchup goes to show precisely that Twain did *not* initially conceive of Hank in ironic terms.

We are left, then, where we began, with an irresolute novel that continues to fascinate us for reasons that its author could not have anticipated or approved. We have largely forgotten the topical issues that so exercised Mark Twain in the later 1880s, and we find it hard to muster the chip-on-the-shoulder American chauvinism to which he crassly appealed. Yet it is Mark Twain and nobody else who created the subversive effects that keep his book alive for us. In my opinion, only the approach that I have dubbed empirical is adequate to the paradox that Twain is at once responsible for and inconvenienced by his novel's ironies. Lacking a prior commitment to formal or thematic wholeness—or, for that matter, to the disunities automatically posited by deconstruction—an empirically minded critic can accept the flawed text as found and inquire into the probable biographical source of its strangeness.

Take, for example, the many signs in *A Connecticut Yankee* that both Twain and his would-be mouthpiece Hank are experiencing difficulty maintaining an egalitarian and Anglophobic posture. Once we have acknowledged the importance of those "anti-intentional" signs, we discover that they have ample counterparts in the external record. Howard Baetzhold in particular has shown that this novel was composed between periods when, in Twain's eyes, England virtually could do no wrong.[25] With at least part of his mind, he himself was an "American claimant," not just to his family's lost Virginia estate but also, still more distantly and tenuously, to the earldom of Durham in the motherland.[26] At the same time, he took satisfaction in his supposed descent from one of Charles I's Puritan executioners. Thus he fused regicidal and ancestor-worshiping impulses in a way that uncannily calls to mind the teetering between sansculottism and vestigial royalism that we find in *A Connecticut Yankee*.[27] Realizing that fact, we will be less inclined to treat the *Yankee*'s signs of pro-aristocratic sentiment as dismissible aberrations.

It would be just as easy, indeed, to maintain that the real aberration in this case was Twain's effort to present himself as a democratic revolutionary. His usual view of aristocracy was not that privilege and rank are evil but that they ought to go to people like himself who had earned them by excelling on a level playing field. As he wrote after visiting with members of the Austrian royal family in 1898, certain princes "make me regret . . . that I am not a prince myself. . . . I have never been properly and humbly satisfied with my condition. I am a democrat only on principle, not by instinct. . . ."[28] Or again, as he scribbled on the flyleaf of a book in 1894, "I am an aristocrat (in the aristocracy of mind, of achievement), and from my Viscountship look reverently up at all earls, marquises, and dukes above me, and superciliously down upon the barons, baronets, and knights below me."[29] What he chiefly admired about America during the gestation of *A Connecticut Yankee* was precisely its function as an arena where, he said, "inequalities are infinite—not limited, as in monarchies; where the inequalities are measured by . . . differences in capacity, not by accidental differences of birth; where 'superior' and 'inferior' are terms which state facts, not lies."[30]

But why, then, did Twain feel impelled in the first place to attempt such a truculently egalitarian novel, and why did his agitation continue to mount during the course of composition? As James M. Cox observed long ago, the *Yankee* is Twain's *Pierre*, a work in which "the writer is drawn more and more into his creation until he can end it all only by fighting his way out."[31] Following the lead of Kenneth S. Lynn, Cox shrewdly proposed that the key to Twain's distress lay in the Paige typesetting machine, his most grandiose and, as time would show, his most disastrous investment. The typesetter was being assembled in the very Colt factory from which Hank Morgan initially emerges, and Twain hoped that it would debut in tandem with his novel, thus ending his literary career in a shower of almost unimaginable wealth—$55 million a year, indefinitely extended. But both projects kept getting postponed, and Twain's financial hopes for *A Connecticut Yankee* and his publishing company became entwined with those of a refractory mechanical leviathan that devoured his ready cash long before it helped to ruin him altogether. In some sense Hank's surreptitiously constructed second England *is* the Paige undertaking, "fenced away from the public view," as Hank puts it, but promising a marvelous transformation of everyone's life.[32]

As Cox perceives, Hank Morgan's expectations for a technological spin-off of democratic reform and universal betterment in living standards correspond exactly to the social effects Twain anticipated from the universal adoption of his typesetter. But there is one telling respect in which Hank and Twain diverge. In the Paige affair Twain acted as a venture capitalist, yet among all the functions that Hank Morgan vertically integrates, from design and manufacture through government licensing and the manipulation of markets, the role of capitalist is never mentioned. In a subsistence economy, the money for his many projects simply materializes from nowhere.

A Freudian might say that venture capitalism is being "repressed" by *A Connecticut Yankee*—but "strategically omitted" would cover the same ground less tendentiously. In either case the tactic appears to be crucial for the protection of Twain's own democratic credentials. Because Hank seeks to prevent the feudal system from continuing to crush its usual victims, he comes across ideologically not as a holder of royal monopolies but as a Lone Ranger of the working class, a man whose most remunerative projects are really a form of philanthropy. Surely Twain flew into his unappeasable rage against aristocracy because he *needed* to make a show of solidarity with the workers— the workers, that is, whose jobs would be imperiled by the very automation that would supposedly propel Twain himself into the top rank of America's plutocracy.

Such a prospect must have made the chronically guilt-ridden Mark Twain feel low and unclean. If he could not own up to his misgivings, at least he could try to smother them in contrived social righteousness. Like his off-and-on friend Andrew Carnegie, he had good psychological cause, first, to blast away at a *remote* source of artificially concentrated power—the ossified but by then largely comic-operatic privileges of royalty and aristocracy; second, to idealize the rude practical genius as a universal equalizer; and third, to confound free enterprise with other forms of freedom that were in fact being jeopardized by the rapid pyramiding of American capital. In positing, then, that the industrial revolution and the French Revolution constituted a single emancipatory act, Twain attempted to wash his hands of the class war in which he almost became, willy-nilly, a capitalist general.[33]

As we see from the novel, however, that attempt was doomed

by Twain's deep cynicism about the improvability of the human race. The *Yankee* reveals, despite its progressive "intention," that its author regarded average folks in every age as inveterate conformists who feel at home in their mind-forged manacles and who, if freed by a Promethean savior such as himself, would promptly set off in quest of a new oppressor. Nothing in the novel quite succeeds in muffling this cynicism: not farcical antics and cartoonlike violence without remorse, not tirades against the most patent forms of credulity and enslavement, not satire of a preindustrial never-never land toward which Twain secretly pined, and not the sentimental staples of the hearth and gallows, each calculated to wring emotion from even the most frozen breast. The final asphyxiating stench of twenty-five thousand rotting corpses may imply, among other things, the revulsion Twain must have felt after such prolonged estrangement from his deepest feelings.

Needless to say, these biographical speculations do not in themselves constitute literary criticism. I offer them, however, in support of those critics who have attended to the *Yankee*'s dissonances without flinching. Like any other substantial literary work, but with more palpable trouble than most, *A Connecticut Yankee* reveals an energetic mind trying to subdue competing claims within an aesthetic scheme that may or may not prove adequate to the task. It is not the business of criticism to prejudge the success of that effort, either by invoking Derridean linguistic fatalism, by bulldozing all obstacles to "intended meaning," or by recasting perceived turbulence as irony. If we reverse the intentionalist protocol, beginning from fissures within the work and then seeing whether they correspond to what is known about the writer's mind, we will find ourselves able to do without aprioristic certainties. And as a bonus that now seems increasingly rare, we will encounter the writer himself, whose life and motives, if he is as imposing a figure as Mark Twain, exercise their own strong claim on our attention.

Pressure under Grace

KENNETH S. LYNN, *Hemingway* (New York: Simon and Schuster, 1987).

I

KENNETH S. LYNN's *Hemingway* is hardly a book that its subject would have enjoyed reading. If the touchy and pugnacious bruiser were still among us, Lynn would surely want to keep a bodyguard at his side for the next several years. Nevertheless, he has written not only one of the most brilliant and provocative literary biographies in recent memory but also the study that Hemingway most urgently needs at this point in his critical fortunes.

Though superficial appearances indicate otherwise, Hemingway's literary stature continues to be subject to the downward revision that began on the day in 1961 when, depressed, paranoid, and stupefied by heavy doses of electroshock therapy, he blew out his brains with a shotgun blast. Throughout the sixties and seventies, feminists and others took their own shots at the tottering idol, whose cult of macho sporting values and stoic mannerisms began to seem hollow and foolish. So much insistence on correctness of attitude in the face of a melodramatically hostile fate; so much self-flattery in the creation of one autobiographical hero after another, always a god to his adoring woman; so much scorn for the weakling, the pervert, the aesthete, the castrating bitch! Wasn't the whole thing—and Hemingway's famous tight-lipped style along with it—a contemptible sham?

Today, when remoteness in time has begun to confer indulgence toward the writer's personal failings, we hear less of such talk. Instead, we find ourselves in the midst of what looks like a Hemingway boom. The 1980s initiated an enormous outpouring of biographies, specialized studies, dissertations, conferences, television specials, and mass-market reissues, along with further posthumous volumes of Hemingway's uncollected or abandoned work, sometimes forced into print with little regard for its quality or even its authenticity.

One may wonder, however, whether this flurry signifies a true reversal of the critical deflation or merely a scholarly and commercial feeding frenzy over the newly accessible Hemingwayana in collections at the John F. Kennedy Library, the University of Texas, and elsewhere. In large measure, what has been restored to us is Hemingway the celebrity—the figure that he himself, the supreme self-publicist of modern letters, created in the thirties and shrewdly marketed through articles and interviews depicting a life of action, courage, and connoisseurship. It says something about our own shallow era that so many of us are happy to revert to that trivial conception of our most influential novelist. In the long run, however, the resuscitation of the Hemingway legend will be seen to have merely postponed an inevitable reckoning. Quite simply, the legend is false, and its certain demise will leave Hemingway once again exposed to his most adamant detractors.

What Hemingway requires is an ideal reader who can discard everything that is meretricious in our image of him but then do justice to the literary art that remains. Put this way, the task sounds straightforward enough. The trouble is, however, that the reality behind the legend is so unpleasant in several respects that biographical debunkers have had no stomach for the work of critical reconstruction. From the former idolator Carlos Baker's reluctantly revelatory *Ernest Hemingway: A Life*

Story to Bernice Kert's *The Hemingway Women* and Jeffrey Meyers's *Hemingway: A Biography,* those who have had the most eye-opening things to say about Hemingway the man have not cared even to attempt critical reformulations.[1]

After Kenneth Lynn's contribution, however, nothing will be the same in any branch of Hemingway studies. Though his ambitious inquiry builds (with acknowledgment) on the work of other biographers, Lynn carries the process of demythification even farther than did Jeffrey Meyers, whose coolly objective and well-researched book has been treated in some quarters as a breach of decorum. We will see that no aspect of Hemingway's conduct, however intimate or embarrassing, escapes Lynn's clinical eye. Yet his intelligence is fully balanced by his humanity. Instead of merely refuting Hemingway's boasts, Lynn offers us our first cogent and sustained explanation of the psychological, familial, and environmental pressures that helped to make the willful yet deeply cautious author what he was. The result is an admirable combination of justice and compassion—but that is not all. In showing that Hemingway secretly entertained broader sympathies than his manly code implied, Lynn is able to return to the fiction with fresh appreciation.

To be sure, the Hemingway who emerges is a troubled and diminished figure in comparison with the mythic presence that once dominated our literary scene. But he is not the exposed fraud we have grown accustomed to meeting in ideological diatribes of recent decades. Rather, he is the Hemingway who once wrote to Scott Fitzgerald, "We are all bitched from the start and you especially have to be hurt like hell before you can write seriously. But when you get the damned hurt use it—don't cheat with it. Be as faithful to it as a scientist."[2]

II

TO ARRIVE AT that vulnerable and exacting artist, we must first learn to forgo the Hemingway legend. But the task is not as easy as it looks. The legend, it is important to grasp, comes in two versions—in effect, one for the credulous mass public and one for relatively wary critics. If the simple version is clearly doomed, its more sophisticated counterpart still has plenty of eloquent defenders.

At the primary level, the legend says that Hemingway was a great sportsman, aficionado, and stoic, religiously devoted to maintaining poise in the face of mortal danger. This is the image cultivated by the surviving Hemingway clan for the sake of its business ventures, including Hemingway Ltd., a corporation formed to market the label "Hemingway" for use on tastefully chosen fishing rods, safari clothes, and (surely the ultimate triumph of greed over taste) shotguns.[3] In contrast, the critics' version of the legend is a limited exercise in damage control. It allows that the hero may have been morbid and fear-ridden but asserts that even his debilities were acquired in a noble, portentous manner—namely, in the traumatizing experience of being hit by shrapnel in World War I. Thanks to the wounding, Hemingway is awarded a red badge of tragic historical consciousness.

Although Lynn provides the most decisive refutation of both accounts, his conclusions about Hemingway the alleged sportsman were already implicit in other biographies. Scholars have known for some time that Hemingway—clumsy, weak-eyed, slow-footed, accident-prone, and, in the words of his third wife, Martha Gellhorn, "the biggest liar since Münchhausen"—always talked a better game than he played. To hear him tell it, no subtlety of sport or combat had eluded his skills or analytic acumen. True specialists, however, were often unimpressed not only by his prowess but also by his claims to expertise.

Did Hemingway, for example, ever acquire the *afición* to which he laid claim from his very earliest days as a bullfight fan? The matador Luis Miguel Dominguín, who spent much time in his company, thought otherwise: "He knew more than most Americans but less than almost all Spaniards." One thing the bloodthirsty Hemingway knew for sure, however, was that the picadors' horses ought to risk being disemboweled; he complained against the introduction of protective pads in 1928.[4]

Hemingway's sense of fair competition was stunted by irrational needs. As a recreational boxer, he became notorious for administering low blows and knees to the groin, mercilessly pounding smaller and weaker friends, sucker-punching one man who was still lacing his gloves, and doing the same to another—indeed, smashing his newly donned glasses—while the latter was *un*lacing a glove. After his eye-hand coordination had been sacrificed to alcoholism, he disgusted his hunting companions by claiming some of their kills as his own. And in recalling deep-sea fishing trips with the later Hemingway— who was fond of shooting at sharks with a machine gun or pistol, and who once wounded his own legs in the process— Arnold Gingrich characterized his overbearing friend as a "meat fisherman" who "cared more about the quantity than the quality," disdained the true angler's concern for proper methods, and was all in all "a very poor sport."[5] In his zeal to throw more punches, ski more recklessly, catch more fish, and slaughter more animals than anyone else, Hemingway was not a sportsman but a man possessed.

If the writer's compulsive side is inescapable, however, its origins are still a theme of lively controversy. Under the influence of Malcolm Cowley, Philip Young, and Hemingway himself—who grudgingly came to find a certain utility in this line of argument—most commentators from the forties until now have traced his psychic problems to the Austrian mortar shell which allegedly shattered both his equanimity and his belief in public causes. As articulated in the backup legend, the famous incident at Fossalta di Piave at once attests to the hero's preternatural valor, imparts an agreeably leftward spin to his grandest themes (the emptiness of politicians' abstractions, the need for a separate peace), and provides a concrete external basis for the not-so-grand ones (night fears, loss of nerve, castration, impotence, nihilism).

Thanks to careful research by Lynn and, before him, Michael Reynolds, this story now stands exposed as a fiction.[6] Hemingway, it seems, grossly misrepresented the immediate aftermath of his wounding, when, with more than 200 shell fragments lodged in his lower body, he allegedly carried a fellow victim 150 yards through machine-gun fire to safety, absorbing several direct hits but somehow picking himself back up and completing the herculean ordeal. The truth appears to be that young Ernest received many flesh wounds from shrapnel, that he showed solicitude for others while waiting to be evacuated, but that during his recovery he embroidered the story to compel maximum awe from parents, friends, and reporters, some of whom were even left with the impression that he had been a member of the Italian equivalent of the Green Berets rather than a Red Cross volunteer dispensing cigarettes and candy from a bicycle.

The most significant distortion, however, was not Hemingway's doing but that of critics enamored of the overworked "postwar disillusionment" or "wasteland" thesis. This banality has served to lend a darker, more mature tinge to the fiction of the Jazz Age, which at its best *(The Great Gatsby, The Sun Also Rises)* is thought to constitute a wise commentary on the moral collapse of the West. Since the books in question reflect scant historical analysis and are patently jejune in some respects, the critics' job has been to catch deeper echoes between the lines. In Fitzgerald's case this has been a losing cause; the carnage had ended before the would-be knight could sail for France in his custom-tailored Brooks Brothers uniform, much less get properly shot, and his novels of the twenties exude an undisguisable combination of naïve, wistful romanticism and sociopolitical indifference. Fossalta, in contrast, has provided the critics with copious servings of Hemingway helper.

Did Hemingway lose his boyish innocence in 1918, acquiring in short order a fissured psyche and a bitter sense of historical disillusionment? Lynn proposes that we need only consult surviving letters and photographs to see that, on the contrary, the teenage adventurer was more elated than shattered by his brush with death. (One of the reproduced pictures, taken shortly after the explosion, discloses a buoyant, handsome youth, not quite nineteen, beaming triumphantly from his hospital bed in Milan.) "It does give you an awfully satisfactory feeling to be wounded," he wrote home. It was, he said in another letter, "the next best thing to getting killed and reading your own obituary"—a line that could have been spoken by Tom Sawyer.[7] Obviously, Hemingway was trying to calm his parents' fears. Even so, the adeptness of his sprightly rhetoric sits poorly with the conventional idea of his thoroughly unnerved, shell-shocked condition.

As Meyers had already perceived, Hemingway's escape without so much as a broken bone "made him feel invincible . . . made him want to challenge fate."[8] Nothing in his subsequent conduct suggests that he returned from Italy with a subdued temper, much less a revulsion against killing or a grasp of the issues and ironies behind the war. No doubt the wounding did render him more "existential," heightening both his bravado and his morbidity. What it assuredly did not do, however, was to equip him with the insight and compassion that his friendliest commentators have wished to lend him. On the contrary, it appears to have launched him on a career of braggadocio and hedonistic thrill seeking (financed by other people's money) that would put him gravely out of touch with the social and political consciousness of later times.

For Hemingway's most compliant critics, however, thoughts of war and death are wonderfully ennobling. Consider, for example, their response to "Big Two-Hearted River," certainly an admirable work, but not necessarily one that reverberates with world historical import. Especially since Malcolm Cowley's influential introduction to *The Portable Hemingway* in 1944, this story of a solitary trout-fishing expedition has been thought to depict its hero's struggle against an underlying panic stemming from the shell shock that figures in other Nick Adams stories written some years later. Hemingway himself belatedly claimed to have adopted this poignant way of reading his tale. "In the first war, *I now see,*" he wrote to Cowley in 1948, "I was hurt very badly; in the body, mind and spirit; and also morally. . . . Big Two-Hearted River is a story about a man who is home from the war. . . . I was still hurt very badly in that story."[9]

In 1981, however, Kenneth Lynn had the temerity to point out that the published text of "Big Two-Hearted River" neither mentions the Great War nor alludes to it in any definite way, and that in this tale Nick Adams neither moves about nor thinks like a man who has recently undergone a physically and spiritually crippling trauma. His escape, through the satisfactions of expert camping and fishing, from an unstated preoccupation is all but complete. As for Cowley's thesis, Hemingway apparently saw in it an opportunity to put his anxieties into the past tense and assign them a public cause. Which reading requires fewer extraneous assumptions? Surely it makes sense, as Lynn urges, to be guided by the story itself rather than by the retrospective gloss that Cowley successfully urged upon the rarely veracious Hemingway.

Lynn maintains that the preoccupation lurking behind "Big Two-Hearted River" had to do not with the war but with Hemingway's mother, who had expelled him from the family home after a bitter quarrel. Lynn could have added that in a rambling, subsequently canceled ending to the story, Nick does mention the war—but in a way that is the very reverse of portentous and traumatized. "The movies ruined everything," Nick muses. "Like talking about something good. That was what had made the war unreal. Too much talking." To judge from the canceled soliloquy, Nick's only nonfishing concerns in that draft of the story were thoughts about the good old days in Michigan, Paris, and Spain and his ingenuous literary ambitions: "He wanted to be a great writer. . . . It was really more fun than anything."[10]

Nevertheless, Lynn's challenge to the "wound" reading has been received as a virtual sacrilege. R.W.B. Lewis's response is typical: "Lynn's critical attitude [toward "Big Two-Hearted River"], however absurd, was only incidental to a larger intention: to insist that American literature in general is and has been sundrenched and happy, and wholly free of the dark Russian morbidity attributed to it by Cowley and his fellows."[11] This gratuitous slur can serve as a gauge of the passions that get involved not just with Hemingway criticism in general but specifically with the Fossalta question. For Lewis, Lynn's failure to be adequately pious about the crushing effects of the war constitutes nothing less than a "nativist" and reactionary program to break the links between the Continent and modern American literature in general.[12]

Hemingway's "postwar disillusionment," such as it was, proved to be a belated and derivative manifestation. *A Farewell to Arms* was published in 1929, long after the acclaimed antiwar novels by Dos Passos and Cummings and in the same year that Remarque's *All Quiet on the Western Front* appeared in English. By then, a bitter view of the slogans of 1914 had become virtually obligatory as a token of tough-mindedness. Moreover, Lynn emphasizes that Lieutenant Frederic Henry's famous embarrassment over "the words sacred, glorious, and sacrifice" is represented not as a wartime revulsion but as a preexisting bias; that is the way he has "always" felt. Lynn's analysis concurs with a brilliant reading by Millicent Bell, which reveals the seeming pacifism of *A Farewell to Arms* to be a curiously private and psychologically regressive affair.

Similarly, Lynn reminds us that some of Hemingway's stories about the prewar Nick Adams already hint at the depressive anxiety with which the wounded Nick will have to contend. Far from maintaining that Hemingway's writings are "wholly free of . . . dark Russian morbidity," Lynn finds them typically saturated in a mood of indefinite resentment, pessimism, and urgency about maintaining control. Indeed, he takes that mood far more seriously than do critics who try to derive it from Hemingway's alleged awareness of failings in modern capitalist civilization. The writer's politics, Lynn repeatedly shows, were suggestible and riddled with inconsistencies. His psychic makeup, on the other hand, was invariable—and deeply strange.

III

THE PRIME ARTICLE OF FAITH for Hemingway's cultists is of course his thoroughgoing maleness. Already in his lifetime, however, that was a topic of considerable speculation. James Joyce saw the brash American as "the sensitive type" trying to pass for tough. A colleague on the Toronto *Star* who knew him at age twenty remarked, "A more weird combination of quivering sensitiveness and preoccupation with violence never walked this earth." "What a book," hissed the novelist's former confidante Gertrude Stein, "would be the real story of Hemingway, not those he writes but the confessions of the real Ernest Hemingway. It would be for another audience than the audience Hemingway now has but it would be very wonderful." And Zelda Fitzgerald, never one for nuances, went much farther, calling Hemingway's he-man posture "phony as a rubber check," characterizing him as "a pansy with hair on his chest," and even voicing a suspicion that he and Scott had been sexually intimate. The idea lacks credibility, but Zelda was prescient in divining that Hemingway's masculine identity was far from secure.[13]

One of Hemingway's most consistent traits was his compulsion to demean the sexual credentials of others—usually people who had wounded his literary or erotic vanity. In stories, novels, and poems he skewered friends and enemies alike, taking pains to make them easily recognizable and portraying them as impotent or homosexual. Four years after Max Eastman had publicly drawn the obvious conclusion from such sniping—that "Hemingway lacks the serene confidence that he *is* a full-sized man"—the wounded lion cornered Eastman in Maxwell Perkins's office, yelled, "What do you mean accusing me of impotence?" and physically assailed him.[14]

But there is evidence that Hemingway did suffer from recurrent impotence in his four marriages, and his pre- and extramarital amours either quickly fizzled or never progressed beyond hand-holding. As soon as he and Pauline had become spouses, he confessed to A. E. Hotchner, "I could no more make love than Jake Barnes." "I wish to hell it were true," said Mary when asked if her husband had been a magnificent lover.[15] Throughout his adulthood Hemingway's relations with women were characterized not by the libidinal freedom of which he bragged but by a babyish, demanding dependency punctuated by sulks, tantrums, and flights to the next would-be protectress.

To say this much about Hemingway's sexual misery is to bring the story up to Kenneth Lynn's point of departure. As Lynn insists, more needs to be established about Hemingway's sexuality if we are to account for the peculiar tremulousness of his fiction. Ever since news of the *Garden of Eden* manuscripts began spreading a decade ago, it has been widely suspected that his secret theme was androgyny—and this has now become the leading motif of Lynn's *Hemingway*.

Androgyny is named just once in Hemingway's published work, in a startlingly sympathetic discussion of El Greco in *Death in the Afternoon*. The painter, Hemingway wrote, "could go as far into his other world as he wanted and, consciously or unconsciously, paint . . . the androgynous faces and forms that filled his imagination."[16] Now, thanks to Lynn's carefully reasoned analysis, Hemingway's own "other world" has become sufficiently distinct to stand beyond conjecture.

Exhibit A, of course, is the posthumous *Garden of Eden,* a work whose dissociated effect can be explained in part, but only in part, by the collage-like job of editing that was required to make it look like a consecutive story.[17] "I was so pleased with it," exclaimed Hemingway's second son, Patrick, who was granted permission to censor any hints of the unsavory. "I'd heard that it was full of these dark sexual secrets, but I found it to be rather a *sunny* book."[18] So it was when Scribner's had got done doctor-

ing it. Yet even this composite, lobotomized text remains manifestly about androgyny.

What made *The Garden of Eden* printable from the family's
standpoint was no doubt the fact that two female characters,
not the Hemingwayesque writer-hero, instigate the story's
kinky games. All the bisexual impulses that are overtly represented belong to David Bourne's maniacal bride, Catherine,
and their mutual friend Marita, a lesbian whom Catherine
praises as "a girl and boy both." Superficially, it is not David's
(or Hemingway's) fault that he and Catherine are taken for
brother and sister, or that Catherine keeps cutting her hair like
a boy's, or that she gets him to dye his own hair—thus turning
him into her same-sex twin—or that her ultimate fantasy in bed
is to trade roles with him. And of course David is just obeying
instructions from Catherine—though with telltale alacrity!—
when he has sex with the boy-girl Marita, who has recently
come from a lesbian encounter with Catherine.

A gullible reader could overlook the motiveless, masturba-
tory quality of this transformational daisy chain and imagine
that Hemingway was merely venting some of his usual misogyny. But as Lynn makes us aware, the same theme of sex-
crossing and even some of the same language can be found in
other fictions dating back to the twenties. In that nominal war
novel *A Farewell to Arms,* another and more celebrated Catherine proposes that she and her man get identical haircuts:

> "Then we'd both be alike. Oh darling, I want you so much
> I want to be you too."
> "You are. We're the same one."

In *For Whom the Bell Tolls* it is the Hemingway stand-in, Robert
Jordan, who takes enough of a recess from preparing to kill
fascists to suggest that he and Maria "go together to the coif-
feur's" and be rendered indistinguishable. While cuddling, they
tell each other, "I am thee and thou are me." And in *Islands in*

the Stream it is once again the woman (does it really matter?) who leads:

"Should I be you or you be me?"
"You have first choice."
"I'll be you."
"I can't be you. But I can try."[19]

Such passages make it difficult to doubt that an imagined switching of sex roles constituted the heart of Hemingway's erotic ideal. And, as Lynn goes on to show, the nonfictional record is entirely consistent with the fictional one.

This is not to say that the strident homophobe Hemingway was disposed toward literally bisexual activities. Whatever he wanted from eros, he sought it from women alone. Lynn shows, however, that the sexual inclinations of women themselves were of more than ordinary interest to him. Hemingway found himself libidinally drawn to lesbians—even to the butch and burly Gertrude Stein, who told her rapt apprentice about women's ways with women and taught him how to crop the hair of his first wife, Hadley. His second wife, Pauline, took female lovers (including Elizabeth Bishop) after Hemingway abandoned her, and in happier days he gloried in her boyishness, just as he had done with his sporting chum Hadley. With all four wives he exhibited the same fetishism of hair length and color, seeking twinlike effects with himself, and in 1947 he startled his Cuban hangers-on by giving his own locks a henna rinse—a practice which, in *Death in the Afternoon*, he had explicitly and contemptuously associated with homosexuality.

As for his most intimate preferences, Hemingway evidently fancied an unclimactic fondling that evoked both infantile passivity and gender confusion. As Hadley once asked in a letter, "Remember how we both tried to be the little, small, petted one the last night on the roof?"[20] At some later point in Hemingway's impotence-ridden sex life, the petting seems to have evolved into what psychiatrists used to label a perversion—that is, a primary replacement for genital intercourse. In a diary entry of 1953, the writer asserted that Mary "has always wanted to be a boy" and that she "loves me to be her girls [*sic*], which I love to be." She had recently initiated him into an embrace that he characterized as "quite new and outside all tribal law."[21]

Hemingway was working on *The Garden of Eden* during that period, and, as Lynn proposes, we can turn to the published text for more enlightenment. After Catherine gets her first cropping ("I'm a girl. But now I'm a boy too and I can do anything and anything and anything"), David lies beneath her and helps to guide her hand lower and lower until he feels only "the weight and the strangeness inside," whereupon she announces, "You're my girl Catherine. Will you change and be my girl and let me take you?"[22] Lynn doesn't spell out the nature of this "taking," but we can find the answer in a mock interview (first singled out for attention by Jeffrey Meyers) that Hemingway improvised for Mary's amusement in 1953:

> Reporter: "Mr. Hemingway, is it true that your wife is a lesbian?"
> Papa: "Of course not. Mrs. Hemingway is a boy."
> Reporter: "What are your favorite sports, sir?"
> Papa: "Shooting, fishing, reading and sodomy."
> Reporter: "Does Mrs. Hemingway participate in these sports?"
> Papa: "She participates in all of them."[23]

The manually sodomized partner, we can infer, was Hemingway himself.

IV

IF ERNEST HEMINGWAY felt himself to be in essence "a girl and boy both," how did he get that way? And what prompted him to encase his androgynous core in a suit of hypermasculine armor? Though any answers must be speculative, Lynn shows us some remarkably affecting correlations between what was done to the writer in his earliest years and the volatile and unhappy man that he became.

Lynn has realized more fully than anyone else thus far that the place to begin looking for explanatory clues about Hemingway's values and predilections is not Fossalta or Paris or Pamplona but Oak Park, Illinois, where he grew up. We now know that he felt himself continually judged against the local standards of sobriety, chastity, decorum, refined culture, and Protestant altruism—standards that had been impressed upon the dutiful cello student and choirboy by both his puritanical and capriciously punitive father and his ambitious, domineering mother. Like Oak Park's other world-class maverick, Frank Lloyd Wright, the mature Hemingway dramatically flouted those standards. In doing so, however, he remained caught in an anxious, resentful quarrel with them.

If Frederic Henry has "always" gagged on words like *sacrifice* and *glory*, that may be because they were instruments of intimidation in his creator's early years; and they remained so as both parents continued to express dismay over their famous son's freedom of language and theme. ("What is the matter?" wrote Grace Hemingway upon first looking into *The Sun Also Rises*. "Have you ceased to be interested in loyalty, nobility, honor and fineness of life?")[24] Once out of Illinois, Hemingway took pains to reverse every feature of Oak Park respectability, even to the extent of encouraging his son Gregory to get repeatedly drunk on hard liquor at age ten and of renting a Cuban prostitute to relieve his other son, Jack, of his hypothetical (but long-departed) virginity at age nineteen. Yet no parent could have been less forgiving than Hemingway's own conscience in damning him for trading on his charm, wasting his time and talent, surrounding himself with flatterers, and marinating his brain in Scotch. Wherever he fled, Oak Park waited in ambush for him.

When Hemingway wrote about scenes from boyhood, they were set not in that priggish Anglophile suburb but in the woods and remote towns of northern Michigan, where he had passed his relatively unconstrained summers. The rural outdoors was his father's masculine territory—the only area where Dr. Clarence ("Ed") Hemingway, in his teenage son's view, had found even a partial refuge from their mutual nemesis, Grace. The author-to-be saw his "Papa" as the cowed and castrated husband par excellence, broken in spirit by a woman who arrogated male authority and who squandered the family's resources on lavish, ego-preening projects. In some of his Nick Adams stories Hemingway alluded to Ed Hemingway's weakness, implicitly put the blame on Grace, and represented his own impressionable self in terms that suggested an already desperate wish to escape a comparable fate.

As Bernice Kert has demonstrated in *The Hemingway Women*, Grace Hemingway possessed several constructive traits that her son chose to overlook. She was more tolerant of boyish mischief than her husband was, and, unlike him, she was more concerned to reward achievement than to lash out against impropriety and sin. Ernest's literary precocity was not just a gift but a tribute to her encouragement and tutelage. For these very reasons, however, his lifelong, virulent, well-documented hatred of the mother he always called "that bitch" must be regarded in a symptomatic light. Like his father, and in a pattern that stretched back and ahead through four unlucky generations, Ernest was constitutionally depressive. In laying his nervous melancholy at Grace's door and arming his mind against all Circes everywhere, the writer was attempting to externalize and forestall a doom that may have been imprinted in his genes.

If nature supplies the flawed clay, however, it is nurture that molds the features into a unique image. Here is where Lynn's *Hemingway* stakes its boldest claim to originality: in showing how pervasively the writer's mind was ruled by his sense of what Grace had done to him. The story is bizarre, and some readers will want to put it down to gratuitous Freudianizing on the biographer's part. But Lynn is not in fact rehearsing oedipal universals or purporting to trace repressed infantile memories; he is merely reconstructing the inferences that Hemingway himself drew as he coped with his mother's conduct, pored over the scrapbook she had compiled about his childhood, and pondered the rumors about her that were common gossip in Oak Park.

Those rumors said that Grace Hemingway enjoyed a lesbian relationship with her young voice pupil and housekeeper Ruth Arnold, who lived with the family for eleven years until Ed, who took the gossip seriously enough to become alarmed, screwed up his courage for once and ordered Ruth out of the house. (The juggernaut Grace was safely off in Michigan at the time.) Ernest Hemingway was twenty years old and in a sullenly rebellious frame of mind when he witnessed the ensuing parental showdown and took his father's side; but throughout his adolescence he must have known what people were whispering. After Ed's suicide the two women stirred further talk, and further resentment from Ernest, by resuming their joint residence in nearby River Forest.

Lesbian or not, Grace had her own obsession with sexual identity. To be sure, the fact that she dressed and coiffed Ernest as a girl for the first two and a half years of his life does not set her apart from many another turn-of-the-century mother. Perhaps that is why previous biographers have attached no importance to such memorabilia as a photograph of two-year-old Ernest in a gown and bonnet, cutely captioned "summer girl." But the biographers should assuredly not have passed lightly by the 1962 memoir written by Hemingway's sister Marcelline, one and a half years his senior. There Marcelline explained that

Grace had wanted the children not just to look alike but "to feel like twins, by having everything alike." As Lynn recounts, Ernest and Marcelline

> slept in the same bedroom in twin white cribs; they had dolls that were just alike; they played with small china tea sets that had the same pattern. Later, the children were encouraged to fish together, hike together and visit friends together, and after Grace deliberately held Marcelline back, they entered grade school together.[25]

And in school, much to Ernest's disgust, Grace once forced the siblings into the same class and did all she could to make them inseparable.

Was Grace Hemingway trying to turn her son into a daughter? Perhaps the answer is both yes and no. Continually experimenting with outfits and hairstyles, she created twin "brothers" as often as "sisters," and at times she showed pride in the sporting exploits of her little man. In all likelihood what Grace wanted, beyond an enactment of some private cross-gender scheme, was a boy whose sexual identity would remain forever dependent upon her dictates and whims. If so, she gruesomely got her wish. The apparent effect of all that dolling and doting was not so much to lend Ernest a female identity as to implant in his mind a permanently debilitating confusion, anxiety, and anger.

Naturally, Hemingway despised Marcelline as fiercely as he came to hate the mother who had glutted him with caresses until she abruptly turned her attention to the next sibling, Ursula. And the strong attachment he subsequently developed to Ursula carried an incestuous intensity, as if he had to validate his maleness through this other sister's love. But the idea of incest, in Hemingway's bemused imagination, was just another means of swapping identities.[26] Later, as an adult, he could only entrust himself to a woman—and then only provisionally, before feelings of entrapment set in—if he mentally conscripted her into the game in which he himself had been initiated by Grace. *Odi et amo.* It is little wonder that Hemingway's writings abound not only in castrating shrews and shattered men but also in sibling-like lovers whose deepest fantasy is to trade sex roles or merge into androgynous oneness.

The virtue of Lynn's account is that it brings into coherence an array of facts—from Hemingway's obsession with lesbianism and hair length through the combination of browbeating and dependency in his love relations—that have hitherto appeared puzzling, though not exactly anomalous. Many commentators have sensed that someone who was not only mesmerized by the castration-defying bravado of the *corrida* but also compelled to sneer at the squeamishness of the unconvinced had to have been caught up in a quarrel with self-doubts. And with increasing certainty after the shotgun blast in 1961, they have known that the writer whose imagination reverted to goring, maiming, crucifixion, exploded body parts, and agonies of childbirth was by no means a simple realist of the out-of-doors. No one before Lynn, however, has established the specific connections between Hemingway's family situation and his fragile personality.

Take, for example, the writer's locker-room, know-it-all side—his claim to definitive expertise on every male topic from boxing and hunting through battle tactics. Lynn shows that such assertiveness would have fit the psychic needs of a boy growing up in the shadow of an older sister with whom he was constantly paired and compared. Likewise, the man who saw betrayal everywhere succeeded the boy who, appealing to one parent for refuge from the other, invariably found the adult ranks closing against him in sanctimonious solidarity. The man who dubbed himself "Papa" while still in his mid-twenties and who sought record-sized kills of fish, beasts, and German soldiers was bent not only on outdoing his woodsman father but on magically repairing the unmanning to which he thought that father (along with himself) had been subjected by Grace Hemingway. And topping everything, the mental hermaphrodite had been systematically deprived of a stable male identity. All in all, we cannot be surprised that even in his final years, family grievances remained uppermost in Hemingway's mind. As he put it so bitterly in *A Moveable Feast*, "With bad painters all you need to do is not look at them. But even when you have learned not to look at families nor listen to them and have learned not to answer letters, families have many ways of being dangerous."[27]

V

THE CRITICAL LESSONS of Lynn's *Hemingway* are chiefly two. In the first place, Lynn enables us to realize why the short story and not the novel proved to be Hemingway's suited genre. The amplitude of a realistic novel calls for broad sympathies and a conscious, integrated understanding of characters and conflicts. A writer whose professed values serve as preventatives against self-insight will find it hard to sustain his characters' development over many chapters or to avoid recourse to stereotypes and posturing. Such, on the whole, was Hemingway's predicament as a full-length novelist; he wavered between being "true to the hurt" and propagandistically disowning it. As Lynn reminds us, even the acclaimed novella *The Old Man and the Sea* seems, on rereading, like a strained and padded effort, bolted together with clunky symbols.

In contrast, Hemingway was temperamentally inclined toward the economy of phrase and gesture required by a ten-page tale, in which, as Lynn puts it, he could "make a virtue of necessity by packing troubled feelings below the surface . . . like dynamite beneath a bridge." Within a short story, Hemingway's characteristic shuttling between mute physical details and irritable, elliptical conversation is hauntingly suggestive. We needn't know, any more than the author himself does, precisely what lurks within the gulf that every sentence barely skirts. (We needn't even know for sure whether "Big Two-Hearted River" is obliquely "about" the war. That is our problem, not the story's.) Hemingway's tales at their best are unforgettable because their actions have the cruel finality of fate itself, without the possibility of recourse to values and theories—not even to Hemingway's own.

The other benefit that discerning readers of Hemingway can draw from Lynn's study is encouragement to trust their instincts, rather than Hemingway's reassurances, when they think they have noticed deviations from the writer's macho norm. In particular, they will find that some of Hemingway's most durable works undercut their own impulse to distinguish simplistically between the he-man and the weakling, the compliant kitten and the castrating bitch.

Consider, as a seemingly intractable test case, "The Short Happy Life of Francis Macomber." Like "Big Two-Hearted River," this powerful story has usually been read in the light of Hemingway's own summary of it, delivered a decade and a half after its composition. "Francis' wife hates him because he's a coward," Hemingway said to an interviewer in 1953. "But when he gets his guts back, she fears him so much she has to kill him—shoots him in the back of the head."[28] But once again Lynn demonstrates that the tale refutes its forgetful teller. Mrs. Macomber is not a murderer; in stating that she "had shot *at the buffalo* with the 6.5 Mannlicher as it seemed about to gore Macomber" (emphasis added), the text unambiguously establishes the killing as accidental. As Lynn insists:

> It is not wifely malevolence that brings Macomber down, but his own dangerous aspiration to be recognized as intensely masculine. Two contrasting aspects of the author are split down the middle in the story. Brutish Robert Wilson, with his double cot and his big rifle, incarnates the Hemingway of the myth, while the doubt-haunted Ma-

comber represents the Hemingway for whom the dark had always been peopled and always would be. Near the end of the fable, the doubter succeeds in winning the approval of the brute. He becomes, in short, the sort of man he is not, and he pays for it with his life. Just as the wife in "Kilimanjaro" is finally relieved of blame by her husband for the tragic waste of his talent, so a critically important narrative detail absolves Margot of responsibility for Macomber's tragedy.[29]

This is much more than a crux resolved; it is one sign among many that Hemingway *could* sometimes identify with a woman's point of view and thus mitigate the tendentiousness of his schematizing.

For a final and more complex example, let us consider Hemingway's best novel, *The Sun Also Rises,* whose "official" reading was laid out by Carlos Baker in 1963. "The moral norm of the book," wrote Baker, "is a healthy and almost boyish innocence of spirit, and it is carried by Jake Barnes, Bill Gorton, and Pedro Romero. Against this norm . . . is ranged the sick abnormal 'vanity' of the Ashley-Campbell-Cohn triangle."[30] In all probability, Hemingway would have endorsed this way of regarding his novel. Yet surely it is much too constraining. Do we in fact experience Brett and Cohn as unredeemably bad? And is the casual anti-Semitism voiced by Bill and Jake somehow "healthier" than Mike Campbell's bullying version? Unless we can find a way of approaching the book that transcends Hemingway's vulgar code, many of us will remain immune to its narrative power.

In one sense Baker was right: from its opening page, *The Sun Also Rises* makes Robert Cohn its embodiment of every trait that violates the Hemingway outlook. We know for certain, moreover, that the sneering at Cohn was inspired by Hemingway's petty but permanently injurious vendetta against his friend and benefactor Harold Loeb, whose romance with Duff Twysden, unlike his own, had been sexually consummated. Yet we now also know from Lynn's biography that everything Hemingway wanted to say about Cohn/Loeb's naïve romanticism and self-pity applied at least as well to his own.

On closer inspection, as several critics have noticed before Lynn, the resemblances between the two "steers" Jake and Cohn seem more impressive than the differences. Furthermore, Jake doesn't simply take pleasure in watching Cohn get humiliated in a setting that he, Jake, has largely staged; he also shows flashes of self-detestation for that very baseness. In Jake Barnes the author has given us his most revealing, if still oblique and alibi-ridden, self-portrait. It is a picture of someone who has good reason to feel himself less than a man, who therefore waxes by turns snappish and maudlin, yet who longs for escape from his private hell into the matador's reticent and impersonal "purity of line." Precisely because Jake *is* Hemingway (indeed, his name in the earliest surviving manuscript was "Hem"), he captures not only his creator's adolescent manifest values but also his mean streak, his fits of remorse, his secret passivity, and his eventually suffocating need to be right about everything. The characterization is far more nuanced than Hemingway could have first intended when he set out to "get" Harold Loeb and create an autobiographical hero who would be disqualified only by a technicality from being Duff Twysden/Brett Ashley's one true love.

And if Carlos Baker's "healthy" Jake escapes black-and-white categories, so does his "abnormal" Brett. According to the Hemingway code, Brett's habit of undermining men's sexual self-respect ought to be unforgivable. In fact, however, her constant yearning to be a "good chap" and mend her ways makes her one of the more appealing figures in the book— more so, surely, than the wooden Pedro Romero, who is novelistically inert precisely because he embodies Hemingway's ideal and nothing else. As Lynn points out, Brett's penitent side was drawn from life—not Duff Twysden's life or Zelda Fitzgerald's but Hemingway's own. Thanks to his capacity for unorthodox identifications, he gave us in Brett what most of his fiction would sorely lack: an independent woman who is not automatically an object of scorn.

There is no need to go overboard here and decide that *The Sun Also Rises* is a wise and compassionate book. As Lynn shows, Hemingway couldn't afford to decide what he finally thought of the sportsman-eunuch-bigot-pimp Jake Barnes, and his novel is not just irresolute but seriously muddled. Readers who think they have found consistently humane ironies in the text—indications, for example, that the author is not crudely anti-Semitic or that his vision of excellence transcends the image of Pedro Romero in his tight green pants—are deceiving themselves. And so, I would add, are those who take this cattiest of romans à clef as a reliable guide to masculine values.

Yet Lynn has revealed that *The Sun Also Rises* is swept by countercurrents of feeling that neither the idolators nor the iconoclasts among Hemingway critics have been prepared to recognize. If this had been a more thoroughgoing "Hemingway novel" in Baker's sense, the final image of Jake and Brett in the taxi—together but forever apart—would have meant nothing to us. Instead, of course, it is a crystalline moment—the nearest approach Hemingway would ever make to the pathos of authentic tragedy.

In replacing the comforts of myth with acute psychological, social, and literary analysis, Kenneth Lynn has not only laid bare that "real Ernest Hemingway" whom Gertrude Stein once fathomed; he has also provided a model of the way biographically informed criticism can catch the pulse of works about which everything appeared to have been said. In short, he has made Hemingway interesting again. For many readers, of course—the potential clientele of Hemingway Ltd.—that contribution will appear superfluous and offensive. In view of the now exposed hollowness of the official cult, however, no one has done more timely justice to what Alfred Kazin once called Hemingway's "brilliant half-vision of life."

SIX

Faulkner Methodized

MALCOLM COWLEY, ed., *The Portable Faulkner* (New York: Viking, 1946).

LAWRENCE H. SCHWARTZ, *Creating Faulkner's Reputation: The Politics of Modern Literary Criticism* (Knoxville: U of Tennessee P, 1988).

CLEANTH BROOKS, *William Faulkner: The Yoknapatawpha Country* (New Haven: Yale UP, 1963).

CLEANTH BROOKS, *On the Prejudices, Predilections, and Firm Beliefs of William Faulkner* (Baton Rouge: Louisiana State UP, 1987).

DANIEL HOFFMAN, *Faulkner's Country Matters: Folklore and Fable in Yoknapatawpha* (Baton Rouge: Louisiana State UP, 1989).

JOHN T. IRWIN, *Doubling and Incest / Repetition and Revenge: A Speculative Reading of Faulkner* (Baltimore: Johns Hopkins UP, 1975).

JOHN N. DUVALL, *Faulkner's Marginal Couple: Invisible, Outlaw, and Unspeakable Communities* (Austin: U of Texas P, 1990).

WESLEY MORRIS, with Barbara Alverson Morris, *Reading Faulkner* (Madison: U of Wisconsin P, 1989).

RICHARD C. MORELAND, *Faulkner and Modernism: Rereading and Rewriting* (Madison: U of Wisconsin P, 1990).

ANDRÉ BLEIKASTEN, *The Ink of Melancholy: Faulkner's Novels from* The Sound and the Fury *to* Light in August (Bloomington: Indiana UP, 1990).

I

ONCE UPON A TIME, a great American novelist—
indeed, the greatest of his century—was languishing in public
neglect, critical disdain, and near poverty, reduced to splicing
and patching the scripts of other Hollywood screenwriters
("schmucks with typewriters," as one of their employers fa-
mously defined them) to make ends meet. Those who knew the
writer's novels, all but one of which were out of print, saw in
him only a minor regionalist, an obscurantist, and a macabre
sensationalist. One day, however, a discerning critic, awakening to the music of the writer's language and the profundity of
his insight, volunteered to assemble a generous sampler that
would guide new readers through his admittedly intricate fictional world—a world he had been constructing in stoic isolation for twenty years. And so it came to pass that a major
injustice was rectified. Thanks to the critic's efforts, everyone
soon perceived the artist in his real stature—a titan of modernism, a Balzacian chronicler of the life and history of his birth-
place, and a tragic, compassionate ironist who had affirmed the
values of family and community by showing what happens
when those values are weakened by callous outsiders.

A fairy tale, this, as flattering to the magic savior as to the
secret prince whom everyone had taken for a lackey. All is
classically one-dimensional here. The writer's greatness looms
as a palpable, indivisible thing that will dazzle all eyes as soon
as they are bidden to look on it, and the critic's motive is as
unclouded as a mountain spring: aesthetic power must be given
its due. Only a child, one supposes, could mistake the story for
a narrative of real events.

But when the names William Faulkner, Malcolm Cowley,
and *The Portable Faulkner* are filled in, most people who know
those names at all, even forty years and more after the fabled
deeds, would have to be counted as believers. The legend has
appealed to them not just because some of its constituent parts

are factual but, more bindingly, precisely because of its mythic reverberation. In America, we like to think that true genius is always ahead of its time and that a season in purgatory therefore counts as one of its validating tests. And those of us who practice literary criticism, whatever our differences of emphasis and method, are all susceptible to the rescue fantasy at the heart of the idealized Cowley-Faulkner linkage. What wouldn't we give to spot a down-and-out master and single-handedly shepherd him to a Nobel Prize?

Reality, however, must have its say. Though Cowley, along with Robert Penn Warren, was indeed Faulkner's leading apologist in the mid-forties, in no sense could he be said to have discovered him. Faulkner had already had many distinguished admirers, among them Conrad Aiken, Katherine Anne Porter, John Crowe Ransom, Eudora Welty, Jean-Paul Sartre, and André Malraux. Cowley's view of him as an idealist and a moralist, pitting the animalistic Snopeses of the New South against the aristocratic Sartorises of the Old, was scarcely original; it drew liberally upon a 1939 essay by the American critic George Marion O'Donnell. Moreover, *The Portable Faulkner*, while it lastingly established Faulkner as having written a fond and harmonious "saga" about such categories as "The Last Wilderness," "The Peasants," and "The End of an Order," by no means effected his rehabilitation all by itself. Between 1946 and the 1950 Nobel award, the book sold a modest twenty thousand copies. The novelist's lean period ended only in 1948 with Random House's publication of the ballyhooed *Intruder in the Dust* and with Faulkner's signing of a well-publicized MGM contract, negotiated by Bennett Cerf, for the movie rights.

It was indeed Cowley who had chiefly prepared the ground for that fresh start by raising Faulkner's standing with critics and common readers. But had he done so for objective aesthetic reasons? During the 1930s, in his proletarianizing days, Cowley had scoffed at *Absalom, Absalom!*, falling in with the left's almost unanimous condemnation of Faulkner as a politically retrograde narcissist and nihilist. His change of heart in the forties had everything to do with his ideological somersault in the same period. As he sloughed off the withered skin of his Stalinism, Cowley experienced what he called "a rebirth of faith in the old values, in love, in friendship, in heroism, in man himself, and a hatred of every social institution that perverts them."[1] And in his search for an American paragon of that Rousseauistic wholesomeness, Cowley thought at once of Faulkner, whose virtual abstention from political involvement in the thirties and whose reluctance to arouse the masses or even to make himself intelligible to them suddenly took on a Jamesian splendor in his eyes.

Faulkner, moreover, could be shown to be steeped in Western masters from Cervantes and Shakespeare through Flaubert and Conrad, and he also bore demonstrable affinities with classic American predecessors from Poe and Hawthorne to Mark Twain and T. S. Eliot. In short, he was ideally ready to be appropriated to the twin causes of universal (not class-based) artistic standards and of American celebration. And so eager was Cowley to align himself with that celebration that he made a partial exception, in Faulkner's case, to his new enmity toward institutions that pervert the human spirit. In his hands the guilt-drenched, slavery-haunted Jim Crow South of Faulkner's imagination underwent a noteworthy pastoral makeover. "He dwells with affection," Cowley wrote of Faulkner's Mississippi in 1944, "on its memories of a great past, on its habits of speech, on its warmth of family feeling; and when he turns from the people to the land itself, he tells how it was blessed. . . ."[2]

One wonders how those Muzak strains sounded to Faulkner himself. The writer needed Cowley's assistance and was grateful for it, but he could not have helped resenting the sweetening of his themes for mass consumption. Indeed, there are signs that he took a dim view of *The Portable Faulkner,* mocking and subtly sabotaging Cowley's attempt to present his work as an organic, affectionate portrait of Southern life.[3] When Cowley, for example, wrote asking if it would be fair to call his work a "myth or legend of the South," Faulkner testily replied that the South "is not very important to me," adding, in a gratuitous discharge of bile, that in his opinion human life is "the same frantic steeplechase toward nothing everywhere and man stinks the same stink no matter where in time."[4] He must have sensed that the incurably superficial Cowley would be only momentarily deterred by such an outburst.

But why, if Faulkner was already respected by a good number of critics and fellow writers, did his promotion to world-class fame have to wait until the late forties? This is the issue addressed by Lawrence H. Schwartz in a recent book that has received less attention than it deserves, *Creating Faulkner's Reputation: The Politics of Modern Literary Criticism*. Schwartz, as a believer in "a materialist interpretation of culture" and "underlying political criteria" for the proper evaluation of literature, evidently feels that Faulkner's elevation at the expense of "social novelists" such as Richard Wright, Erskine Caldwell, and John Steinbeck constituted an ideologically motivated injustice.[5] Few readers will share that grievance, and some will wonder why Schwartz accepts Faulkner's apparent indifference to "the social" at face value. Nevertheless, *Creating Faulkner's Reputation* casts a revealing light on the forces that conjoined not only to repair the novelist's fortunes but also to induce nearly everyone—including, eventually, even Faulkner himself—to misinterpret his writings as expressions of benevolent humanism mingled with Southern pride.

As Schwartz insists, Cowley's belated self-baptism in the American mainstream was not an isolated therapeutic act. It anticipated a wider convergence, on the part of literary intellectuals and academics, toward the political and cultural center as revisionary thoughts about the Soviet Union were given more urgent impetus by the cold war and its penalties for deviation. In the forties and fifties, Schwartz argues, ex-Communists from the left and Southern traditionalists from the right joined hands on a safe common ground of high art and diffuse moral seriousness, thus transforming not just our understanding of Faulkner but the entire ethos of American criticism.

Part of this record is by now thoroughly familiar—namely, the cultural left's retreat into a no-fault, nondenominational "radicalism" emphasizing modernist aesthetic difficulty and dark pronouncements about the existential dilemmas and Freudian anxieties of "modern man." Less well known, but equally significant, is the path that led from the candidly reactionary Agrarian manifesto of 1930, *I'll Take My Stand*, to the institutional ascendancy of critical formalism, which was to play a major role in devising a Faulkner to suit a quietistic age.

Unlike their opposite numbers on the left, the twelve founding Agrarians—among them Allen Tate, Donald Davidson, Andrew Lytle, John Crowe Ransom, and Robert Penn Warren—had no need to trim their ideological sails in the forties. Their original muddled platform, spurning the vulgar industrial world, calling for renewed social hierarchy and paternalism, and clinging to a white-yeomanly, airbrushed picture of the Old South, had collapsed of its own absurdity shortly after it was announced. But this is not to say that the Agrarian and, a little later, the New Critical vision of literature lacked a sociopolitical cast. "All great, or really good writers," as Tate put it in a letter to Davidson, "must have a simple homogeneous sense of values, which incidentally are the kind of values we wish to restore." The whole notion of treating art as a higher realm of knowledge and self-referential order was intended as a slap at modern "materialism," a capacious term stigmatizing all departures from what Tate called "classical Christian culture."[6]

In the Agrarians' eyes, it was materialism—rather than, say, slavery and its aftermath—that accounted for the modern decline of their beloved Southland. As Tate put it in an essay, "the southern subject is the destruction by war and the later degradation of the South by carpetbaggers and scalawags and a consequent lack of moral force and imagination in the cynical materialism of the New South. . . ."[7] If that sounds like Faulkner, it is because all but the youngest among us have been schooled, quite unknowingly, in an Agrarian interpretation of his value system.

Significantly, the original Agrarians were in no rush to claim Faulkner for their cause. It is true, as Cleanth Brooks has recently shown, that not only Warren but Ransom and Davidson as well had generously reviewed some of the early novels. Yet the Faulkner whom the Agrarians had encountered in person—moody, uncommunicative, openly adulterous, and, according to Tate's wife, Caroline Gordon, invariably drunk—hardly seemed the model chalice bearer for "classical Christian culture." Nor could they feel comfortable with the only novel of his that other American readers could be counted upon to know, *Sanctuary*—a classic not of the library but of the drugstore rack, remembered chiefly for a bloody corn cob that lacked any trace of sacramental portent. Before George Marion O'Donnell and later Cowley succeeded in universalizing and prettifying his themes, then, most of the Agrarians were unwilling to stake much of their credit on his greatness.

By the postwar era, as Schwartz recounts, the points of irreconcilable conflict between Agrarian/New Critics and ex-Marxist intellectuals had narrowed to an extraordinary degree. All were congregating in the academy, none were pressing activist causes, and for varying reasons they all could make their peace with both literary nationalism and international modernism as it was personified, however fastidiously, in "Mr. Eliot." Since there was much in Faulkner's work that could have caused unreconstructed Agrarians and Marxists alike to accuse him of political waywardness, this blurring of old antagonisms was crucial for the coming Faulkner boom. By the 1950s, moreover, a widespread revulsion against Soviet artistic regimentation had given Faulkner's stock still another lift, creating greater sympathy for his eccentric stylistic flights, his distrust of utopian agitators, and his individualistic probing of (formerly character- ized as his morbid wallowing in) private regressions and fixa- tions.

Vast in scope, morally engaged without being propagandis- tic, studded with complex image patterns, and intractable to ready explanation, Faulkner's newly republished writings beck- oned as an inexhaustible-looking supply of raw material for what John Crowe Ransom, without derogatory intent, called Criticism, Inc. Thus Faulkner was destined to become the object of "an outpouring of critical attention," as one observer has noted, "such as no other writer, it may be, in the whole history of letters has received so near the time of his work, and such as only a few writers have received at any time."[8]

The main image of Faulkner to emerge from all that early attention, however, would necessarily reflect both the domi- nant critical style of the universities and the specific politics of the Southern-born professors who largely shaped that style. For many years, and with surprisingly few exceptions, the academy contented itself with a formalist-Agrarian Faulkner—formalist, because his works were assumed to possess a unifying "moral vision," and Agrarian, because the alleged content of that vi- sion flattered Southern traditionalism without counting its cost in misery. The result was a body of criticism that occluded Faulkner's improvisation and interior debate, reduced his often daring characterizations to illustrated moral lessons, and subtly adulterated and softened his anguish over Southern history.

II

THE LEADING BOOK in this vein also happens to have been, thus far, the most influential, as well as the most widely assailed, of all Faulkner studies: Cleanth Brooks's *William Faulkner: The Yoknapatawpha Country* (1963). Teachers still pull it from the shelf when they need to sort out Faulkner's bewilder- ing social world, and even today one can discern its residual effect on critics who resent the main drift of contemporary criticism. To them, Brooks is not an ideologue but merely an affectionately objective critic who happens to know Faulkner's South firsthand. What Brooks actually gave us, however—and what became the leading strain of Faulkner criticism for a whole generation of teachers and students—was in effect the Agrarian party line.

For Brooks, Faulkner is primarily a spinner of instructive tales about the Old South and the New as they are typified in a single northern Mississippi county. In characteristic Agrarian style, the critic holds that the admittedly exploitative plantation system coexisted with a nobler, poorer South made up of independent white farmers whose values—courage, honor, perseverance, loyalty to family and village and religion—derived from a life of working the soil that their hardy forefathers had cleared from the wilderness. The chief offenses against those values, Brooks believes, can be found not in slavery, which was at least partially redeemed by its paternalism, but in secular Northern materialism, especially as it corrupted the helpless South after 1865.

According to Brooks, Faulkner's novels relate the lingering consequences of that incursion while nevertheless showing how local solidarity has managed to survive as both a fact and a standard. "Community" thus becomes the central Faulknerian value in Brooks's hands, and "fanaticism" the error that inevitably brings about misfortune. In his view, for example, *Light in August* teaches us to beware the self-destructiveness of outsiders, like Joe Christmas and Joanna Burden, who lack a stable local identity and so cannot temper their extremism with mundane and humanizing involvements. And *Absalom, Absalom!* purportedly depicts a similar tragic flaw in Thomas Sutpen, whose fierce disregard of his neighbors leads to his eventual fall and, still worse, reveals him to be not a Southerner at all but a generic American innocent driven by abstract (i.e., Northern) notions.

As many recent critics have shown, these are highly dubious

interpretations. The main reason for Brooks's dwindling appeal, however, lies not in this or that misreading but in the high price we must pay for assenting to his notion of community. Brooks would have us see an absolute opposition between Faulkner's criminals and zealots on one side and, on the other, the solidly rooted burghers and farmers of the town of Jefferson and its surrounding acres. But that provincial enclave as Faulkner depicts it looks like anything but a showcase of Southern virtue. It is rather a bastion of segregation, chicanery, night-riding, lynching, and the routine oppression of women; and its antebellum record, in Faulkner's rendering, is no better, beginning with the theft of the land from gullible Indians and culminating in the incestuous union of Carothers McCaslin with his own half-white slave daughter and his racist spurning of the resultant child/grandchild. Brooks quite gratuitously assumes, and asks that we, too, assume, that all those crimes and vices are outweighed in Faulkner's scale of values by the bare fact of social cohesion among the conforming whites.

For a long while now, *William Faulkner: The Yoknapatawpha Country* has been an object of faint praise and increasingly fierce denunciation. Brooks, however, has continued to fill out his original picture of Faulkner, serenely addressing himself to various works and problems that had found no place in his first study. After *William Faulkner: Toward Yoknapatawpha and Beyond* (Yale UP, 1978) came *William Faulkner: First Encounters* (Yale UP, 1983) and then, in 1987, *On the Prejudices, Predilections, and Firm Beliefs of William Faulkner*. Those books show an understandable decline of critical energy but no retreat from a position that now appears indefensible.

It would be pointless, then, to dwell on the shortcomings of Brooks's most recent collection of talks and essays. Suffice it to say that he remains determined to regard Faulkner's novels as the fictionalized illustration of holistic ideas, especially those that show off Southern virtue to best advantage. "A great literary artist such as Faulkner," as he puts it, "helps the rest of

the country and the rest of the world to understand us better."
Some of the values thus paraded appear to unravel in the very
act of being named—for example, "the feminine principle,"
which Faulkner is said to have treasured because male energies
"require being checked and channeled into fruitful enterprises."[9] Brooks's deeper liability, however, remains what it
always was, the formalist's overeagerness to sift homilies from
texts that could otherwise yield any number of disruptive implications.

By today, the formalist standpoint is upheld chiefly by critics
who think of it as a last stand against the deliberate subordina-
tion of Faulkner's meaning to leftist ends. Take, for instance,
Daniel Hoffman's new *Faulkner's Country Matters: Folklore and
Fable in Yoknapatawpha*. Hoffman's findings are mostly recycled
commonplaces about "intertwined themes" that supposedly
unify even the most heterogeneous of Faulkner's works. Thus,
for example, he purports to discover that *Go Down, Moses* is
unified by "the Quest and Initiation of Isaac McCaslin"—as if
that "Quest" could somehow be extended to cover such dispar-
ate chapters as "Pantaloon in Black" and "Go Down, Moses,"
in which Ike figures not at all. Hoffman's tone becomes truculent, however, when he looks up from his desk to observe what
is bearing down on him: a tidal wave of theory, as he sees it,
issuing from "a contemporary sense of grievance, perceived
injustice in the treatment of race or sex, to be assuaged at the
expense of the integrity of fiction."[10]

Hoffman fails to notice that his version of "the integrity of
fiction" is no less permeated with theory (a theory, however,
now half a century old) than the critical tendencies he opposes.
So anxious is he, moreover, to avoid the excesses of ethnic and
feminist victimology that he ends by ascribing to Faulkner an
unquestioning attachment to the ideals of the antebellum
planter class. *"Noblesse oblige* is expected of the aristocrat," he
says, applauding Colonel Sartoris's supposedly altruistic re-
building of his railroad after the war, "a courtesy toward those

whom Providence has decreed he should lead." And again: "This aristocracy had, in the nature of things, certain high and undeviating obligations toward those it owned or led."[11]

Such magnolia-scented declarations make Hoffman sound like more of a Southern chauvinist than Brooks himself. Methodologically, however, he is not departing from Brooks's precedent but merely instancing its bankruptcy. Both formalists attempt to pacify the unruly Faulknerian world by extracting certain favored opinions from it and investing them with an imagined power of aesthetic unification. That strategy seemed natural thirty years ago, when nearly all American critics still looked to literature for transcendent order and wisdom. Providence and "the nature of things" notwithstanding, however, the formalist image of Faulkner has lost all persuasiveness.

III

IT HAS TAKEN remarkably long. For whatever reasons, Faulkner critics waited until the mid-1970s to mount a significant assault on the formalist-Agrarian account of their subject—and this despite the general radicalization of academic consciousness from the mid-sixties onward. Even today, Daniel Hoffman is by no means alone among Faulknerians in resisting the idea that literature is a site of struggle whose primary conflicts, both intrapsychic and social, deserve to be brought to light rather than homogenized into notions of fixed authorial "values." But for more than a decade now, the most innovative as well as the most overreaching Faulkner studies have pointed in that direction.

As one might have expected after so many years of acquiescence to an intellectually numbing paradigm, not every early effort to throw off the formalist yoke was well considered. Faulknerian antiformalism began boldly, but also perversely, with the 1975 publication of John T. Irwin's *Doubling and Incest / Repetition and Revenge: A Speculative Reading of Faulkner*. That book ambitiously set out to trace certain features of Faulkner's plots to his sense of historical belatedness and self-fragmentation, but it ended by reducing everything it touched to the trite determinism of the Oedipus complex.

After declaring at the outset that the truth of Freud's writings is problematical, Irwin embraced every psychoanalytic notion from the castration complex through the death instinct as universally valid and explanatory not just of Faulkner but of virtually all cultural expression. He maintained, for example, that the ram in Abraham's sacrifice is really the penis, the birth of Jesus is incestuous, and the Crucifixion, likewise, is "a sexual act that, because Jesus is both the priest and the victim, is incestuous."[12] Through the exercise of such allegorical license, Irwin fashioned a tautological argument about Faulkner that withdrew from the tangible, if partisan, social reference of Agrarianism into an ahistorical and fatalistic hall of mirrors.

A more promising start toward a nontranscendent account of Faulkner was made in the late seventies and early eighties by ideologically aware academics such as Myra Jehlen, Carolyn Porter, and Eric J. Sundquist.[13] These critics departed from the mainstream tradition by showing less interest in Faulkner's early "modernist masterpieces" *The Sound and the Fury* (1929) and *As I Lay Dying* (1930) than in the works that address the race question most directly: *Light in August* (1932), *Absalom, Absalom!* (1936), and *Go Down, Moses* (1942). The latter novels, they saw, deal centrally not with "community," as Brooks had maintained, but with racism, miscegenation, and the crippling effects of Lost Cause nostalgia. Faulkner, in short, could be shown to have come to grips with both the torment and the hypocrisy of the modern white South, attempting as it did to cope with its heritage of guilt and bitterness while continuing to stifle an increasingly restive black underclass.

Not surprisingly, then, the most theoretically self-conscious of the newest Faulkner studies—represented, in the books at hand, by John N. Duvall's *Faulkner's Marginal Couple*, Wesley

Morris's (and Barbara Alverson Morris's) *Reading Faulkner,* and Richard C. Moreland's *Faulkner and Modernism*—are militantly committed to uncovering Faulkner's sympathies with the blacks, women, and other subaltern figures who were "marginalized" by the racist and patriarchal Southern order. And two of those works, at least, make a substantial contribution to that end.

Yet readers who are not already steeped in the idiom of current vanguard criticism will find much that is puzzling and forbidding in these volumes. All three critics take us "beyond text and intention," as Morris puts it, stripping the authorial mind of its once presumed wholeness and autonomy and thus freeing themselves to insert fragments of the literary record into the analytic systems of such "human scientists" as Jacques Derrida, Michel Foucault, Pierre Macherey, Jacques Lacan, and Julia Kristeva. In Morris's words, quoting Macherey, "the writer's work must be open to displacement, otherwise it will remain an object of consumption rather than an object of knowledge."[14] Instead, then, of eschewing John Irwin's vacuous Freudian gnosticism, Duvall, Morris, and Moreland replicate and embellish it with uncritical zeal.

Thus Morris, citing Irwin, solemnly invokes the death instinct to account for Quentin Compson's obsessive repetitions. Moreland in his turn correlates Faulkner's historical sense with Kristeva's theory of "the infant's primary repression or abjection of the mother and the attendant oedipal investment of the abjected maternal with its psychological and historical 'powers of horror.' " Duvall associates Joanna Burden's false pregnancy with the Virgin Mary's supposed "impregnation by the fart," thus revealing poor Joanna to be in effect "a male homosexual." When Lena Grove's search for Lucas Burch instead yields Byron Bunch as a surrogate father for her unborn child, Duvall reasons that "in this minimal difference of the signifier—*r/n*—Lucas may be seen as the self-castrating male (for what is the *r* but a castrated *n*?)—who denies both patronymic and paternity." And here is how Morris explains the significance of Addie Bundren's thought, in *As I Lay Dying*, that, of her five children, she has given her husband three "that are his and not mine":

> Three, of course, is also the oedipal number, and here Vardaman's being in excess returns us to oedipal economics. As a symbolic machine for harnessing reproductive power in the service of the father, the oedipal triad can be rewritten as $2 + 1 + x$ where x is an infinite series of one more. The value of x depends on natural resources (scarcity) and artificial factors of regulation (the marketplace), in other words, on the relationship between the reproductivity of the female body and the symbolic code, or between the aesthetic and the political dimensions of Faulkner's narrative. Addie's one more demystifies Oedipus, deconstructs the imposing mythology of Oedipus read as $3 + 1$ where 1 is a transcendental guarantee of oedipal authority and conclusiveness; 1 is the One.[15]

In one sense, we could say that the motive for such theoretical fugues is simply fashion: this is how things are done in the most prestigious English departments these days. But in another sense, Moreland, Morris, and Duvall can be seen as taking extreme precautions against any backsliding into formalism. As Duvall, justifying his recourse to abstruse terminology such as "destinator" and "destinatee," remarks:

> I would say that these words (and the models they imply) usefully estrange the act of reading; when the text is made strange, the critical context can no longer seem natural. And in the gap between that which used to seem natural and the new perception that commonsense opinions may not be sense at all but the determined products of discur-

sive formations, the critic can begin to understand his or her insertion into ideology.[16]

In plainer English, Duvall is saying that you should welcome every means of thwarting naïve identification with Faulkner or any other writer; the proper business of criticism is not empathetic commentary but a demonstration of the ways in which both literature and the critical tradition itself have been "determined" by hidden interests.

The trouble is, however, that this goal collides absolutely with the critic's other aim of making the writer out to be a friend of the oppressed. Under the old formalist dispensation, the occasionally reactionary attitudes of a writer like Faulkner could be acknowledged but neatly quarantined as "extrinsic" to the ennobling vision that supposedly inspired a given work. But for a poststructuralist, no element of discourse is ever out of bounds. Moreover, his relentlessly reductive techniques of analysis tend inherently to discount the writer's humanity while exaggerating his thralldom to the appalling prejudices of his contemporaries. To forestall revulsion against a monster of their own creation, then, some critics now resort to a saving counterstrategy: they will endow the orphaned text with an insurrectionary unconscious of its own, and thus—just like their formalist adversaries, but with far more methodological fanfare—they will find it amenable to their politics after all.

Consider an especially delicate problem, Faulkner's treatment of women, which unfriendly observers have characterized as consisting of open misogyny punctuated by occasional homage to dim-witted earth mothers. It is hard to disagree; any present-day reader will find the egregiousness of Faulkner's sexism hard to overlook. Through much of his career, he showed himself largely unable to conceive of women except in relation to their "purity." That value, already placed in doubt at adolescence by the outcropping of "mammalian ludicrosities"[17] such as Dewey Dell Bundren's and by what both Quentin Compson and Joe Christmas think of as "periodic filth," is variously doomed (like Caddy Compson's) to be squandered on the wrong man, or grotesquely embalmed within a Rosa Cold-field or an Emily Grierson, or undervalued by a rape-prone Temple Drake, or comically trampled by a pneumatic and oblivious Eula Varner. Like Addie Bundren's corpse, the female body—as the narrator of *Light in August* puts it, "the lightless hot wet primogenitive Female"[18]—is less a thing in itself than a source of big trouble for men. The final line of *The Wild Palms*—" 'Women, shit,' the tall convict said"[19]—though meant to be droll, conveys something of the author's own chronic exasperation.

Just a decade or so ago, feminist critics, in deference to Faulkner's widely acknowledged genius, were still inclined to be diplomatic about this awkward record. Perhaps overgenerously, for example, Judith Bryant Wittenberg ascribed much of Faulkner's apparent sexism to that of the rural society he faithfully depicted; she concluded that on balance he was "neither pro- nor anti-female, but rather an absorbed student of the endlessly variegated human scene." And Judith Fetterley showed how a feminist could discount Faulkner's surface values, note his insight into the structural and psychological roots of gender prejudice, and redistribute sympathy without regard for the preservation of Southern chivalry.[20]

By today, however, as John Duvall relates in *Faulkner's Marginal Couple: Invisible, Outlaw, and Unspeakable Communities,* "new wave feminist theory" of a more drastic stripe has pervaded our thinking. According to Duvall, "writers of the earlier part of this century seem hopelessly backward in their sense of women and men, so much so that calls for moratoriums on reading their texts almost seem correct."[21] Now Faulkner's works must yield distinctly liberating implications, not just neutral or sympathetic ones, if they are to avoid being dismissed as valueless.

But in this more inquisitorial climate, the author is not the only one for whom apologies may need to be made. A critic, too, can feel that he has already damaged his credibility by having entered the world as a male. Duvall, for instance, hesitates to cloak himself in the name of feminist, since, as he feels obliged to disclose, he "will never have a baby." He compensates for this handicap, however, by professing his faith that all gender differences beyond the minimum "sexual hardware"—even hormones, one supposes—are culturally constructed and by making the following pledge: "I resolutely oppose thinking that tells me I have a more primordial bond with my male dog than with a human female because my dog and I both have testicles or that my wife's behavior can be compared to a cow's because each has a uterus."[22] Duvall does not tell us which Faulkner critics subscribe to such cross-species masculinism—and of course none of them do. In its very crudity, however, the statement conveys a sense of the trend-conscious male academic's anxiety to be considered politically unstained.

Someone in Duvall's predicament, if he is to write about Faulkner's women at all, stands in need of a straw man to topple. Given the polarized history of Faulkner criticism, his choice is inevitable: the eighty-four-year-old but ever-serviceable Cleanth Brooks. Duvall therefore begins not by building on the considerable body of extant feminist insights into Faulkner but by resuscitating and challenging Brooks's version of the proper Faulknerian family, whereby "man makes the choices and lives up to the choices" while woman is "characteristically fostering and sustaining."[23]

It is easy, then, for Duvall to muster indignation about the failure of Brooks's model to match what one actually finds in the fiction: a significant number of soft-spoken, passive men like Ernest Talliaferro, Horace Benbow, Byron Bunch, and Henry Stribling, and plenty of decisive, forceful women such as Margaret Powers, Drusilla Hawk, Joanna Burden, Charlotte Rittenmeyer, and Laverne Shumann. Especially in "the ideologically disruptive non-Yoknapatawpha material," Duvall adds, Faulkner's plots often conjoin two such "deviants" in a successfully functioning "counterhegemonic" pair. Hence his thesis: that "although Faulkner's texts operate in a horizon of misogyny, the alternative communities created by marginal couples in those texts provide alternate [*sic*] narratives for rethinking hegemonic myths of love and bourgeois marriage."[24]

There are indeed numerous unions between strong women and weak men in Faulkner's work. The pattern is so common as to suggest an oblique confession of sexual inadequacy on the part of the shy, diminutive, much-rejected, unhappily married, incest-haunted, and alcoholic novelist. Just what can be considered emancipatory about those quirky fictional relationships, however, is harder to establish. When Faulkner's women behave "mannishly," they would appear to represent for him not a model for general liberation but innate female unruliness and a sign that lamentable emasculating forces have been set loose in the social world.

To keep this dismal realization at bay, Duvall idealizes every "outlaw" relationship insofar as possible and then ascribes any residue of negative elements to warping patriarchal influence. This allocation of blame seems at least partly appropriate to the tensions between Joe Christmas and Joanna Burden in *Light in August*, a novel which is "about" the transmission of zealotry and hatred from generation to generation, but it is largely gratuitous in the cases of Charlotte Rittenmeyer and Harry Wilbourne in *The Wild Palms* and of Temple Drake and Popeye in *Sanctuary*. Granted, Duvall has perceptive things to say about the stifling, incestuous possessiveness of Judge Drake and of Popeye's briefly glimpsed mother. But *Sanctuary* generates little sympathy for any of its characters, and Temple is hardly an exception. Though Duvall is quite right to charge Faulkner critics with typical eagerness to blame the rape victim for her rape, he won't admit how much encouragement they receive from the sardonic *roman noir* itself.

Even in his treatment of *Light in August*, Duvall's insistence on Joe Christmas's "deep and real love"[25] for Joanna Burden sentimentalizes where Faulkner himself conspicuously does not. The tumultuous Joe-Joanna affair is one of Faulkner's boldest psychological explorations, a power game played out between self-despising loners who are settling old scores on one another's bodies in a manner that commingles puritanism, racism, exhibitionism, and voyeurism. But Duvall, contemplating a spectacle of sadomasochistic carnality and revulsion that ends in two attempted murders, sees little more than another precious "alternative community"; he even goes so far as to deny that the consummated murder deserves to be called such.[26]

What *Faulkner's Marginal Couple* finally offers us is a mirror image of the much-refuted Brooksian moralism that its author holds up to scorn. Ideological fashions aside, there is nothing to choose between strip-mining Faulkner's works for wholesome communities and for incipiently revolutionary ones. Both tasks obey an arcadian impulse; each seeks a haven from the novelist's chronic gloom and often merciless humor. Duvall, no less than Brooks, would have done better to bear in mind what Faulkner wrote to Else Jonsson in 1955: "But human beings are terrible. One must believe well in man to endure him, wait out his folly and savagery and inhumanity."[27]

IV

AT FIRST GLANCE, the jargon-filled studies by Wesley Morris and Richard Moreland may appear to be as remote from Faulkner's sensibility as Duvall's *Faulkner's Marginal Couple.* Yet Morris and Moreland do set themselves apart from Duvall in one redeeming way. Instead of turning Faulkner's texts into a semiotic machine for dispensing congenial implications, they keep in mind a sobering biographical reference point: the writer's motives and preoccupations as a man of his time and place. There is a human Faulkner—fallible, biased, but also surprisingly capable of growth—to be discovered at the end of these critics' twisting paths. And this simple fact, which no one would have thought worthy of remark in a critical study until quite recently, enables Morris and Moreland to pass beyond ideological shadow-boxing and reach some conclusions of general interest.

As their titles imply—Morris's is *Reading Faulkner;* Moreland's is *Faulkner and Modernism: Rereading and Rewriting*—the emphasis of these books falls not on meaning in the usual sense but on the experience of immersion in Faulkner's unstable world. The essence of that experience is a cognitive and emotional jostling produced by Faulkner's refusal to provide us with an "omniscient" perspective outside the characters' and narrators' own struggles. What the critics see, in contrast to the school of Brooks, is that in struggling to arrive at an adequately complex account of the modern white Southern mind, Faulkner was plunging into the thicket of his own confusions.

But Morris insists on a crucial difference between the novelist and such similarly troubled characters as Quentin Compson and Ike McCaslin: temperamentally, Faulkner always felt himself to be an outsider and a rebel who despised half-truths. Though he was no more capable than Quentin of straightforwardly rejecting the South or of siding unambiguously with the victims of Southern laws and customs, his sense of alienation goaded him not only into indicting his ancestors for their misdeeds but also into sniffing out and exposing all the mental tricks that safeguarded his townsmen's complacency.

The Faulkner described by Morris could call to mind Nathaniel Hawthorne, who also began in the shadow of illustrious ancestors whose public deeds appeared to mock his own early aestheticism and introversion. As victims of downward family mobility, both Hawthorne and Faulkner needed to appropriate their forefathers' prestige yet also to get out from under their intimidating authority. Hence both writers' ambivalent gestures of dissociation from family crimes whose heinousness they found it convenient both to broadcast and to embellish. In this dialectic between pride and shame, the oppressed—Haw-

thorne's seventeenth-century Quakers, Faulkner's blacks—
served not as objects of a primary sympathy but merely as
witnesses against the ancestors' predations.[28]

Yet throughout the misery-stricken thirties, Faulkner, unlike
Hawthorne, did progressively emerge from the familial bell jar
and awaken to the claims of the defenseless. Once he had fully
realized that miscegenation was the key not only to his predecessors' hypocrisy but also to the deepest fears of his contemporaries, he found himself drawn to characters like Joe Christmas,
Clytie Sutpen, and Charles Bon—liminal figures whose ostra-
cism highlights a general pathology in white Southern culture.
And in *Go Down, Moses,* with the wrenching portraits of
Lucas and Mollie Beauchamp and of the unnamed near-white
woman of "Delta Autumn" who grandly refuses to renounce
her doomed love for Edmonds McCaslin, he seemed to put his
prejudices in abeyance and, however briefly, to feel the full
humanity of the despised other.

In the same period, correspondingly, Faulkner hardened his
resistance to romantic nostalgia, whether of the Lost Cause or
the Agrarian variety. As he explicitly proclaimed while working
on *Absalom,* a comprehensive irony toward the fallen present is
a form of sentimentality no less contemptible than flight into
costume drama.[29] The opportunism of the Snopeses, he saw,
was akin not only to Thomas Sutpen's but also to that of the
Sartorises, Compsons, and McCaslins; the Old South and the
New formed a continuum that could be examined without
special pleading for any class, family, or epoch. By the end of
the Depression, Morris and Moreland both show, Faulkner had
achieved a formidable maturity, objectivity, and breadth of
social and historical understanding.

Though Morris discusses this development trenchantly,
some of its nuances seem to escape his notice. Too often, he
appears content merely to insist that the academy's favorite
themes of race, class, and gender can be found in even the most
apolitical-looking of Faulkner's works. The result is a certain

redundancy, a loss of discrimination between very different texts, and a hard-edged "materialism" of emphasis that sometimes ignores what is distinctively Southern about those texts. Morris's contention, for example, that Thomas Sutpen "is nothing more than a businessman ruthlessly obsessed with the trappings of success" dismisses the specific force of the plantation myth in *Absalom, Absalom!*, collapsing the distance—still important to Faulkner—between Northern and Southern forms of inhumanity.[30]

Richard Moreland does better, partly by attending more closely to Faulkner's language and partly by allowing his emotions as well as his intellect to stay fully engaged. A criticism that goes no further than indicting real and fictional white oppressors, Moreland sees, will stall at the phase of consciousness represented in *Go Down, Moses* by Ike McCaslin's neurotic and horror-stricken renunciation of his patrimony. Faulkner himself came to understand that merely "facing the facts" of collective guilt is no solution, since it perpetuates the depersonalization of the underclass. As Moreland perceives, the power of *Go Down, Moses* derives not merely from its grim unearthing of Carothers McCaslin's abominations but also from its disarming tenderness. The theme it finally broaches—implicit in earlier works, but never directly approachable—is interracial love, founded in a lifelong Southern intimacy that racist customs cannot altogether transmute into hatred and fear.

Moreland is especially keen on the subject of Faulkner's humor, which, once again, could not find full expression until he had seen through Lost Cause nostalgia, adjusting his gaze downward from ancestral authority, metaphysical irony, and fashionable despair to ordinary human venality—the perennial stuff of comedy. In *Absalom, Absalom!* he was still critiquing, without fully laying to rest, the self-exculpating idea of Southern historical change as, in Moreland's words, "a cataclysmic collapse from purity and order into chaos or fated ruin."[31] But by *The Hamlet* (1940), perhaps the most underrated of his works, he could take a relaxed and canny view of the way one form of institutionalized injustice had evolved into a more "liberal," economically rationalized one, the tenant-farming and monopoly-store treadmill. The reduced social distance between exploiters and the exploited under that system, in which contractual obligation and cunning figured more prominently than aristocratic birth, gave Faulkner an opening to revive and refine the tradition of southwestern humor, whose typical focus is not class oppression but a chain of particular deceptions.

Critics of *The Hamlet*, like several of the characters within it, have been quick to mythify its villain Flem Snopes as a principle of evil, or, in Agrarian terms, as a figure for carpetbagging capitalism as it preyed upon the economically helpless New South. But Flem is in fact the son of Ab Snopes, the thoroughly Southern antagonist of the patrician Colonel Sartoris in "Barn Burning"; and Ab himself, apparently headed for tragedy in "Barn Burning," reappears in *The Hamlet* as a perennial survivor whose ability to intimidate his social betters has become a source of reluctant general admiration. Faulkner is not choosing sides; there is nothing at stake for him between Flem and his equally greedy but less agile prey Jody Varner, any more than there was between the shit-smearing, barn-burning Ab and the insufferable Colonel Sartoris. And as Moreland shows in detail, Faulkner comically belittles the good townsmen of Frenchman's Bend who make Flem the scapegoat for their own legalism, money fetishism, and infatuation with sharp dealing.

Thus the tension and outrage that we normally associate with Faulknerian narration are largely missing from *The Hamlet*, and Faulkner himself, like the itinerant storyteller V. K. Ratliff, finds cause for narrative drollery everywhere. In most critics' eyes, these are the makings of minor literature—perhaps the first signs of Faulkner's long decline. Yet *The Hamlet* was followed by the dazzling *Go Down, Moses,* a work which resumes the interrupted theme of the color line at its highest pitch of intensity. In their comic and tragic ways, Moreland argues, both of those books display Faulkner at his mature best, in command of a fully articulated social world.

v

WHAT SHOULD WE SAY, however, about the books that came after *Go Down, Moses*—especially those in which Faulkner, precisely because he had outgrown his obsessiveness, was free to cultivate the liberal sentiments that his newfound Northern admirers expected of him? Those works constitute a test for critics like Moreland and Morris: will they be able to acknowledge a possible divergence between ideological congeniality and literary power? It is not reassuring to find Morris warming, however warily, to the garrulous *Intruder in the Dust* (1948), which earns his admiration for its "alternative community consisting of blacks, women, and children."[32] And most readers will want to think twice before accepting Moreland's high estimation of the labored *Requiem for a Nun* (1951), which implausibly rehabilitates Temple Drake as a born-again feminist and scourge of racism.

But politically driven evaluations are hardly confined to Faulkner's last phase. Consider the near consensus of advanced academic opinion, since about 1980, whereby the preeminently "social" *Absalom, Absalom!* is more highly regarded than the merely "private" and "oedipal" *Sound and the Fury* and *As I Lay Dying*. Surely it ought to matter, however, that *Absalom* is a book more easily studied than read. Its characters, as its first reviewers saw quite clearly, are at best half-realized sketches of the people they purport to be; its plot is riddled not just with mysteries but with uncontrolled absurdities; and its prose, in which, to quote Rosa Coldfield, "the prisoner soul, miasmal-distillant, wroils ever upward sunward,"[33] reverts to the logorrhea of Faulkner's apprentice period. Such Swinburnian bloat might justifiably cause one to pine for the cutting language of a Jason Compson or the bleeding language of a Benjy.

American formalists and most of their adversaries are united, it seems, in a determination to equate artistic success with thematic "maturity," "historical seriousness," and so forth. Yet Faulkner is often at his most memorable when not being public-spirited—as, for example, when he is pitilessly recounting the antics of those surreal yokels, the Bundrens, or when he explores the mind of a young neurotic who is fixated on nothing more exalted than his sister's muddy drawers. If Faulkner is to be given his full due, such critics as Morris and Moreland (to say nothing of John Duvall) need to be supplemented by others who won't flinch from the literary sparks given off by sheer willfulness and compulsion.

In fact, Faulkner has always had such critics, though few of them have been Americans. As early as the 1930s, well before Malcolm Cowley's campaign to monumentalize the genial chronicler of Yoknapatawpha County, commentators in France had been drawn to him for just the qualities that Cowley and later Brooks sought to minimize: his pessimism, his wild experimentation, and his unflinching treatment of sex, whiskey, bigotry, and violence as staples of American life. And since the early 1970s another French critic, André Bleikasten of the University of Strasbourg, has been publishing remarkably intuitive and free-ranging analyses of certain novels, uninhibited by either an Agrarian or an anti-Agrarian agenda but informed by comprehensive knowledge of the Faulknerian critical tradition on both sides of the Atlantic.[34] Now Bleikasten has revised, consolidated, and doubled the range of those studies in a large book, *The Ink of Melancholy: Faulkner's Novels from* The Sound and the Fury *to* Light in August. It is, I believe, unsurpassed as an act of sustained engagement with Faulkner's language. In addition, it can serve as a bracing antidote to an American criticism that, in Bleikasten's words, habitually "confuse[s] the merits of a literary work with the tangible magnitude of its themes."[35]

This is not to say that we could turn to Bleikasten, if we wished, for a theory-free impressionism. Though he claims to stand outside all systems and schools, he has drawn upon every trend in the French "human sciences" from phenomenology through Althusserian Marxism to Lacanian psychoanalysis. Indeed, he evidences much the same credulousness toward psychoanalysis as we have seen in Duvall, Morris, and Moreland.[36] For the most part, however, Bleikasten keeps to what he calls "a lighter, more mobile and more alert reading" than we have grown resigned to, a critical style adapted to the fact that "Faulkner's texts are not deposits of fixed and final meaning for us to decipher; they are discharges of mental energy, fields of turbulence, records of battles won and lost. . . ."[37]

Since he is more concerned with those fields of turbulence than with position taking, Bleikasten finds no need to shrink from the racism and sexism that keep surfacing in some of Faulkner's most compelling work. In a book like *Light in August,* he argues, women and blacks tend to serve as interchangeable figures for the viscous pit of otherness that constitutes their author's ultimate nightmare. Though Bleikasten knows that a critic might minimize that nightmare by ascribing it, in certain works, to a Horace Benbow or a Gail Hightower rather than to Faulkner, he perceives that the represented horror tends to pervade the text.

Reading Bleikasten, we become aware that in their understandable reaction against both the bromides of Agrarian formalism and the social disdain of Eliotic modernism, recent American commentators have oversold the socially conscious Faulkner. Despite Wesley Morris's account of it, for example, *As I Lay Dying* is not finally a story about the economic predicament of Depression-era poor whites. It is closer to being what Bleikasten calls "an almost timeless fable" about "the naked scandal of existence"[38]—a scandal which it confronts with an irreducible, farcically tinged astonishment that leaves little room for sociological diagnosis or sympathy for the downtrodden.

As for modernism, Bleikasten's distance from the squabbles

of the American academy allows him to see that, whether or not Faulkner ever completely outgrew his early infatuation with *The Waste Land,* he long remained a participant in the broader modernism that runs from Mallarmé and Rimbaud to Rilke, Stein, and Beckett. Faulkner shared with those writers a belief that the meanings to which the human race clings "are little more than the precarious fictions of our desires and the erratic impositions of our wills."[39] Hence, Bleikasten senses, his practice of hinting at inexpressible realities while allowing the engine of rhetoric to jump its mimetic rails.

Bleikasten misses no chance to show how Faulkner, at least in his most inventive mode, continually defies his readers' complacency. The final leap to either Christianity or nihilism in *The Sound and the Fury,* he admonishes, "is never made, nor should it be attempted by the reader." The master trope of *Light in August,* the circle, "absorbs everything it touches into its enigmatic, apparently meaningful, yet ultimately purposeless patterns of repetition and deferment and threatens us with the empty perfection of the cipher." And again, the alarming, yet patently calculated, breaches of plausibility in *As I Lay Dying* suggest a typically modernist intent "to weave a text and to tear it to pieces, to build a fiction and to ruin its pretensions."[40]

And then there is *Sanctuary.* The language of liquefaction and exudation that runs like an open sewer through its pages leads to the following stark inferences on Bleikasten's part:

> Bodies are not sanctuaries. No presence, no mystery dwells in them—unless it be that of their generation and death. What dignity could one find in these leaking sacks of skin? Bodies do not know how to contain and control themselves. Everything urges them to spill their slimy little secrets. Sweat, spittle, vomit, blood—through all these oozings and flowings and outpourings flesh bespeaks its incontinence and inconsistency, announces its carrion future. In the last resort, the language of the body comes

down to this reiterated admission of its shame and misery—a nauseous epiphany, aptly epitomized by "that
black stuff that ran out of Bovary's mouth."[41]

Though it quotes Faulkner, such a phenomenological tour
de force is less an act of analysis than one of parallel creation
in Faulkner's honor. Yet after receiving assurance from
Cleanth Brooks that the novelist was never cynical or nihilistic,
and after hearing from John Duvall that *Sanctuary* "illustrates
how all males become implicated in a sexist ideology that
makes possible violence against women," we can appreciate
Bleikasten's wish to part company with the prim American
tradition.[42] Here is one critic who has digested Faulkner's
uniqueness without having to regurgitate a sermon.

Between Morris and Moreland on one side and Bleikasten
on the other, we have two incompatible-looking cases for the
importance of Faulkner's achievement. Yet each case is persua-
sive in its own terms. Need we choose, then, between seeing
Faulkner as an elliptical, allusive, alienated modernist and,
alternatively, as a reflective teller of local tales, circling about a
core of morally charged themes as he rethinks his relation to
Southern defeat, persecution, and suffering?

There can be no doubt that the novelist shifted toward the
latter self-conception during his sustained creative burst of
1929–42. But he did so gradually and incompletely, meanwhile
creating radically hybrid works that are somehow both confid-
ing and contrived, voluble and sly, vertiginously poised between the realistic and the weird. This is the Faulkner who
keeps us continually off balance, as he will fail to do in later
novels like *The Town* and *The Mansion*. "It is a unique role that
the reader must play," as Hugh Kenner has remarked, "seeing
folk material imitated, synthesized, by the devices of the twentieth-century avant-garde, being aware that that is what is
going on and yet responding as if he were what he cannot be,
a sympathetic member of a vanished community."[43]

When Kenner spoke those words at a conference in 1978, he offended career Faulknerians, who saw that he was implicitly chiding the writer for failing to match the thoroughgoing experimentalism of the master modernist, Joyce. The resentment was warranted; avant-gardism is hardly a touchstone of novelistic excellence, and there are ways in which Faulkner makes Joyce look petty and cold. Still, Kenner was right about the experience of reading. Faulkner often flew blind, juxtaposing wildly different sets of conventions to see what might result. And that, surely, has helped to keep him fresh even for academics as the Faulkner industry enters its fifth decade of all-out production. It will never be said of Faulkner, as Faulkner said of Hemingway, that "he stayed within what he knew. He did it fine, but he didn't try for the impossible."[44]

SEVEN

The Critics Bear It Away

FLANNERY O'CONNOR, *Collected Works*, ed. Sally Fitzgerald (New York: Library of America, 1988).

ROBERT H. BRINKMEYER, JR., *The Art and Vision of Flannery O'Connor* (Baton Rouge: Louisiana State UP, 1989).

RALPH C. WOOD, *The Comedy of Redemption: Christian Faith and Comic Vision in Four American Novelists* (Notre Dame: U of Notre Dame P, 1988).

FREDERICK ASALS, *Flannery O'Connor: The Imagination of Extremity* (Athens, Ga.: U of Georgia P, 1982).

I

HOBBLED AND ENFEEBLED by a disease that would kill her at age thirty-nine, but determined not to be a drain on her mother's household economy, Flannery O'Connor, in her dozen years of fame, was inclined to seize every chance to earn a modest honorarium on the college lecture circuit. Venturing as far as Notre Dame or Wesleyan or as near as her hometown alma mater, Milledgeville's Georgia State College for Women, she would read a story or deliver one of her standard, virtually interchangeable, talks about "The Grotesque in Southern Fiction" or "The Church and the Fiction Writer" or "The Catholic Novelist in the South." And to hear her tell it, the questions from the floor were almost as predictable as the lectures. "Everywhere I go," she once observed, "I'm asked if I think the universities stifle writers. My opinion is that they don't stifle enough of them."[1]

It is easy to picture what she had in mind. Always punctilious in her dealings with strangers, O'Connor was more bothered than most authors by hapless apprentice manuscripts and pleas for help. They made it that much harder for her to husband scarce energy for her fiction while answering every letter she received—even the one from a young man who proposed collaboration on a novel "as good as *Gone with the Wind,*" and the one from "a real West Virginia mountineer" who praised her for writing "sinsationally, wow, ha ha," and still another from an eligible Cincinnati bachelor "who has not read anything of mine," she told a friend, "but doesn't really see how I can say a good man is hard to find."[2] Those interruptions at least gratified O'Connor's comic sense, but unsolicited student prose may have provided the severest test of her forbearance.

The truth is, however, that O'Connor had no cause to disprize university writing programs, for she herself, despite the marked individuality of her work, was the first prominent American author to have been significantly shaped by one. Scholars who examine her early manuscripts, housed at what is now called simply Georgia College, are always taken aback by their awkwardness.[3] As she freely acknowledged, she came into her own as an artist only after undergoing a full New Critical initiation at the University of Iowa's Writer's Workshop under the tutelage of Paul Engle and Andrew Lytle, with Brooks and Warren's then ubiquitous *Understanding Fiction* providing the models.

Like so many college-trained writers who have succeeded her, O'Connor never wrote without a sense of the critics looking over her shoulder. Nor, in her shorter fiction at least, did she ever stray from the regnant creative-writing mode. Even the most impressive and original of her stories adhere to the classroom formula of her day: show, don't tell; keep the narrative voice distinct from those of your characters; cultivate understatement; develop a central image or symbol to convey your theme "objectively"; and point everything toward one neatly sprung ironic reversal. No one has ever put it all together with greater deftness.

A cynic might say, then, that in lionizing O'Connor the American university has not so much acknowledged a literary genius as bestowed a posthumous laurel on its most diligent student. Whatever the reason, O'Connor now holds a niche in the anthologies nearly as secure-looking as Hemingway's or Faulkner's and more so than those of, say, Anderson, Fitzgerald, Lewis, and Dos Passos. Virtually every American survey course sets aside a day for one of her crystalline, eminently teachable stories such as "Revelation," "A Good Man Is Hard to Find," or "Good Country People." The violence of action and freakishness of portraiture that troubled many of her earliest readers scarcely raise an eyebrow today, while the ironies, paradoxes, Doppelgängers, and image patterns that she so painstakingly implanted in her texts stand available for moralized "close reading" of exactly the sort that she herself mastered at Iowa four decades ago.

As this description may imply, however, the question of O'Connor's stature is hardly settled for good. Is she really to be acknowledged as the preeminent fiction writer of the postwar period? No less an honor must have been intended by the publication, last year, of her *Collected Works* in the prestigious Library of America series—the closest thing to a formal canonization that our dispersed and eclectic culture can now bestow. But to contemplate not a story or two but her whole body of fiction wedged against those of such demigods as Melville and James and Twain is to face the issue of her plentitude, or lack of it, in a suddenly glaring light. Placed in such company, O'Connor's works for all their brilliance cannot conceal a certain narrowness of emphasis and predictability of technique.

O'Connor's sensibility, as she well knew, was maladapted to the incremental, circumstantial, untranscendent development that typically sustains a novel between its moments of peak signification. Her two quirky novels, *Wise Blood* and *The Violent*

Bear It Away, are considerably alike in theme and structure if not in texture. Both of them, especially *Wise Blood,* are top-heavy with obvious symbols. More damagingly, neither succeeds in enlisting most readers' sympathy with, or even their credence in, the final turn toward salvation that the author imposes on her spasmodic, one-dimensional, Christ-fleeing protagonist. And even the individually dazzling stories, once we have been alerted to the world view that animates them, can all be seen to be performing the same religious maneuver—namely, a humbling of secular egoism to make way for a sudden infusion of God's grace. That is not, one would think, a device with a great deal of literary mileage left in it, either inside or beyond the university.

Indeed, the current iconoclastic mood of academic trend-setters might suggest that even within the world of "English," O'Connor's stock is due for what Wall Street calls a correction. After all, the religious neoorthodoxy of the post–World War II university has long since evaporated. A demystifying sensibility cannot help but be restless with O'Connor's latent premise of a fixed theological backdrop to human action, with God and Satan vying for possession of the individual soul and with the author standing helpfully by to mete out rebukes to the impious. Meanwhile, the recent revival of forthrightly ideological habits of reading portends a related kind of trouble. In a time of rapidly expanding ethnic and egalitarian sentiment in the universities, O'Connor's provincial conservatism, especially with regard to the race issue, will probably come to seem harder to discount.

Academic second thoughts about O'Connor already appear to be astir, although, curiously, it is her would-be protectors who chiefly manifest them. Here and there, one notices, her penchant for settled judgments is being treated as a worrisome problem. But today, no less than in the prime of the New Criticism, the professorial instinct when a difficulty looms is not to face it squarely but to reach for a methodological wand that can make it disappear. In the fifties that protective principle was "organic unity" or "ironic vision"; now it is some form of deconstructive loosening whereby the offensive content can be represented as neutralized or altogether negated by subversive textual forces.

Consider, for example, an article in the December 1989 number of *American Literature,* the flagship journal in its field: James M. Mellard's "Flannery O'Connor's *Others:* Freud, Lacan, and the Unconscious." Until recently, Mellard claims, O'Connor's religious explications of her own works placed her high among those modern authors "who have had their way with critics." But today, he says, any "metaphysics of presence" whatsoever, to say nothing of an explicitly Catholic variety, is anathema to us; we can't allow ourselves to heed "irrelevant" authorial directives along such lines. What should we do instead?

> The solution, I suggest, is to displace O'Connor's way toward something else, some other Other, the Otherness that postmodernists such as Lacan find inside human texts—and the text that *is* human—rather than outside in some metaphysical space. In a critical turn that no doubt would have utterly dismayed O'Connor, we are enabled to see that a reading through Lacan, rather than Freud, leads to another notion of the Other. The Other of her art is not necessarily any God of theology, and it may yet be the Other of psychoanalysis and the unconscious.[4]

Thus the critic, for O'Connor's own presumed good, proposes to disregard the "higher" thematic content of her works and insert a suitably lower one in its place. Where God was, there shall the Lacanian unconscious be. And though this appropriation may appear violent, it turns out, Mellard says, "to include a vindication of sorts for O'Connor." Once we have chosen to regard the unconscious, rather than Christ, as the proper goal of reconciliation toward which everything finally points, "the end results for the subjects of her fiction remain very much the same."[5] There is benefit here, then, for both of the affected parties: O'Connor gets to keep the positive and negative moral judgments that she passes on her characters, and we get to replace the embarrassing theological basis of those judgments with something congenially secular, subterranean, and Continental.

To illustrate how the academy's now-favorite offshoot of Freudianism can be supposed to pervade O'Connor's fiction, Mellard devises a standard Lacanian reading of "A View of the Woods." Characters, scenes, and even single words are said to reverberate in what Mellard calls "wonderfully Lacanian ways,"[6] with cryptic (if often farfetched) reference to castration, the mirror stage, the *moi*, the law, the Other, the Name of the Father, and the Imaginary and the Symbolic. And with this much compliance extorted from the text, O'Connor's obsolete Christian theme can be confidently recast in more palatable terms. In killing his nine-year-old granddaughter, the story's seventy-nine-year-old protagonist is not, as O'Connor thought she meant, thereby resisting salvation but rather expressing narcissism and an oedipal fixation on his mother.

It may be doubted, however, whether such patent critical tampering really constitutes a vindication of O'Connor's art. The very extremity of Mellard's tactics appears to bespeak discomfort with her fiction in its unadulterated state. Moreover, the critic can hardly be said to have disposed of the problem that originally troubled him. Though he has managed to spurn O'Connor's obnoxious Christian glosses, his Lacanian reading reinstates a "metaphysics of presence" no less rigid than the redemptive meaning it is supposed to dislodge. If one is worried about allowing complex literary texture to congeal into allegory, what is there to choose between one Name of the Father and another?

Mellard appears to realize that his master key for thematic substitutions will appear trivial unless he can provide a show of biographical justification for it. Freud, he therefore alleges, actually *was* O'Connor's psychic "Other"—the figure she most feared, since his explanatory system covered the same terrain as her own while eliminating any recourse to theism. But this hypothesis requires as much license with the facts as does the critic's reading of "A View of the Woods." Thus, for example, when O'Connor rejects a correspondent's surmise that Sheppard in "The Lame Shall Enter First" is really a representation of Freud, Mellard finds that she is "protesting too much,"[7] denying her all-consuming fear of "possession" by her true psychological master. Mellard cannot afford to consider that O'Connor may simply be right: Freud and Sheppard bear no resemblance worth mentioning.

This is not to deny, however, that Freud played a part in O'Connor's moral and psychological thought. She realized that he had anticipated her idea that human beings are deluded by their mental estrangement from drives that must nevertheless find expression. But in O'Connor's world view, the "natural" human core that gets sublimated and perverted is not libido but an innate love of the Creator. Since to a third party the Christian and psychoanalytic systems of explanation would appear equally undemonstrable and reductive, it is culturally parochial to say, as Mellard does, that the spiritual strivings of O'Connor's characters must "really" refer to the castration complex, the mirror stage, and so forth. O'Connor emerges from Mellard's attempted salvage operation looking as intractable as ever to a postmodern, poststructuralist makeover.

A parallel effort to save the author from her announced values can be found in the latest of the twenty-two books on her to have appeared thus far, Robert H. Brinkmeyer's *The Art and Vision of Flannery O'Connor*. Unlike Mellard, Brinkmeyer is at heart an old-fashioned thematic critic, seeking only to discover what makes O'Connor's works coherent and successful in their own terms. Significantly, however, he too regards her Catholic principles as a potential threat to her stature. In particular, he worries about an apparent unyieldingness in her, a tendency to

"suppress and punish" those characters who defy her supernaturalism.[8] Unless that impression can be effectively coun-
tered, Brinkmeyer feels, we must resign ourselves to thinking of
O'Connor as a minor artist.

For a remedy, Brinkmeyer turns to a truncated, moralized
version of the great Soviet critic Mikhail Bakhtin's now modish
idea of "the dialogic imagination." O'Connor, he asserts,
grasped the unfruitfulness of aesthetic "monologism," whereby
"artists do not interact with their characters but manipulate
them to illustrate and validate their own visions." She saved
herself from this error, Brinkmeyer claims, by imaginatively
entertaining two radically incompatible versions of Christianity, channeling all her "fundamentalism" into her narrators
and then turning those narrators into objects of Catholic judgment. The outcome, he says, is an endlessly extended Bakh-
tinian interplay of voices, affirming neither one theology nor its
rival but only the desirability of keeping the self in a constant
state of revision. This sounds plausible enough until one returns
to O'Connor's works and begins looking for those satirized
"fundamentalist" narrators. They are nowhere to be seen. Instead, we find a uniformly urbane and laconic manner of story-
telling that generates abundant irony, but never detectably at
the expense of "the narrator." Brinkmeyer has simply invented
a scapegoat figure so that O'Connor herself can be absolved of
the cardinal sin against his own age: the harboring of "a univo-
cal and finalized consciousness."[9]

The lesson of suspended judgment and perpetual flux that
Brinkmeyer draws from O'Connor's works, furthermore, is
foreign to everything she passionately believed. She faulted her
contemporaries not for monologism but for being, in her
words, "swept this way and that by momentary convictions,"[10]
and she detested nothing so heartily as Brinkmeyer's ideal of
self-development for its own sake. Her fictional universe is one
in which, as she herself put it, "everything works toward its true
end or away from it, everything is ultimately saved or lost."[11]

Though there is much that is disturbing and even ambiguous about O'Connor's world, critics who seek to justify her in postmodern terms would do well to cease evading her intellectual and emotional loyalty to a single value system.

II

IN THE ENTIRE BODY of Flannery O'Connor's available statements, both public and private, one finds not a whisper of dissent from the central teachings of Roman Catholicism—from the Incarnation, the Resurrection, and the reality of heaven, Satan, and the angels to the belief that the church is God's sole medium for dispensing both redemption and divine truth. The literally present body and blood of Christ in the Eucharist, she declared, "is the center of existence for me; all the rest of life is expendable."[12] Nor did she experience her hereditary faith—she was a fourth-generation Georgia Catholic—as inhibiting her art in any way. On the contrary, she considered Christian dogma at once "an instrument for penetrating reality"[13] and a preventative against the relativism that was threatening, she felt, to leave modern fiction insipid and directionless.

Those who know O'Connor only through one or two popular stories are unlikely to realize the intensity of her Christian commitment. One need only scan her letters, however, to grasp the point. The first of her two collections of tales, *A Good Man Is Hard to Find,* consisted, she accurately wrote to Sally Fitzgerald, of "nine stories about original sin, with my compliments."[14] And the "standard of judgment" informing those stories, she insisted to another friend,

> concerns specifically Christ and the Incarnation, the fact that there has been a unique intervention in history. It's not a matter in these stories of Do Unto Others. That can be found in any ethical culture series. It's the fact of the

Word made flesh. As the Misfit said, "He thrown everything off balance and it's nothing for you to do but follow
Him or find some meanness." That is the fulcrum that lifts
my particular stories.[15]

When even Christian readers kept perceiving her as a nihilist,
moreover, O'Connor began making her redemptive theme
more explicit, so that she could be "known at last to the Bap-
tized."[16] Both *The Violent Bear It Away* and several of the stories
in *Everything That Rises Must Converge* were reworked with that
goal expressly in mind.

This built-in doctrinal emphasis has given an initial advantage to O'Connor's Christian critics, who tend to make up in
theological alertness for what they sometimes lack in literary
sensibility.[17] Most of us would recoil, for example, from one
believer's proposal that the escaped bull in "Greenleaf" sym-
bolizes "the justice of God in its destructiveness and the love of
Christ in its function of saving Mrs. May by revealing the truth
to her"[18]—this in the act of goring her to death!—but O'Connor's overriding concern with redemption impelled her, time
after time, to impart just such last-moment visions to her protagonists. Though not itself divine, the bull is indeed meant to
be recognized as an instrument of God's stern benevolence. Or
again, take the gruesome remark of the serial killer, "The
Misfit," as he stands over the bullet-ridden corpse of the
Grandmother in "A Good Man Is Hard to Find": "She would
of been a good woman if it had been somebody there to shoot
her every minute of her life."[19] It may seem like lunacy to assert,
as the pious critics regularly do, that this sadistic outburst embodies O'Connor's own view of the matter. Yet her numerous
surviving remarks about the story leave little doubt that she,
too, wanted us to grasp that, as one critic puts it, "had death
been perennially present to remind the Grandmother of her
total dependence on God, she would have trusted in his grace
rather than her own gentility."[20]

This last comment comes from Ralph C. Wood, who allots

O'Connor two chapters in his unflaggingly devout new book, *The Comedy of Redemption: Christian Faith and Comic Vision in Four American Novelists.* (The other three writers are Walker Percy, John Updike, and Peter De Vries.) Those chapters contain some of the best-informed and most discerning theological criticism O'Connor has yet received, and they press the case for a strictly Christian understanding of her work as far as it can plausibly go.

For Wood as for the other Christian exegetes, O'Connor is fundamentally a comic writer. Her droll puncturing of her characters' self-satisfaction is underwritten by a larger comic sense deriving from the good news of Catholic eschatology. What the secular reader may perceive as barren "Southern Gothic" terrain, by turns banal and terrifying, is actually, Wood claims, suffused with prevenient grace—a divine pressure on the wills of characters whose entanglement in original sin has left them psychologically alienated from their Saviour. Through violence or humiliation or both, they must learn that it is futile to hide from an infinitely caring God.

From this point of view, the grace that is implied at the end of both of O'Connor's novels and most of her stories cannot be faulted as a deus ex machina device; it resolves an underground spiritual battle at work from the outset. According to O'Connor's comic vision, her heroes never stand a chance of possessing the worldly independence they think they want. Instead, they get liberated into the only freedom that counts: the freedom to obey. As O'Connor declared about *Wise Blood,* for some readers "Hazel Motes's integrity lies in his trying with such vigor to get rid of the ragged figure [Christ] who moves from tree to tree in the back of his mind. For the author, his integrity lies in his not being able to."[21]

So far, so orthodox. As Wood feels obliged to concede, however, the quality of "Christianity" apparent in O'Connor's relation to her characters must give us pause. Outside her fiction, she insistently avowed her allegiance to Vatican II theology, whereby God is regarded as continually expressing his benevolence within ordinary life. Such an outlook ought to prompt depictions of a world in which charity and compassion make at least a modest daily showing against sin. But the fiction tells a quite different story. With few exceptions, O'Connor's characters can be divided into the stupid, the wicked, and the insufferably pretentious. However they may be presumed to stand with God, they strike *us* as objects of unremitting condescension. There is something suspiciously cruel, moreover, about a divine love that manifests itself chiefly in catastrophic, often annihilating, interventions against smugness. O'Connor's God would seem to manifest himself only in exercises of power less reminiscent of the New Testament than of Jahweh at his most dyspeptic. As Wood observes with mournful delicacy, "O'Connor the Christian writer does not always discern that God's resounding Yea always precedes and follows his devastating Nay."[22]

Like other Christian interpreters before him, Wood attempts to save the day by drawing finer theological distinctions. For him, O'Connor is not a Manichean who despises the world but only a latter-day Jansenist—a sympathizer, that is, with the branch of Catholic thought that rejected humanism, conceived of Christ as stern and inscrutable, and emphasized suffering and penitence as the only road to holiness. But this, as O'Connor recognized whenever she herself commented on Jansenism, is no defense at all, since the mainstream church has always accused the Jansenists precisely of being Manicheans. Thus she strenuously and repeatedly disavowed any belief in Jansenist principles. Indeed, she even risked an opposite heresy by endorsing the mystical "evolutionary Christianity" of Teilhard de Chardin, whereby organic matter itself supposedly contains an inherent salvational teleology.

Yet at bottom the satirically minded O'Connor was anything but a mystic. It seems reasonable to conclude that in embracing Teilhard's pseudoscience, she was doing what she could to neutralize, not exactly a *contemptus mundi*, but a temperamental impatience with what she took to be a virtually universal inanity. If so, her case is much like that of Graham Greene as she described it in a letter. Greene's convictions, she wrote, are Catholic but his sensibility is Manichean; and of course, she pregnantly added, "you write with the sensibility."[23]

O'Connor's own Manicheism expresses itself not only in the portrayal of an undignified human species but also in an emphasis on redemption so uncompromising as to be dubiously Christian in spirit. In her rendered world, mere suffering elicits no authorial sympathy; nor, more tellingly, does the infliction of suffering incur her unequivocal blame. Both Hazel Motes and young Tarwater commit murders along their paths to acceptance of their Saviour, yet in neither case are we given reason to feel that this grave sin appears as such to either the hero or his author. What does count absolutely for O'Connor is faith in Christ, arrived at by any means necessary; and the active imagination of evil that facilitates that faith is thus a higher virtue for her than ordinary decency. The Misfit, in his deranged obsession with the truth or falsity of the Resurrection story, appears closer to O'Connor's heart than the whole innocuous family that he massacres.

One of the earliest critics to drink in that truth without gagging was the novelist John Hawkes, who asserted in 1962 that O'Connor, like Blake's Milton, was of the Devil's party without knowing it.[24] Though he and O'Connor became friends, they could never settle that issue between them. They were classically talking past each other—O'Connor the clear-principled intentionalist, secure in her knowledge of what she wanted her fiction to convey, versus Hawkes the phenomenologist of the sentence, insisting that only a diabolical consciousness could have created such pitiless grotesques as a young mother whose face is "as broad and innocent as a cabbage," or an old woman "about the size of a cedar fence post," or a confidence man with "an honest look that fitted into his face like a set of false teeth."

The Hawkes-O'Connor debate has not subsided in the quarter-century since O'Connor's death. It is the vortex into which nearly every other question about her work gets inevitably drawn, and there is never a shortage of volunteers to replace the original antagonists. Thus today a Christian interpreter like Wood must try his best to fend off a secularist like the French critic André Bleikasten, who maintains, in the best Devil's-party tradition, that O'Connor's fictions show merely a token interest in spiritual growth, that her freaks are just freaks and not "prophet-freaks," and that the tyranny she exercises over her characters' fates derives from her identification with a counter-terrorist deity who settles her private scores against the world.[25]

The Devil's-party school has performed a valuable function in returning O'Connor criticism to earth—in preventing all the talk of grace from obscuring the actual antics, as Hawkes put it, of "soulless characters who leer, or bicker, or stare at obscenities on walls, or maim each other on a brilliant but barren earth."[26] Ultimately, however, this way of reading misses a crucial fact: O'Connor is most "diabolic" precisely when she is being most militantly Catholic.

This connection can be plainly discerned in her less guarded prose—as, for example, in a letter in which she calls the church's position on birth control "the most absolutely spiritual of all her stands. . . . I wish various fathers would quit trying to defend it by saying that the world can support 40 billion. I will rejoice in the day when they say: This is right, whether we all rot on top of each other or not, dear children, as we certainly may."[27] This Bosch-like nightmare, with humanity conceived as a putrefying heap which is nonetheless bound to its torment by divine law, is closer to the church's historic social vision than most modern Christians can bring themselves to acknowledge.

At the heart of O'Connor's value system, it would seem, lies neither charity nor sympathy with the Devil but rather a stern fanaticism, a scorn for the liberal attempt to dispense with supernatural aid. As she put it in one of her least noticed but most revealing statements, her introduction to a memoir of a little girl who had died from a hideous cancer, our age attempts to govern by "a tenderness which, long since cut off from the person of Christ, is wrapped in theory. When tenderness is detached from the source of tenderness, its logical outcome is terror."[28] O'Connor thus casts a cold eye on the whole modern world, whose recent cataclysms are just what it deserves, in her opinion, for having taken up with the Enlightenment's fatal substitution of reason for revelation. From this reactionary standpoint, it would be better not to address pain and injustice at all than to do so in a secular way.

O'Connor's absolutism doubtless served to sharpen the edge of her satire. At the same time, it also helps to explain why she had so little access to novelistic empathy and why she could not be shaken by the momentous events occurring just beyond her porch in the fifties and sixties. Even the Christians among us, I should think, must feel the shortcomings of a perspective that narrows all social problems to the abiding question of whether an individual can believe that Jesus died for his sake. Precisely when she is being (from her point of view) most expansive, casting her eyes upward to a realm of awesome illumination, O'Connor is most vulnerable to the charge of resorting to parochial and quietistic reflexes.

The wrenching issue in O'Connor's time and place was, of course, civil rights, and she was far from oblivious to it. It figures prominently in several of her later stories, most notably "Revelation" and "Everything That Rises Must Converge." More generally, black-white relations are of signal importance throughout her work—never more so than in the penultimate tale she wrote, "Judgment Day." The fact that that story deals with interracial friendship as well as interracial violence has been highlighted by critics seeking to mitigate the casual racism that crops up in some of her correspondence about "the niggers" on her mother's farm. And indeed, the black characters in her fiction generally do come off better than the whites—more humane, more intuitively sensible, and of course markedly less susceptible to the status anxiety and self-aggrandizement that she loved to pillory.

The problem in O'Connor's handling of race, then, is not a lack of insight into her black characters—not, at least, into those who occupy traditionally subservient roles. Given the social and political tensions of her time, her refusal either to demonize or to sentimentalize "the Negro" bespeaks an admirable insistence on applying a single standard of judgment to everyone. The problem lies with what she leaves unexpressed—namely, any appreciation of the stakes for human dignity at play in the civil rights movement. In story after story, the only white characters who even pretend to care about black emancipation are hypocritical, self-deluded fools who presumably would be better occupied looking out for their own salvation. By default, then, we are left to gather that any active concern to break down the South's apartheid must be a form of vanity—and therefore, ultimately, of resistance to God. O'Connor's deity, it could be inferred, won't stand for venial hubris but shrugs at massive and systematic oppression.

Ralph Wood puts the best face on this coldness by telling us that O'Connor found it "more courageous . . . to write about liberal self-satisfaction than about racist injustice."[29] But it took no courage for a white Georgian in the fifties and sixties to belittle the civil rights movement, as O'Connor usually did. It wasn't courage, for instance, that prompted her to declare in an interview, "White people and colored people are used to milling around together in the South, and this integration only means that they are going to be milling around together in a few more places."[30] Nor was courage required for her to reject a correspondent's suggestion that she entertain James Baldwin in Milledgeville: "It would cause the greatest trouble and disturbance and disunion. In New York it would be nice to meet him; here it would not. I observe the traditions of the society I feed on—it's only fair. Might as well expect a mule to fly as me to see James Baldwin in Georgia."[31] As she put it in another letter, her real feelings amounted to "a plague on everybody's house as far as the race business goes."[32] Surely there is a link to be drawn between such vexation and the transcendentalizing tactics of her fiction, whose predictable fadeout to the horizon obviates any need to make a final reckoning with racial guilt.

O'Connor's religious critics, harboring their own predilection for ennobling glimpses of the beyond, remain largely blind to this problem. Insofar as they perceive any dissonance between the author's Christian tenets and her actual social complacency, they cope with it by scouring her oeuvre for instances of positive assurance that everyone, black and white alike, is eligible to be saved—as if the only issue were how O'Connor feels about the next world rather than the one we actually know. And when they find such an instance of general salvationism, they incautiously award the highest aesthetic status to the work that embodies it.

Here again Wood is representative:

> At its worst . . . her fiction is animated by a baleful desire to lash modernity for its unbelief, and thus to depict this late stage of human history as uniquely damned and devoid of grace. At its best, however, O'Connor's work overcomes this incipient dualism. She discerns that the Kingdom of Heaven is not borne violently away by frustrated atheists; it is gratuitously given to the unsuspecting children of God.[33]

Thus Wood exalts O'Connor's own dubiously chosen favorite among her stories, "The Artificial Nigger," in which the protagonist undergoes an explicitly Christian expansion of sympathy and, for once, is rewarded with a no less explicit assurance that he is saved:

> [Mr. Head] realized that he was forgiven for sins from the beginning of time, when he had conceived in his own

heart the sin of Adam, until the present, when he had denied poor Nelson. He saw that no sin was too monstrous for him to claim as his own, and since God loved in proportion as He forgave, he felt ready at that instant to enter Paradise.[34]

The trouble is, however, that these lines, which Wood singles out for praise, belong to one of the few trite, dramatically unearned, propagandistic passages in all of O'Connor's mature fiction.

In context, furthermore, this gratuitous epiphany takes on another troubling aspect. As O'Connor wrote to a friend, the Sambo figurine that occasions Mr. Head's vision is meant to suggest "the redemptive quality of the Negro's suffering for us all."[35] "It points," as Wood emphasizes, "to a suffering that has been willingly, patiently borne."[36] But this reversion, in the year of *Brown v. Board of Education,* to the exemplary passivity of Uncle Tom must strike us as a regressive political act—and doubly so when the lesson turns out to be not the need for black freedom but access to heaven for "us all." Far from demonstrating O'Connor's compassion or silencing doubts about her sensitivity to the race issue, "The Artificial Nigger" epitomizes her penchant for beating retreats from social struggle to allegedly eternal meaning. And it does so by means of a lame device, a too obviously "planted" symbol that is supposed to initiate a spiritual metamorphosis in an otherwise earthbound character.

III

BY NOW, I imagine, readers who care about Flannery O'Connor for her distinctively literary qualities—her extravagant yet piercingly apt imagery, her subtle wit, her eye for the maliciously revealing detail, her infallible sense of pace and timing, her knack of sliding seamlessly between the petty and the sinister—must be thoroughly exasperated. They could gather that I have been depreciating her fiction for its failure to pass a crude litmus test for liberal sentiments. My aim, however, is just the opposite: to show that we can never recognize the strongest examples of her fiction, or let them work their magic on us, if we keep demanding that they also flatter our opinions.

That mistake is shared in roughly equal measure by O'Connor's Christian and anti-Christian critics. For James Mellard, O'Connor is too profound to be taken for a mere Catholic; she must rather be attuned to the abysmal Lacanian powers in which he invests his own faith. For Robert Brinkmeyer, in contrast, O'Connor has to be an acolyte of the unfinished, experimental self—the therapeutic ideal of a more mobile and narcissistic epoch than her own. James Wood is able to avoid such fatuity because he can gladly embrace O'Connor's values and purposes as she herself understood them. But even here, we notice, the critic has situated his pulpit over a trap door. Precisely because Wood broadly shares O'Connor's theology, he cannot grant that her most successful art tends to be that which is least doctrinally explicit, allowing basic and sometimes terrifying uncertainties to remain in fruitful play.

O'Connor's fiction regularly presents us with a grimmer, more "godforsaken" world than we could have guessed from her collected remarks about it. At the same time, however, that world is suffused with a portentousness whose undeniable source is the author's religion—her orientation to a looming metaphysical presence that casts an ironic shadow on nearly everything her characters attempt to do. Her best writing is that in which "mystery," as she called it, drastically intrudes on the mundane without requiring us either to embrace a dogma or to suspend our belief in naturalistic causation.

Take, for example, the most celebrated of O'Connor's tales, "A Good Man Is Hard to Find," which is at once plausible in each detail, cumulatively horrific, and refractory to straightforward interpretation. Is The Misfit a psychotic, a sinner, a lost pilgrim, or the Devil himself? And in calling him "one of my own children"[37] just before she is killed, is the Grandmother surmounting her earlier vanity and expressing a Christ-like grace, or is she simply continuing to plead selfishly for her life? Instead of trying to resolve such indeterminacy, we need to accept it as a product of conscious artistic tact. To be sure, O'Connor eventually offered her own, predictably orthodox, answers to our questions about the story's meaning.[38] It is too seldom remembered, however, that she gave those answers as a *reader* of her work, looking backward with an eye to doctrinal vindication. As an author, she aimed not at conspicuously "Catholic fiction," which she loathed, but at the Jamesian ideal of felt life, and more often than not she brilliantly attained it.

Where the religious critics go most seriously astray is in assuming that O'Connor must have chosen the bare ingredients of her artistry—her characters, settings, actions, and tone—with a didactic end already in mind. She herself was not so naïve about her sources of imaginative energy. The most influential of her distant literary forebears, she knew, was the sensationalist Edgar Allan Poe, whose taste for incongruity and horror she had already acquired in childhood. And she also acknowledged (though not fully enough) the revolutionary example of Nathanael West, the stylistic and thematic godfather of *Wise Blood* and the chief model for all her subsequent experiments in the grotesque. O'Connor adopted wholesale West's surreal comic violence, his deadpan manner, and (in *Wise Blood*) his episodic sense of plot and his theme of the contorted religious quest. Theological reassurance, however, was one thing she couldn't have taken from him. It ought to give the Christian critics pause to reflect that the most formative experience of her career was her literary encounter with a cynical Jewish atheist who saw no hope for humanity from any quarter.

O'Connor's real reason for authorship, she said more than once, was simply that she was good at it. In her view, a writer could only follow her imagination wherever it led and then hope to exert some ethical control over the result. As she was fond of pointing out, St. Thomas himself believed that "rectitude of the appetite" was unnecessary to art.[39] Thus she was not as surprised as she pretended to be when people told her that her works revel in violence and spite. Catholicism, as she construed it, was not a matter of being good or even devout but of knowing that the church and its sacraments could be called upon when needed. They were especially needed, she thought, to turn her gift for demolition to godly ends, but she was shrewd enough—and also sufficiently confident of divine approval— not to mollify the pitiless caricature and jarring metaphors that turned her otherwise taciturn prose into a minefield of harsh surprises.

Such a mixture of faith and cool professionalism is evidently too untidy for most of O'Connor's critics, who must either reduce her work to homiletics or denounce her religious protestations as a sham. Yet there have been refreshing exceptions that deserve our notice. In 1972, for example, Miles Orvell's *Invisible Parade: The Fiction of Flannery O'Connor* provided a supple appreciation of her tragicomic mode, relating it at once to her temperamental wavering between Jansenist severity and Teilhard's evolutionary optimism, to her immersion in diverse literary models from Poe and Hawthorne through Faulkner and West, and to her consequent struggle to mediate between allegory and satire, romance and realism, an inner circle of Catholic readers and a wide audience of unbelievers. Undogmatically and convincingly, Orvell showed where the fiction manages to achieve a universal appeal—not, in a word, where O'Connor deviates from her convictions but where she most rigorously shuns the temptation to be didactic.

In 1982, again, Frederick Asals advanced Orvell's critical enterprise in the subtlest and, to my taste, the most impressive book on the subject published to date, *Flannery O'Connor: The Imagination of Extremity*. For Asals, what sets this author apart is not the fictionalization of theology or a taste for the outrageous but something more peculiarly literary, "the tautness of *concordia discors.*"[40] Asals sees O'Connor as a master of tension between bizarre action and understatement, the cosmic and the quotidian, laughter and terror. Her secret, he believes, was the sense she cultivated of how to indulge her bleakest imaginings while simultaneously subjecting them to forms of control that were both aesthetic and ascetic.

Asals is especially helpful because, unlike the horde of critics who expound a static deductive vision on O'Connor's part, he traces her growth toward the relative serenity of her later work. This is not to say that he undervalues *Wise Blood* as a precocious tour de force. On the contrary, he praises its uniquely exuberant fusion of comic and repellent images. But he also shows that after 1952, O'Connor made a concerted effort to bring her repugnance for everything physical under ironic control:

> The central thrust in all of Flannery O'Connor's later fiction is to explode [a] complacent escapism or pseudo-transcendence by insisting again and again that existence can only be *in* the body, *in* matter, whatever horrors that may entail. To recall that in its deepest implications *Wise Blood* moved precisely in the opposite direction is to point to the profundity of the shift that occurred in her imaginative thinking. For if the narrative eye of the novel can discover no spirit in the matter at which it gazes, the author of the later work firmly suggests that there is no point in looking for it anywhere else.[41]

In addition, however, Asals perceives that O'Connor never really discarded her dualistic outlook. Instead of attaining to the full Christian humanism that she liked to profess, she could only press her complacent characters either "downward toward the level of animals and things or upward toward the mania of numinous possession."[42]

For all her private loyalty to the church's hopeful teachings, then, the world of O'Connor's fiction remains radically askew. Readers immersed in that fiction without a lifeline to the doctrinal assurance found in her lectures and letters tend to feel an existential vertigo at the very moments where the Christian critics want them to feel most worshipful. And this response cannot be dismissed as a mere error, a product of incomplete knowledge. O'Connor's works, we must understand, are not finally about salvation but about doom—the sudden and irremediable realization that there is no exit from being, for better or worse, exactly who one is.

If we ask why this should have become O'Connor's central theme immediately after the publication of *Wise Blood*, an obvious answer suggests itself. She was still working on that novel when she was nearly killed by her first siege of lupus. Though the immediate crisis passed, the onset of semi-invalidism canceled her hopes for an independent, normal, physically active life in the literary Northeast, where she felt with good reason that she had earned a place. In effect, she was abruptly handed a life sentence of exile, disease, and a social role, as she once memorably expressed it, of covering the stain on the sofa at her mother's parties. To pursue her art in those conditions without succumbing to anger and self-pity required a daily heroism whose traces she assiduously hid from everyone. Yet the experience also ended by imparting a moral complexity and poignancy to the satiric aggression that had roved unchecked through the pages of *Wise Blood*.

It is no accident that O'Connor's mature writing dwells on both the friction and claustrophobia of adversary family relations and on the humbling of false autonomy, especially of intellectual pride. To survive in Milledgeville without a paralyzing bitterness, she needed to assimilate her case to a general sense of the human plight, finding amusement not just in the Mrs. Turpins and Mrs. Hopewells who surrounded her but also in the Hulgas and Asburys and Mary Graces who embodied her own impotent urge to rebel, abstain, escape, obliterate. Her finest works make an impression of almost superhuman detachment, not because she is fair to all tendencies but because none, least of all her own, are exempted from mocking judgment.

The same kind of stoic impersonality, we could gather, chilled O'Connor's relation to her God, who must have seemed to test her daily in the manner of Job. She kept her formal beliefs intact but, revealingly, saved her most acerbic sarcasms for the idea of "an emotionally satisfying faith."[43] To make her constricted circumstances bearable and to face death with equanimity, she had to hold tight to a self-abnegating conformism, mortifying the skeptical and individualistic side of her intellect even while she was working discreetly to mitigate smugness and cultural isolationism within the church.[44] And perhaps it was this same need to keep reconciling herself to a cruel and unanswerable God that gave her best stories their air of ruthless drivenness, of allowing merely moral issues to drop out of the equation.

Girding herself against the sentimental indulgences of "the novena-rosary tradition,"[45] as she called it, O'Connor ended by coming dangerously near to exhausting her single thematic vein of individual pride and the "mystery" that must always strike it down. If she is indeed a great modern writer, it is not by virtue of amplitude of vision, depth of feeling, or social range but rather through the perfecting of a single hard-edged mode. Yet if her outlook remains one-directional and obsessive, it is hardly more so than that of, say, Hemingway or Lawrence. Her path was less original than theirs, more bounded by academic as well as ecclesiastic rules, but it was also free of their bullying egoism and self-deception.

The primary question for criticism, in any event, should not be what the author failed to include but whether the works hold up on their chosen ground. We cannot regret, then, that O'Connor avoided using her stories and novels to untangle her twisted feelings about segregation. Rather than open that Pandora's box, she was shrewd enough to portray the prejudice of others in a few efficient strokes—as when the self-infatuated Grandmother patronizes a "cute little pickaninny" by the roadside, or when the supercilious liberal Asbury tries to fraternize with one of his mother's farmhands but unselfconsciously calls him "boy," or when the hoglike Mrs. Turpin thanks Jesus because "He had not made her a nigger or white-trash or ugly."[46] We don't need to approve of O'Connor's own racial views in order to see how deadly accurate she was about the way bigotry springs from the commonest forms of status anxiety.

Nor, finally, need we come down definitively on one side or the other of the "Devil's party" debate. If the issue still remains open for the righteous and didactic Milton, the same will surely hold for a writer schooled in the discreet and elusive aesthetics of the objective correlative. "I belong to that literary generation," O'Connor once recalled, "whose education was in the hands of the New Critics or those influenced by them, and with these people the emphasis was on seeing that your thoughts and feelings—whatever they were—were aptly contained within your elected image."[47] Such reticence fostered ambiguity even where the "thoughts and feelings" may have been clear as glass. And O'Connor's, by her own reckoning, were not. "If you live today," as she said in a letter, "you breathe in nihilism. In or out of the Church, it's the gas you breathe." And elsewhere she reflected, "I doubt if anyone ever touches the limits at either end of his personality. We are not our own light."[48]

The exact balance in O'Connor's mind, then, between entertaining the void and taming it with the Cross, between making artistic concessions to her readers' godlessness and secretly trying it out as an imaginative hypothesis, can never be determined. Instead of claiming her for a party of either stripe, we need to recall that her first loyalty as a writer of fiction was to the cause of vivid, resonant, radically economical art. It is a measure of her success that we are still grasping at formulas that might explain, or even explain away, her electrifying power.

EIGHT

Mr. Updike's Planet

JOHN UPDIKE, *Roger's Version* (New York: Knopf, 1986).

I

WITH THE POSSIBLE EXCEPTION of his friend Norman Mailer, no living American writer has been more closely watched than John Updike. After eleven novels and thirty books overall, however, our most prolific and various man of letters remains curiously out of focus and resistant to consensus. According to Joseph Epstein among others, Updike lacks anything much to say and is thus habitually thrown back on "overwriting and sex, and overwriting about sex"; he "simply cannot pass up any opportunity to tap dance in prose."[1] That is the Updike for whom, according to Gilbert Sorrentino, reality appears "a poor drab thing that awaits his gilding."[2] But on the other side we find a formidable array of critics, most of them English professors, who consider Updike a powerful social chronicler, a master of physical texture and psychological nuance, a profound moralist, a symbolist, a Christian philosopher, in short a living classic whose accession to the Nobel podium is already overdue. Who is kidding whom?

Updike's residence in limbo is the more surprising because we have a vast body of information and analysis to go on. Despite his vaunted reclusiveness, Updike has republished three books' worth (more than seventeen hundred pages) of essays, reviews, and interviews that exhaustively document his opinions, beliefs, tastes, antecedents, and artistic phases. Seizing on that treasure horde and rejoicing in the availability of a contemporary American author who combines linguistic dexterity with moral seriousness, the critics have thus far produced no fewer than seventeen volumes of exegesis and praise, expounding their hero's theological affinities and scouring his fictional corpus for myths, parallels, symbols, rituals, pastoral conventions, social reflections, and uplifting homilies. For several recent years we even had a *John Updike Newsletter* devoted to preserving every scrap of memorabilia relating to that larger-than-life figure whom the editor suggestively dubbed "the Man."

With so much data at hand, why the blurred image? In part the problem can be traced to mixed signals from Updike. In his autobiographical reflections he sometimes depicts himself as a modernist wordsmith, a down-home avatar of Proust and Joyce who lives for the aesthetic frisson. Elsewhere, though, he plays the religious philosopher, aligning himself with such theological heavyweights as Berdyayev, Kierkegaard, and Karl Barth. In still other passages he turns debonair and implies, in light verse as well as prose, that we should count him among the long-vanished Algonquin wits. But keep reading and sooner or later you will find him insisting that he is merely another "dumb American" harboring the usual lowbrow prejudices. It is largely by chance, if you believe this last Updike, that he works for *The New Yorker* instead of selling Toyotas in the sticks.

None of this multiplicity would matter if the fiction itself were not ambiguous in key respects. Take, for example, the novel that has provoked the most polarized responses, *Couples* (1969). It has been plausibly represented both as suburban pornography—a sesquipedalian *Peyton Place*—and as a grave modern parable of the lapse from Edenic innocence, a Christian critique of post-pill licentiousness. There are ample objective grounds for both interpretations.

Uninstructed readers have naturally enough seen the plot of *Couples* as a neutrally rendered daisy chain of wife swapping, leading to what Updike himself has called the "happy ending" of Piet Hanema's marriage to Foxy Whitman.[3] The academics, on the other hand, have predictably focused on the countersacramental patterns and ironic allusions which are indeed there to be unearthed. This double perception has given Updike a splendid free ride; not many authors get to please the horny and the sanctimonious at one stroke. Eventually, however, we must wonder if the novelist was writing from any unified perspective.

But a chronic lack of consistency may itself be understandable in consistent terms. Most of Updike's novels do revert to a few central, urgently autobiographical preoccupations. It is not that he literally fictionalizes his own life history—though he sometimes does so—but that each of his serious novels gives oblique representation to his longings and discontents. The apparent evolution of those mental states, as they can be inferred from both fictional and nonfictional writings, can help explain why the novels occasionally become confused in both their thematic and their structural features. Though such analysis courts the risk of mistaking artistic license for confession, the risk seems worth taking. On the whole, Updike has tended to be more candid than his euphemistic interpreters have been, and we will see that even his attempts at irony, as the *Couples* example suggests, point to misgivings about his manifest values.

Updike's academic critics are right on at least one key point: his religious stance is indispensable to any broad comprehension of his work. Updike has always been a visible Christian, and he is more insistent about theological niceties today than when he started out. The enduring, autobiographically urgent, themes of his work are Christian-existential: a fear (bordering on phobia) of eternal nonbeing; an attempt to reconcile both spiritual and erotic striving with awareness of the implacable heartlessness of the natural world; and a resultant struggle to believe in the grace of personal salvation. If Updike often seeks literary respite from those obsessions—one thinks especially of the *Bech* books, *The Coup,* and *The Witches of Eastwick*—he never escapes them for long.

Over the years, however, Updike's doctrinal emphasis has grown more eccentric and brittle as the range of his sympathies has contracted. This is what his adoring critics, with few exceptions, would rather not acknowledge. In their zeal to keep him within the pietistic fold, they have generally failed to see that as his career has progressed, he has radically divorced his notion of Christian theology from that of Christian ethics. It is precisely that dissociation, I believe, which accounts for the main interpretative dilemmas posed by his most problematic fiction.

In Updike's youthful writings, righteous belief and righteous conduct marched confidently hand in hand. Witness the *caritas* of John Hook in *The Poorhouse Fair* (1959) and of George Caldwell in *The Centaur* (1963), figures who, it is important to grasp, were modeled on Updike's grandfather and father, respectively.[4] That conjunction of faith and virtue, however, soon unraveled, with fateful consequences for Updike's capacity to control his readers' sympathies.

We can see the new, morally emancipated Updike quite clearly in his credo poem, "Midpoint," of 1969:

> *Our guilt inheres in sheer Existing, so*
> *Forgive yourself your death, and freely flow.*
> *Transcendent Goodness makes elastic claims;*
> *The merciful Creator hid His Aims.*[5]

What this meant in practice was that Updike would not feel bound by standard notions of sin. Instead, he would seek in sheer experience, and above all in sexual experience, continual reassurance against the terror of nothingness which has haunted him, so he tells us, since his preadolescent years. As he put the matter succinctly in the same poem,

$$ASS = \frac{1}{ANGST}{}^{6}$$

That is, sex—the more the better—had become Updike's answer to Kierkegaard, his preferred means of validating his existence through immersion in the tangible.

Needless to say, what Updike had in mind here was not the obligations of the marriage bed. As his fictions repeatedly implied, the seeker's wife was almost by definition a death bearer who would clip his metaphysical wings and, by entrapping him in bland and benign routine, allow the doomsday clock to tick irreversibly away. Somebody else's wife, on the other hand, would be another story. Thus Updike wryly recast the ninth (Lutheran) commandment as follows: "Don't covet Mrs. X; or if you do, / Make sure, before you leap, she covets you."[7] Since the time of *Couples,* that has been pretty much the extent of Updike's ethical vision.

But no one could imagine that Updike's leave-taking from his first wife and children in 1974, after twenty-one years together, was effected without remorse. The many stories and novels that dwell upon that trauma tell us that his Christian upbringing and his sense of fair play would not leave him in peace. Nevertheless, we can also gather that he fiercely resisted the condemnatory internalized voice of his Pennsylvania forebears, steeling himself, perhaps like the philandering Tom Marshfield in *A Month of Sundays,* to register "no distinct guilt but rather a sort of scrabbling restiveness, a sense of events as a field of rubble in which he is empowered to search for some mysterious treasure."[8]

That struggle, I believe, was directly responsible for the anaesthetic tone and the moral inconclusiveness of Updike's novels about disintegrating marriages—books that stew in a pervasive yet unacknowledged atmosphere of self-reproach. The author made no effort to disguise the unprovoked, perverse quality of his heroes' yearnings for escape. Readers thus found it hard not to side with the long-suffering wives—Janice in the *Rabbit* books, Angela in *Couples*, Ruth in *Marry Me*—who had to put up with the compulsive Updikean man-child. But at the same time, for obvious reasons, Updike could not afford to register the full asininity of a Piet Hanema or a Jerry Conant, "heroes" who are routinely unfaithful, maddeningly indecisive and self-absorbed, yet nonetheless religiously priggish.

The oddest-looking element in this picture was surely Updike's and his heroes' dogged insistence on conservative Protestant theology. His zeal for salvational dogma, it is clear, waxed in direct proportion to his abandonment of sin as a judgmental category. But that development looks less paradoxical if we reflect that orthodoxy can itself be a means of discharging guilt, and doubly so when the favored tenets minimize the importance of virtuous conduct. Indeed, Updike's whole project of mooting ethical injunctions looks like an overreaction to self-judgment on the single point of adultery. A truly untroubled existentialist would hardly think to take such casuistic pains.

In any case, it is certain that one after another of Updike's wandering husbands ardently champions Updike's doctrinal hero, Karl Barth, heaping abuse on the Christian liberals' retreat from the Cross to charitable works and kindly feelings— the values invariably associated with the deserted or soon-to-be-deserted wife. The more Updike's characters misbehave, the more stridently they proclaim, with Tom Marshfield, "Ethical passion [is] the hobgoblin of trivial minds. What interests us is not the good but the godly. Not living well but living forever."[9] We know from many sources that this is precisely Updike's own most cherished priority.

Updike appears to have taken comfort from Karl Barth, with whatever violence to Barth's intent, in four mutually reinforcing respects. In the first place, Barth, too, downgraded ethics, though hardly in the spirit of Updike's libertines. Second, Barth welcomed human imperfections, since without them the Creator and his Creation would be indistinguishable and we mortals would lack a motive to accept our Saviour. Third, Barth characterized God as "Wholly Other" from us and thus as immune to influence by our good deeds. And last, Updike has clung to what he calls Barth's "virtually antinomian doctrine of all-inclusive Grace."[10] In Barth, then, Updike has found a means of talking back to a prickly conscience and a set of reasons for believing that, regardless of his conduct, he may yet be counted among the saved.

But this dry account fails to capture the most striking features of Updike's adaptation of Barthianism, namely, its pugnacity and its grim coldness. As he has Tom Marshfield reveal, "In Barth I heard, at the age of eighteen, the voice my father should have had."[11] The father who was equivocally honored in George Caldwell had impressed Updike as a chronic Mr. Nice Guy victim, one who could have used stiffening by what Tom calls Barth's "wholly masculine, wholly informed, wholly un-frightened prose."[12] "For fifteen years," Updike has written of the years when his father was still alive, "I'd watched a normal, good-doing Protestant man suffering in a kind of comic but real way. I think it left me rather angry. There is a lot of anger in my books, really. Their secret ingredient."[13] The chief target of that anger has been "limp-wristed theology" and "androgynous homogenizing liberals"[14]—the apparently feminine, sympathy-bestowing element that is supposedly anathema to the Barthian outlook.

In his zeal to stifle that tenderness in himself and to deflect the idea of punishment for sin, Updike has come to take morbid satisfaction in God's imagined indifference to our goings-on. As he said in "Midpoint,"

> *It little counts in History's level eye*
> *Just how we copulate, or how we die.*
> *Six million Jews will join the Congolese*
> *King Leopold of Belgium cleared like trees. . . .*[15]

A casual reader might take the poet to imply that we forsaken mortals had better care for one another. On the contrary, the context makes clear that we should seize our pleasure where we can, embrace the full horror of "History" as an expression of God's will, and worship the power that thus casually torments and crushes us. As Joyce Carol Oates shrewdly observed some years ago, "how odd that the author of *Pigeon Feathers* should be evolving, before our eyes, into the Mark Twain of *The Mysterious Stranger.* . . ."[16]

Sometime in the sixties, then, Updike's piety begins to sound like that of a village crank. He does still aver that the Apostles' Creed, asserting the Creator's oneness with the Redeemer, states the essence of his Christianity.[17] But he seems less and less able to put together the God of mass liquidation and the Man of Sorrows; the redemptive end of the bargain evidently strikes him as a wild and ever more desperate uncertainty. The result has been the growth of a belligerent, almost hysterical callousness. At the base of Updike's supernaturalism we seem to discern, not Barth's vision of general forgiveness, but the logic of the cowering Neanderthal: if I can make my heart as hard as that of the lightning hurler, perhaps he will acknowledge me as one of his own and spare me from destruction.

No wonder, then, that in *Couples* Piet Hanema's spiritual unease is resolved as soon as the divine arsonist, in a novelistically callow move on Updike's part, has incinerated Tarbox's church of mere Sunday fellowship. When "the supernatural proclaimed itself" in the conflagration, "Piet wondered at the lightness in his own heart, gratitude for having been shown something beyond him, beyond all blaming."[18] The link between raw heavenly force and blamelessness is crucial: a God who is himself so willful surely couldn't be bothered peering into bedrooms in search of straying husbands.

Updike's none too convincing efforts toward guilt management eventually entailed stylistic and structural corollaries that were as far-reaching as the thematic ones. The immediacy of his early manner had been buoyed by a near-pantheistic sense of "a quiet but tireless goodness that things at rest . . . seem to affirm."[19] The writer, then, could be construed benignly as "a middleman between the ideal world and this,"[20] one who would strive for prose effects that Henry Bech once called "a tightness perhaps equivalent to the terribly tight knit of reality."[21] In works like *Rabbit, Run* (1960), *The Centaur* (1963), and *Of the Farm* (1965), that affinity for sheer texture was itself a kind of redemptiveness, a promise that even the most ordinary small-town experience could blossom into plenitude. But by 1969, as Updike's anxiety over salvation was becoming more clamorous, he already looked with nostalgia toward the "primitive rapport I lately lack."[22] Both the inherent goodness of experience and Updike's communality of outlook with his readers now seemed dubious.

After the sixties, therefore, Updike began experimenting with a cooler, more sardonic artistic posture, filling his novels with Nabokovian guessing games. Now the main idea was to keep his readers off balance, leaving them unsure whether they weren't being cast as the victims of a practical joke. Consider, for example, the factual discrepancies in Colonel Ellelloû's narration of *The Coup* (1978)—should we believe a word he tells us?—or the three alternative endings to *Marry Me* (1976), in which realism suddenly collapses into perspectivism as the author skips away. These private and somewhat defiant high jinks were remote from that earnest mode of mimesis-cum-symbols which once sent the second-echelon New Critics into full and apparently permanent mobilization.

Along with the turn toward mannerism came other significant changes in subject and emphasis. In some cases the questing husband gave way to a more cynical protagonist—a Tom Marshfield, a Colonel Ellelloû—whose conduct was utterly unrestrained and whose first-person narrative rushed along with manic afflatus. Yet most of the opinions voiced by such figures remained manifestly Updike's own. Thus he began to give us a combination of rant and facetiousness, with the latter serving as a kind of alibi for the former. That is, by making his hero a virtual madman and then casting doubt on the veracity of the narrative, Updike could let fly with all the dour and spiteful reflections that had found no outlet, or perhaps no need for it, in his early works.

Perhaps the most striking change in the seventies, however, was a new hard-edged, biologically literal apprehension of sex. Throughout most of the previous decade, sexual and religious aspiration had still been a single blur for Updike. But nobody's adolescence can last forever. A writer whose inclination has been to confuse a damp crotch with a burning bush is likely to wake up some years later and wonder what he could possibly have had in mind. The post-*Couples* Updike has finally understood that hormones are great weavers of illusion—and he seems resentful of the fact. Though he writes incisively about the ironies of desire, he is also susceptible to revealing outbursts of misogyny.

The key text here is Updike's most unguarded book, *A Month of Sundays* (1975). For Tom Marshfield, the eternal feminine comes down to this: "My wife, *ma femme,* this cunt indentured to me. Sad to say, lib-lubbers."[23] The sentiment, it will be protested, belongs only to the protagonist, not the author. Yet that same truculent synecdoche, "cunt," has always been Updike's preferred term for his own erotic grail, and we hear his voice behind Marshfield's more temperate remark, "I wonder, truly, if 'love' . . . is not a reifying rather than de-reifying process, and 'sex object' not the summit of homage."[24] To conceive of a wife as an indentured cunt is merely the obverse side of such "homage."

A Month of Sundays also extends this defiant mood to both politics and religion. Indeed, what Marshfield has to say about theology sounds like a coda to his view of women: "Away with personhood! Mop up spilt religion! Let us have it in its original stony jars or not at all!" In his eyes, liberal Christianity and liberalism generally have become synonymous with a sexless, maudlin, meddlesome empathy that would ensnare us within the "random grid" of the material world.[25] Our task instead must be to fly that world.

As preparation, Marshfield advocates a militant political quietism, a "vigorously pro-Caesar" stance: "Somewhere Barth says, 'What shall the Christian in society *do* but attend to what *God* does.' What God does in the world is Caesar." Only by full acquiescence in established power, in other words, can the salvation-minded Christian ready himself for "a way out of the crush of matter and time."[26] The citation of the seemingly infallible Barth makes it clear, as usual, that the sentiments expressed come with Updike's imprimatur.

In a memorable phrase, Updike once told us that he regards his novels as "crystallizations of visceral hopefulness."[27] "I think a writer can portray a victim," he said elsewhere, "without forgetting that there is a primitive star . . . that keeps him running after something. . . ."[28] But some of Updike's recent spokesmen-heroes appear to have been running *from* everything except their hobbies and their hobbyhorses. His sensibility, it appears, has appreciably calcified, leaving him at once morally obtuse, politically inflexible, and crabbedly protective of beliefs that boil down to me-first salvationism. And lest we conclude that those were passing symptoms from a time of crisis, along comes *Roger's Version* (1986), the coldest and most self-conscious of all his novels, to reinforce the picture.

II

T O J U D G E F R O M its reviews, *Roger's Version* has been delighting some readers, annoying rather more of them, and bewildering most. The book is puzzling partly by design; as we will see, it is an elaborately cunning work whose secret coherence is meant to be perceptible only to the initiated. In that sense it constitutes a further instance of that dry and slightly sadistic manner that Updike cultivated after the sixties. But there is much else about *Roger's Version* that appears blocked and self-defeating. Its broadest theme is the threat of chaos—mental, cosmic, sexual, sociopolitical—and its underlying impulse is to fend off that threat by any available means, from aesthetic trickery to dogmatizing to hostile suspicion of the unwashed.

The most conspicuous feature of *Roger's Version* is a protracted, abstruse theological dispute between two Christians who both invoke science in their support. Roger Lambert, a fifty-three-year-old ex-minister and current divinity professor, holds the approved Updikean belief in a "Wholly Other" God—one whose very remoteness permits us to accept an impersonal materialistic understanding of this world below. In opposition, Dale Kohler, a twenty-eight-year-old computer jockey, fancies that he sees God's engineering in the big bang and in the statistically implausible aftermath that culminated in human consciousness. The debate is labored and stilted, but it can be skimmed; we know that Roger the Barthian has got to win.

Thus Updike administers yet another fictional drubbing to the windmills of facile and erroneous religion. The only novelty in this regard is that the enemy is not a Unitarian do-gooder but a rapt young Jesus freak who feels the immanence of God in nature and, not coincidentally, is good in bed—specifically, with the protagonist-narrator's wife. Before the novel is over he will have been not just silenced but shattered in spirit. We can surmise, then, that resentment of enthusiasm, in both the religious and the sexual implications of that term, connects the two plots of *Roger's Version* and brings them to a single vindictive end.

In Updike's and Roger's judgment, the trouble with Dale's natural theology is that it all but abolishes the gap between God's mind and our own. Updike requires the physical universe to be utterly, penitentially, inhospitable to our "anthropic" longings, so that we will have no recourse but to make an otherworldly commitment. It would be unthinkable, besides, to turn God into a kind of contractor who has left vulgar fingerprints on his handiwork for all to see. Thus Dale's arguments, stuffed awkwardly full of scientific detail that Updike has borrowed with acknowledgment from popular treatises, exist to be defeated. And they are knocked over quite easily by a double-team assault: Roger takes care of the heresy, and then a scientist-neighbor, Myron Kriegman, shows how infantile it is to insert the idea of God into every lacuna in our current knowledge.

In a negative way, the novel's decisive verdict against a trackable God leaves clear sailing for a Barthian God of "Revelation and Redemption."[29] Yet it is only through rhetorical sleight of hand that Updike can intimate where we must turn for solace once we have registered the full impact of scientific materialism. A God of Revelation and Redemption is of course far more "anthropic" than the Creator of Equations envisioned by Dale Kohler. Barth maintained that the very notion of a first cause was meaningless without Jesus Christ as revealed in Scripture,[30] and his account of Creation as a covenant with the unborn to secure general salvation through the Cross was, to put it mildly, prescientific in spirit.

In concentrating all our attention on the faultiness of Dale's humanistic line, Updike is employing the same stratagem as Barth himself was charged with using by an anti-Barthian in *A Month of Sundays:* "It's atheism. Barth beheads all the liberal, synthesizing theologians with it, and then at the last minute whips away the 'a' and says, 'Presto! *Theism!*' "[31] That Updike can see through such a parlor trick and yet be reduced to practicing it himself strikes me as a sign of gravely eroded confidence.

A similar combination of self-doubt and cornered assertiveness shines through the author's whole presentation of Roger Lambert. To be sure, Updike seems to place considerable distance between himself and this leering cynic, pedant, pornography addict, and schemer. In his later fiction, however, we have observed that extreme denigration of a narrator can supply the requisite "cover" for authorial ventriloquism. Such is plainly the case here. Moreover, in a broader sense the whole of *Roger's Version* is "Roger-like." That is, the novel treats its readers much as Roger himself might wish to do, discharging upon us an unrelieved dose of mean opinion, fussy learning, prurience, and manipulation.

Roger's "sullen temper" and chronic "uprising of bile," just like Tom Marshfield's in *A Month of Sundays*, allow him to voice Updike's own long-familiar views on every topic from hypocritical campus protest and knee-jerk feminism to the spinelessness of nondenominational Christianity. Indeed, he even goes so far as to paraphrase Updike's poetic assertion of God's indifference to gassed Jews and starving Africans. The effect of this mixed portrait—bad character but "correct" ideas—is less ironical than it is emotionally confused, as if Updike were at once mortified by his nearness to this "cold, play-it-safe bastard" and driven to keep venting grievances through him.[32]

Prominent among those grievances is sexual disillusionment. In Roger Lambert, it could be said, we pay a visit to the grave of Updike's early hedonism. Fourteen years earlier, Roger has risked all for love, losing his ministry by divorcing one wife so as to marry the sexual athlete Esther. But by now, sex appears to him merely as "a grand surprise nature has cooked up for us, love with its accelerated pulse rate and its drastic overestimation of the love object, its rhythmic build-up and discharge; but then that's it, there isn't another such treat life can offer, unless you count contract bridge and death."[33]

As that sentence illustrates, the jaded Roger can be brilliantly mordant. He is hardly in peak condition, however, for the inevitable Updikean round of musical beds. His wife Esther, we immediately learn, has long since become sexually as well as conversationally bored with him. Though he assures us that he lusts after Verna, the sluttish daughter of his half-sister, he is notably timorous in comparison with the young man who is daily, strenuously cuckolding him. Despite Updike's perfunctory effort to award Roger an epiphany on Verna's mattress—we are halfheartedly asked to believe that one fumbling act of "incest, adultery, and child abuse"[34] somehow gives him an intimation of God's existence—Roger at fifty-three has lost his sexual nerve.

But even a dud can have a dirty mind. Our hero's remaining libido is channeled largely into picturing what his juniors—his own wife, Esther, and Dale Kohler—are up to. Thus, tellingly for a student of Updike's once-Lawrentian love ethic, it is proxy sex between the still-vigorous that transfixes both hero and author in this work. And we as readers are conscripted to be its captive audience.

In the past, Updike has sometimes been unjustly charged with pornographic writing. His furtive adulterous couples have usually felt themselves inconvenienced in pathetic, even comic, ways that interrupt the effect of literary masturbation. But Roger's depictions of Esther and Dale constitute pornography proper, the close-up representation of sex without reference to the mind and heart, without antecedents or consequences:

> I pictured a white shaft: tense, pure, with dim blue broad veins and darker thinner purple ones and a pink-mauve head like the head of a mushroom set by the Creator upon a swollen stem nearly as thick as itself, just the merest little lip or rounded eaves, the *corona glandis,* overhanging the bluish stretched semi-epiderm where pagan foreskin once was, and a drop of transparent nectar in the little wide-awake slit of an eye at its velvety suffused tip. Esther's studious rapt face descends, huge as in a motion picture, to drink the bitter nectar and then to slide her lips as far down the shaft as they will go, again and again. . . .[35]

Huge as in a motion picture: we scarcely know whether we are supposed to read the scene or to rent it.

If Roger is merely imagining such Vermeer-like tableaux, they can be accepted as contributions to the portrayal of his twisted mind. Note, for example, the affectlessness of that description and its characteristically ironic flourishes of theology and pedantry. But Updike wants his hero to be not only prurient but accurately so. In a reckless stroke which jeopardizes the novel's pretensions to aesthetic coherence, he has Roger lay claim to a special gothic power, a telepathic faculty of distant viewing.

Without effort, it seems, Roger can scroll off before his inner eye not only Dale's adulterous trysts with Esther but also Dale's exotic computer calculations within an unfamiliar building and even the childhood memories that Esther recalls as she arrives at Dale's apartment. Is this X-ray vision authentic? We are given hints that would lead us to think so. But in that case Updike has sabotaged the verisimilitude so carefully established in every other element of his story. The effect is as if that plodder Harry Angstrom were to take up with one of the Eastwick witches and thenceforth devote himself to causing thunderstorms through incantation.

There is, however, a hidden reason for this anomalous deviation into "romance." *Roger's Version* is among other things a cryptic attempt to reproduce *The Scarlet Letter* in modern terms. Thus Roger (Chillingworth) must be made to spy on Esther (Hester) and (Dimmes) *dale*. Even though Updike appears to be misreading Hawthorne here—the original Roger was not visionary but merely astute at drawing inferences—we can at least grant that Updike is not mixing genres through inadvertence.

Once we have been alerted to the *Scarlet Letter* parallel, much that appears odd about *Roger's Version* does begin to make sense. The novel's title refers in part to Chillingworth's perspective on his cuckoldry, and Updike has seeded clues to the ur-drama throughout his text. Thus *The Scarlet Letter* is evoked in Roger's "odd and sinister empathy" and "secret bond" with Dale, in the red-haired Esther's secular and sensual disposition, in the custody issue over Verna's nature child Paula (Pearl), in Roger's perverse taunting of both Esther and Dale with hints of what he knows, in Dale's "inner worm" of remorse, in his nocturnal "self-mortification," even in his catching sight of a possibly divine sign—the pattern of a hand on a computer screen—whose real import may be that he is losing hold of reality. We see, too, that Roger Redux shares his prototype's strategy of forestalling a confession by his "friend and enemy" so as to keep "the wound . . . festering."[36]

Given all these points of sameness, the differences constitute Updike's wry commentary on both *The Scarlet Letter* and our own altered times. He impishly hints, for example, that if Arthur Dimmesdale had had free sexual access to Hester, he would have found himself overmatched and finally broken by her appetites. In the age of Dr. Ruth, Updike appears to say, a Roger Chillingworth could get his revenge simply by letting matters run their course.

Such implications supply a kind of privileged entertainment for readers who notice them. Yet we must ask whether Updike has really saved his novel from emotional torpor by turning it into a cryptogram. The superimposition of one story on another exemplifies that general shift toward superciliousness found in his novels since the seventies. Indeed, *A Month of Sundays* was itself a burlesque of *The Scarlet Letter*, complete with characters named Professor Chillingworth and Ms. Prynne. *Roger's Version* works its Hawthornian magic with a steadier and subtler hand, but the same doubt persists: how can we reconcile the joking spirit of the narrative with the Barthian gravity of the message? The strand of allegory, undetectable by most readers and thus of dubious novelistic value, only reinforces the impression that Updike no longer feels at home in the here and now.

Inevitably, that discomfort bears social as well as philosophical and aesthetic implications. Just as *Roger's Version* retreats from metaphysical anxiety into dogma and from the risk of uncontrolled experience into mirror games and magic, so it conjures a menacing picture of contemporary American life and withdraws toward a petty, fearful exclusivism. In an inconspicuous but unrelenting way, the book manages to cast malevolent suspicion on every group that strikes the author as potentially disruptive.

The action of *Roger's Version* spreads across a Boston-like city whose slums and upper-middle-class enclaves are drastically, perhaps terminally, disconnected. The threat of criminal black incursion hangs like smog over the Lamberts' tidy home on Malvin Lane (another, too cute, reference to a Hawthornian Roger), and the protagonist's involvement with the ghetto-dwelling Verna brings the black menace psychologically closer. Beyond Roger's academic dignity, what is threatened is the once-smug WASP mentality which, like Roger himself, has lost "whole octaves of passion" and now appears helpless to cope not only with technically apt Asians and "grounded" Jews unhobbled by the Puritan legacy but also with that supposedly violent, licentious, imperfectly quarantined black race which, Roger vilely thinks, "travels from cradle to grave at the expense of the state, like the aristocrats of old."[37]

Is this Updike's own considered opinion? Nothing in the novel could persuade us otherwise. *Roger's Version* is not just the author's *Scarlet Letter* but his *Heart of Darkness* as well. The "messy depths" that Roger encounters on the black side of town, suggesting a "random human energy too fierce to contain in any structure," are at once an emblem of his inner condition, a counterpart to the untamably alien physical universe, and a reminder of the socioeconomic chaos that goes unrecognized by most Americans, who prefer to live "inside Reagan's placid, uncluttered head as inside a giant bubble."[38] Updike implies that his propertied white readers had better wake up—not, however, to social injustice, but to the fact that their homes, jobs, and persons cannot be indefinitely safeguarded against the covetous have-nots.

Unfortunately, this show of class-based misanthropy cannot be dismissed as a passing aberration. A general ill will toward the marginal has informed Updike's outlook at least since the time of *Rabbit Redux* (1971) and probably much earlier. Remember, he has always given fair warning that he is "not essentially advanced over Harry Angstrom."[39] Some of the low remarks that his protagonists toss off about spoiled youth, loud and ugly Jews, freeloading, animalistic blacks, butch feminists, degenerate hippies, and whining peaceniks find counterparts in cartoonlike figures who pass through his works, from the demonic Skeeter and the spaced-out Jill in *Rabbit Redux* to the pudgy, obnoxious Myron Kriegman in *Roger's Version* and the ghetto girls whom Roger must hurry past, "fat, with fat Afros and fat rubber-dark rounded arms and fat false pink pearls."[40] We could almost mistake these outsiders for the damned—those, that is, who will not be golfing with Updike in the great country club in the sky.

As we noted at the outset, there are many Updikes—more than enough to keep us guessing which if any of them is primary. Oddly, however, the best candidate for that role goes largely unrecognized, so poorly does he gibe either with the worldly satirist of the Bech stories, the genially urbane *New Yorker* essayist, the light versifier, the Red Sox fan, or the critics' sacramental sage. Only through sporadic outbursts can we make out that other figure—morbid and curmudgeonly, starved for a missing grace, playing an unfunny hide-and-seek with his readers, reluctant to confide his anguish yet driven to express both a lurking nihilism and a doctrinal obsession that barely keeps that nihilism at bay. If Updike has often preferred to dwell in the sunny outskirts of his mind, perhaps the reason may be found in a certain bleakness at the center.

Notes

[1] William J. Bennett, *To Reclaim a Legacy: Report on the Humanities in Higher Education* (Washington, D.C.: NEH, 1984); Allan Bloom, *The Closing of the American Mind* (New York: Simon, 1987); Lynne Cheney, *Humanities in America: A Report to the President, the Congress, and the American People* (Washington, D.C.: NEH, 1988); and Roger Kimball, *Tenured Radicals: How Politics Has Corrupted Higher Education* (New York: Harper, 1990).

[2] See chapter 8 ("Dialectical Immaterialism") of my *Skeptical Engagements* (New York: Oxford UP, 1986).

[3] The name "New Americanists" is no longer simply mine. See Donald Pease, "New Americanists: Revisionist Interventions into the Canon," *boundary 2* 17 (1990): 1–37. Unfortunately, this article, written as an introduction to an edited book of the same title, reads like a parody of hothouse-radical discourse. For example: "New Americanists have changed the field-Imaginary of American Studies. The political unconscious of the primal scene of their New Historicist readings embodies *both* the *repressed relationship between* the literary and the political and the *disenfranchised groups previously unrepresentable in this relationship*" (31; italics as found).

[4] See Paul Lauter et al., eds., *The Heath Anthology of American Literature*, 2 vols. (Lexington: Heath, 1990). For a comprehensive critique of this ambitious collaborative book, which seeks to reconceive the field by giving ample representation to ethnic, social, and political groups that have been previously neglected, see Richard Ruland, "Art and a Better America," *American Literary History* 3 (1991): 337–59.

[5] See John Patrick Diggins, *The Rise and Fall of the American Left* (New York: Norton, 1992).

ONE

The Sins of the Fathers *Revisited*

¹New York: Oxford UP; the University of California Press reprint appeared in 1989.

²*Sensational Designs: The Cultural Work of American Fiction 1790–1860* (Chicago, 1985) 35.

³Tompkins 197.

⁴Tompkins 198.

⁵As an arresting test case, consider a recent piece of Hawthorne commentary, James Bense's "Nathaniel Hawthorne's Intention in 'Chiefly About War Matters,' " *American Literature* 61 (1989): 200–214. Bense appears to have discovered that all known readers of Hawthorne's essay have until now radically misconstrued it by failing to see that its dissenting footnotes are Hawthorne's own creation, not that of a nervous editor, and that the ensemble is a Swiftian hoax, a satire on censorship. Common sense tells me that if Bense is right, "Chiefly About War Matters" was a satire from the day it was finished, even though its real genre escaped notice for more than a century. Tompkins, however, would be obliged to say that the satire came into existence only in 1989 and is largely an artifact of the critic's school of thought. Could anyone, including Tompkins, really believe that?

⁶That was to be the path taken, with fruitful results, by Gloria C. Erlich in *Family Themes and Hawthorne's Fiction: The Tenacious Web* (New Brunswick: Rutgers UP, 1984).

⁷On this point, see especially David R. Reynolds, *Beneath the American Renaissance: The Subversive Imagination in the Age of Emerson and Melville* (New York: Knopf, 1988). The book is discussed on pages 40–45 of this book.

⁸See especially David Leverenz, *Manhood and the American Renaissance* (Ithaca: Cornell UP, 1989); and T. Walter Herbert, *Dearest Beloved: The Hawthornes and the Making of the Middle-Class Family* (Berkeley: U of California P, 1992).

⁹On this point, see especially Henri F. Ellenberger, *The Discovery of the Unconscious: The History and Evolution of Dynamic Psychiatry* (New York: Basic, 1970); and Frank J. Sulloway, *Freud, Biologist of the Mind: Beyond the Psychoanalytic Legend* (1979; rev. ed. New York: Basic, 1983).

¹⁰The most sophisticated defense of this outlook can be found in

Paisley Livingston, *Literary Knowledge: Humanistic Inquiry and the Philosophy of Science* (Ithaca: Cornell UP, 1988).

TWO

Whose American Renaissance?

[1] Geoffrey Hartman, *Beyond Formalism* (Yale UP, 1970) 356.

[2] See, for example, the recently published, and excellent, one-volume *Columbia Literary History of the United States,* ed. Emory Elliott (Columbia UP, 1988).

[3] See especially Bercovitch, "The Problem of Ideology in American Literary History," *Critical Inquiry* 12 (1986): 631–53; the phrases quoted below are from p. 634.

[4] "The Problem" 635.

[5] *Literary History of the United States,* ed. Robert Spiller et al. (1946; rev. ed. New York: Macmillan, 1959) xviii.

[6] Lionel Trilling, *The Liberal Imagination* (1948; New York: Anchor, 1950) 20.

[7] See Nina Baym, "Melodramas of Beset Manhood: How Theories of American Fiction Exclude Women Authors," *American Quarterly* 33 (1981): 123–39.

[8] Trilling 9.

[9] Matthiessen xi.

[10] Matthiessen 7, 4.

[11] Matthiessen 459.

[12] Michaels 97–98.

[13] Michaels 96.

[14] Matthiessen 535; italics added.

[15] Pease 247.

[16] Bercovitch and Jehlen 3.

[17] Bercovitch and Jehlen 3.

[18] See Richard Slotkin, *Regeneration through Violence: The Mythology of the American Frontier, 1600–1860* (Middletown, Conn.: Wesleyan UP, 1973); and *The Fatal Environment: The Myth of the Frontier in the Age of Industrialization* (New York: Atheneum, 1985).

[19] Bercovitch and Jehlen 433–34.

[20] In a close-textured, judicious book that challenges conspiratorial and economic-determinist approaches to history, Lawrence Buell makes ex-

actly this point with respect to a favorite text of the New Americanists, *Uncle Tom's Cabin*. Antebellum writers were socialized, Buell says, "in such a way as to activate the moral imagination, to give it the status of an autonomous rhetorical and thematic force, and this in turn converted it into a history-shaping influence, as in Stowe's case." The impact of *Uncle Tom's Cabin* ceases to be comprehensible as soon as we decide "to 'unmask' that autonomy as a social reflex of the bourgeois era." See *New England Literary Culture: From Revolution through Renaissance* (New York: Cambridge UP, 1986) 19.

[21] Bercovitch and Jehlen 5.

[22] Bercovitch and Jehlen 10.

[23] Bercovitch and Jehlen 259, 252.

[24] Bercovitch and Jehlen 251.

[25] Bercovitch and Jehlen 252–53.

[26] Bercovitch and Jehlen 43.

[27] Pease 24.

[28] Pease 10.

[29] Pease appears unaware that Hawthorne himself practiced corrupt partisan politics in his surveyorship of the Salem Custom House. See Stephen Nissenbaum, "The Firing of Nathaniel Hawthorne," *Essex Institute Historical Collections* 114 (April 1978): 57–86. Nissenbaum shows that though Hawthorne fervently wished to place himself above the political fray, he was obliged to serve as a "Democratic party enforcer" (70) in a kickback scheme.

[30] Pease 82.

[31] Pease 71.

[32] *The Scarlet Letter,* ed. Harry Levin (Boston: Houghton, 1960) 93.

[33] Pease 262, 203.

[34] Pease 274.

[35] Thus one of the *Ideology* essayists, the orthodox Althusserian J. H. Kavanagh, defiantly states that his reading of "Benito Cereno" will not be constrained by Melville or the text but only by his own wish "to challenge a dominant ideology"—that is, to make the story "available for a certain form of [Marxist] teaching practice" (Bercovitch and Jehlen 360).

[36] Tompkins xi.

[37] Tompkins xvi.

[38] Tompkins 16.

[39] Tompkins 142, 145.

[40] Tompkins 162.

[41] Tompkins also refrains from mentioning Warner's prize-winning essay, *American Female Patriotism* (New York: Edward H. Fletcher, 1852), a dialogue whose authoritative persona argues against female suffrage, maintaining that women and children occupy the same class, "as belonging decidedly to the Home Department, and fit for no other" (47).

[42] Tompkins 30–31.

[43] Tompkins 35.

[44] Reynolds 193.

[45] Reynolds 104.

[46] Reynolds 107.

[47] Reynolds 109; italics as found.

[48] Reynolds 328.

[49] Reynolds 491, 264.

[50] Reynolds 102.

[51] Reynolds 39.

[52] At times Reynolds sounds like one of Poe's or Hawthorne's monomaniac investigators, a man who sees nothing but his own obsession wherever he turns. The fall of the house of Usher, he says, entails "the fall of the artistic control and unity that Poe feared would accompany modern sensational writings, whose typical narrative patterns he knew to be as crooked as the zigzag fissure that splits apart Usher's mansion" (236). Likewise, Hawthorne's little Pearl "remains the wild embodiment of the Subversive imagination as long as her parents remain within the amoral value system of nineteenth-century sensationalism" (267). And "just as the bartender [in the Spouter-Inn] pours poisonous drinks to rambunctious sailors . . . so in a sense the dark-temperance mode 'pours' *Moby-Dick* by providing Melville with a variety of subversive images" (156).

[53] Reynolds 77; italics as found.

[54] Fisher 98–99.

[55] Edmund Wilson, *Patriotic Gore: Studies in the Literature of the American Civil War* (1962; rpt. Evanston: Northwestern UP, 1984) 5.

[56] "Her assumption, in writing *Uncle Tom*, is that every worthy person in the United States must desire to preserve the integrity of our unprecedented republic; and she tries to show how Negro slavery must disrupt and degrade this common ideal by tempting the North to the moral indifference, the half-deliberate ignorance, which encourages inhuman practices, and by weakening the character of the South through the

luxury and the irresponsibility that the institution of slavery breeds"
(Wilson, 9).

THREE

The Parting of the Twains

[1] Gillman 179.

[2] Gillman 3, 11.

[3] Gillman 8.

[4] See Louis J. Budd, *Our Mark Twain: The Making of His Public Personality*
(Philadelphia: U of Pennsylvania P, 1983); and Everett Emerson, *The
Authentic Mark Twain: A Literary Biography of Samuel L. Clemens* (Philadelphia:
U of Pennsylvania P, 1984).

[5] Quoted by Gillman 32.

[6] Gillman 38, 31.

[7] Gillman 100.

[8] Quoted by Gillman 97.

[9] Quoted by Gillman 124.

[10] Gillman 11.

[11] Gillman 158.

[12] Gillman 94, 90, 67, 187.

[13] Gillman 94, 131, 17.

[14] Gillman 187.

[15] Gillman 88, 93, 95.

[16] Gillman 180.

[17] On this point, see Forrest G. Robinson, *In Bad Faith: The Dynamics of
Deception in Mark Twain's America* (Cambridge: Harvard UP, 1986).

[18] Among the critics of *Pudd'nhead Wilson*, for example, the one who
least insists on unifying patterns is Hershel Parker, an old-school intentionalist who nevertheless demonstrates that Twain's failure to make a
clean break with the ur-text *Those Extraordinary Twins* left *Pudd'nhead Wilson*
incoherent in several important ways. See *Flawed Texts and Verbal Icons:
Literary Authority and American Fiction* (Evanston: Northwestern UP, 1984)
115–36. Susan Gillman takes passing note of Parker's argument but cannot absorb its implications. On her level of analysis—that of Twain's
participation in the cultural unconscious of the Gilded Age—everything
in *Pudd'nhead Wilson* fits together nicely.

[19] See Budd, *Mark Twain: Social Philosopher* (Bloomington: Indiana UP,

1962); Baetzhold, *Mark Twain and John Bull: The British Connection* (Bloomington: Indiana UP, 1970); and Gribben, *Mark Twain's Library: A Reconstruction*, 2 vols. (Boston: Hall, 1980).

[20] Indeed, in his relegation of all meaning to the realm of illusion, Twain became a "poststructuralist" before his time—a fact, ironically, that our own poststructuralists have trouble perceiving, since *their* determinism tells them not to credit him with enough intellectual autonomy to have arrived at such insight.

[21] Cummings 16.

[22] Quoted by Cummings 16–17.

[23] Quoted by Cummings 22, 32.

[24] Quoted by Cummings 31, 201, 28.

[25] Quoted by Cummings 31. See also, however, Stan Poole, "In Search of the Missing Link: Mark Twain and Darwinism," *Studies in American Fiction* 13 (1985): 201–15. Poole's article supplements Cummings by giving a more nuanced account of the "soft" and "hard" Darwinisms that were at play in Twain's culture. In Poole's view, even Social Darwinism was such an ambiguous phenomenon that Twain could readily adapt it to humanitarian and anti-establishment purposes.

[26] "An Indian thug," Darwin reported in *The Descent of Man,* "conscientiously regretted that he had not strangled and robbed as many travellers as did his father before him." In *What Is Man?* Twain made the same point with his own illustration: "I knew a kind-hearted Kentuckian whose self-approval was lacking—whose conscience was troubling him, to phrase it with exactness—*because he had neglected to kill a certain man*—a man whom he had never seen" (quoted by Cummings 58–59).

[27] See Walter Blair's summary in his introduction to the magnificent edition of *Huckleberry Finn* edited by Blair, Victor Fischer, and others and issued by the Mark Twain Project (Berkeley: U of California P, 1988) xxiii–xlv.

[28] Cummings 128–29.

[29] Cummings 151, 15

FOUR

A Yankee in the Court of Criticism

[1] Quoted by Horst H. Kruse, "Mark Twain's *A Connecticut Yankee:* Reconsiderations and Revisions," *American Literature* 62 (1990): 464–83 (the quotation is from pp. 476–77).

[2] Quoted by Roger B. Salomon, *Twain and the Image of History* (New Haven: Yale UP, 1961) 103.

[3] Henry Nash Smith, *Mark Twain's Fable of Progress: Political and Economic Ideas in "A Connecticut Yankee"* (New Brunswick: Rutgers UP, 1964) 65.

[4] In this regard it is especially telling that, in James D. Williams's words, "the story that the Boss repeats fifteen times at the monastery—until the audience 'disintegrates'—was initially about a 'celebrated jumping frog of Calaveras County.'" See "Revision and Intention in Mark Twain's *A Connecticut Yankee*," reprinted in the Norton Critical Edition of *Connecticut Yankee*, ed. Allison R. Ensor (New York: Norton, 1982) 361–68 (the quotation is from p. 365). Hereafter cited as "Norton."

[5] Salomon 116.

[6] Twain's immersion in Taine's *Ancient Regime* helps to explain this anomaly. Taine, who despised both the Revolution and the abuses that made it inevitable, judged the eighteenth century more harshly than the tenth. When new, feudalism had afforded a measure of security to the wandering *villanus*, but its vestiges survived into modern times only as a set of high-handed aristocratic privileges. On this point see Rodney O. Rogers, "Twain, Taine, and Lecky: The Genesis of a Passage in *A Connecticut Yankee*," *Modern Language Quarterly* 34 (1973): 440.

[7] Norton 297.

[8] John M. Ellis, *Against Deconstruction* (Princeton: Princeton UP, 1989) 139.

[9] See pp. xix–xx, 20, 37–38 of this book.

[10] See *Validity in Interpretation* (New Haven: Yale UP, 1967), and *The Aims of Interpretation* (Chicago: U of Chicago P, 1976). Later statements by Hirsch have substantially blurred the boundary between meaning and significance, thus giving legitimacy to at least a measure of "modernized" interpretation. Even in its most liberalized form, however, Hirsch's intentionalism retains its "symptomatic" approach to elements that *contradict* a work's one true meaning; only modern "applications" or "exemplifications" of that meaning are considered acceptable. See "Meaning and Significance Reinterpreted," *Critical Inquiry* 11 (1984): 202–25.

[11] Norton 434–52.

[12] Norton 435.

[13] Norton 441.

[14] Norton 441, 449, 452.

[15] Norton 435. Carter's attitude here stands in apparent contrast to that of Hirsch, who tells us that criticism proper begins precisely when we pass

from meaning to significance—that is, from objectively reconstructing intention to asking how the work bears on our own concerns. Yet by calling features that oppose intended meaning "symptomatic," Hirsch inevitably lends them an air of pathology. It is no surprise that his followers tend to overlook his token hospitality to "significance," since they sense—correctly, I believe—that all the polemical force of his theory is concentrated at the other end of the spectrum.

[16] All the information in this paragraph comes from Horst Kruse's important article (note 1 above). For a discussion of Twain's plagiarism and his devious efforts to disavow it, see David Ketterer, " 'Professor Baffin's Adventures' by Max Adeler: The Inspiration for *A Connecticut Yankee in King Arthur's Court?*" *Mark Twain Journal* 24 (1986): 24–34.

[17] See, e.g., James M. Cox, *"A Connecticut Yankee in King Arthur's Court: The Machinery of Self-Preservation,"* Norton 390–401; Kenneth S. Lynn, "The Volcano," reprinted in Norton 383–89; Clark Griffith, "Merlin's Grin: From 'Tom' to 'Huck' in *A Connecticut Yankee,*" *New England Quarterly* 48 (1975): 28–46; Judith Fetterley, "Yankee Showman and Reformer: The Character of Mark Twain's Hank Morgan," *Texas Studies in Literature and Language* 14 (1973): 667–79; Lorne Fienberg, "Twain's Connecticut Yankee: The Entrepreneur as a Daimonic Hero," *Modern Fiction Studies* 28 (1982) 155–67; and David R. Sewell, "Hank Morgan and the Colonization of Utopia," *American Transcendental Quarterly* n.s. 3 (1989): 27–44.

[18] "The 'serene volcano' is only the most striking image of a concealed destructive force. . . . While working clandestinely to destroy Merlin's tower, [Hank] demands that everyone be kept a quarter of a mile away. By the time he comes to repair the Holy Fountain, the inviolable space of his authority has expanded to a half mile. Once, as the innovative entrepreneur, Hank assailed barriers and tore them down. However, long before the novel's climactic struggle, waged across acres of sand and miles of electrified barbed wire, Hank is busy erecting bastions in his own defense and territories of barren waste to shield himself from his foes" (Fienberg 164).

[19] This is the position argued by Steven Knapp and Walter Benn Michaels in "Against Theory," in *Against Theory: Literary Studies and the New Pragmatism,* ed. W.J.T. Mitchell (Chicago: U of Chicago P, 1985) 11–30; and "Against Theory 2," *Critical Inquiry* 14 (1987): 49–68.

[20] It was certainly within Mark Twain's habitual practice to lay just such traps. The preeminent example is the "evasion" episode of *Huckle-*

berry Finn, which is good sport for those whose sensibilities are as immature as Tom Sawyer's but subtle, instructive torture for the rest of us. See pages 72–73 of this book.

²¹ All of the points in this paragraph are indebted to Sewell's penetrating article (note 17 above).

²² Griffith 44.

²³ Fetterley 673.

²⁴ Fetterley 675–77.

²⁵ See Howard G. Baetzhold, *Mark Twain and John Bull: The British Connection* (Bloomington: Indiana UP, 1970).

²⁶ We cannot be altogether surprised, then, to find that Twain, when writing to Howells from England in 1897, professed himself "appalled" at the way "the wide extension of the suffrage" had "damaged [England's] manners, & made her rather Americanly uncourteous at the lower levels" (quoted by Baetzhold 182).

²⁷ The ancestor in question was Geoffrey Clement. See Mark L. Sargent, "A Connecticut Yankee in Jane Lampton's South: Mark Twain and the Regicide," *Mississippi Quarterly* 40 (1986–87): 21–31. As Sargent observes, Twain saw himself as "a hybrid of the Roundheads and the Southern gentry" (24).

²⁸ Quoted by Baetzhold 169.

²⁹ Quoted by Baetzhold 172–73.

³⁰ Quoted by Louis J. Budd, *Mark Twain, Social Philosopher* (Bloomington: U of Indiana P, 1962); reprinted in Norton 405.

³¹ Norton 390.

³² Alan Gribben notes the secrecy of the Paige assembly process and draws the parallel with Hank's plans; see "Mark Twain, Business Man: The Margins of Profit," *Studies in American Humor* n.s., 1 (1982): 24–29. This article also shows that the volatility, grandiosity, aggressiveness, and lack of follow-through in Hank's enterprises were fully matched by Twain's own. If there is a difference, it is that whereas Twain bullied his business associates and suffered from chronic suspicion of betrayal by them, his fictional counterpart *is* betrayed without cause. Surely this is further evidence that Twain's portrait of Hank was not fully ironic.

³³ Twain's advocacy of trade unionism in this same period would appear to run counter to his economic self-interest. In fact, however, he was lukewarm about specific causes such as the eight-hour day, and in any case he seems to have thought of the Paige typesetter as a virtual robot that would scarcely require tending. What's more, the same troubling

savagery of spirit that invades *A Connecticut Yankee* can be found in his writing about the labor movement. In "The New Dynasty" (1886), for example, he manages to make the labor czar of the future, who will "oppress the thousands" for the sake of the millions, sound like a cross between John L. Lewis and Tamburlaine. What we see here is not so much a sympathy with the working class as a yearning for an irresistible Mysterious Stranger who will put everything in order. (See Norton 284–89.)

F I V E

Pressure under Grace

¹Carlos Baker, *Ernest Hemingway: A Life Story* (New York: Scribner's, 1969); Bernice Kert, *The Hemingway Women* (New York: Norton, 1983); Jeffrey Meyers, *Hemingway: A Biography* (New York: Harper, 1985).

²*Ernest Hemingway: Selected Letters,* ed. Carlos Baker (New York: Scribner's, 1981) 408.

³See Lance Morrow, "A Quarter-Century Later, the Myth Endures," *Time* 25 (August 1986): 70.

⁴Meyers 525, 192.

⁵Meyers 256.

⁶See Michael S. Reynolds, *Hemingway's First War* (Princeton: Princeton UP, 1976). This study and Reynolds's other scrupulous books, *Hemingway's Reading: 1910–1940* (Princeton: Princeton UP, 1981) and *The Young Hemingway* (New York: Oxford UP, 1986), have notably helped to restore the writer to human scale.

⁷Lynn 91–92; Meyers 33.

⁸Meyers 35.

⁹Malcolm Cowley, "Hemingway's Wound," *Georgia Review* 38 (1984): 229–30 (emphasis added).

¹⁰See *The Nick Adams Stories* (New York: Scribner's, 1972) 237, 238.

¹¹R.W.B. Lewis, "Who's Papa?" *The New Republic* 2 (December 1985): 34.

¹²Ironically, however, Lewis had already accepted (from Jeffrey Meyers's biography) the largely unflattering picture of Hemingway's personality that has now been fully developed by Lynn. "With his incessant rages and quarreling, his cruelties, his stupefyingly boring literary and sexual boasting," wrote Lewis, "Hemingway emerges as perhaps the least sim-

patico figure in the annals of twentieth-century letters" (34). It is precisely because he finds himself saddled with an otherwise monstrous Hemingway, one gathers, that Lewis wants to keep the war myth intact.

[13] Lynn 162, 114, 170, 286.

[14] Lynn 398, 401.

[15] Meyers 195, 530.

[16] Lynn 402.

[17] *The Garden of Eden* is the most egregious example of a long-standing policy on the part of Scribner's and the surviving Hemingways: to reorder or even reconceive the writer's unfinished work, to encourage readers to believe that the resultant text closely matches the manuscripts, and to deny scholars access to those manuscripts until the royalties are safely in the bank. Readers of the published *Garden of Eden* were not told that their "new Hemingway novel" of 247 pages had been excavated by the unmentioned editor, Tom Jenks, from miscellaneous segments of a 1,200-page draft containing two tragic endings, neither of which was deemed sufficiently upbeat for inclusion in the published book. (Two further abortive drafts totaling 700 pages were apparently ignored.) Nor could anyone tell from the book that in the manuscripts Hemingway's autobiographical hero, David Bourne, does not in fact remain a fresh young writer but grows to the unromantic age of sixty and touchingly suffers from the same anxieties and self-recriminations that tormented his creator in his pathetic final decade. See Barbara Probst Solomon, "Where's Papa?" *The New Republic* 9 (March 1987): 30–34.

[18] Quoted by Eric Pooley, "Papa's New Baby," *New York* 28 (April 1986): 60.

[19] Lynn 389, 487, 488, 418.

[20] Lynn 142.

[21] Quoted by Lynn 533.

[22] *The Garden of Eden* (New York: Scribner's, 1986) 15, 17.

[23] Mary Welsh Hemingway, *How It Was* (New York: Knopf, 1976) 368.

[24] Lynn 357.

[25] Lynn 41.

[26] See especially "The Last Good Country," a long story—really a fragment of an abandoned novel—in which Nick Adams, hiding from game wardens, flees into a virgin forest and sets up camp with his adoring young tomboy sister, "Littless" (*The Nick Adams Stories*, note 10 above). As Lynn argues, Littless is almost certainly based on Ursula. Before the story is over, Littless will have sat on Nick's lap and caused an erection, kissed

and teased him with sexual talk, confessed that she wants to grow up and marry him, and cut off her her hair to please him: "Now I'm your sister but I'm a boy, too." We can surmise that the larger work remained unfinished for the same reason that *The Garden of Eden* did: it said too much. Some idea of Ursula apparently remained entangled in Hemingway's peculiarly limited but intense eroticism.

[27] Lynn 587.

[28] Quoted by Lynn 432.

[29] Lynn 436.

[30] Carlos Baker, *Hemingway: The Writer As Artist* (Princeton: Princeton UP, 1963) 82–83.

SIX

Faulkner Methodized

[1] Quoted by Schwartz 105.

[2] Malcolm Cowley, "William Faulkner's Human Comedy," *New York Times Book Review* 29 (Oct. 1944): 4.

[3] See Cheryl Lester, "To Market, to Market: *The Portable Faulkner,*" *Criticism* 29 (1987): 371–92.

[4] Lester 381, 391.

[5] Schwartz 209, 139, 3.

[6] Quoted by Schwartz 143, 91.

[7] Quoted by Schwartz 92.

[8] Richard H. Brodhead, Introduction to *Faulkner: New Perspectives,* ed. Brodhead (Englewood Cliffs, N.J.: Prentice, 1983) 2.

[9] Brooks, *On the Prejudices . . .* 59, 91.

[10] Hoffman 88, 163, xiv.

[11] Hoffman 39, 23.

[12] Irwin 128, 129, 134.

[13] See Myra Jehlen, *Class and Character in Faulkner's South* (New York: Columbia UP, 1976); Carolyn Porter, *Seeing and Being: The Plight of the Participant Observer in Emerson, James, Adams, and Faulkner* (Middletown, Conn.: Wesleyan UP, 1981); and Eric J. Sundquist, *Faulkner: The House Divided* (Baltimore: Johns Hopkins UP, 1983).

[14] Morris 6, 7.

[15] See Morris 211, 168; Moreland 200; Duvall 140, 53, 35.

[16] Duvall 133.

[17] William Faulkner, *Novels 1930–1935,* ed. Joseph Blotner and Noel Polk (New York: Library of America, 1985) 110.

[18] *Novels 1930–35:* 483.

[19] William Faulkner, *Novels 1936–1940,* ed. Joseph Blotner and Noel Polk (New York: Library of America, 1990) 726.

[20] See Wittenberg, "William Faulkner: A Feminist Consideration," in *American Novelists Revisited: Essays in Feminist Criticism,* ed. Fritz Fleischmann (Boston: Hall, 1982) 325–38 (the quotation is from p. 327); and Fetterley, *The Resisting Reader: A Feminist Approach to American Fiction* (Bloomington: Indiana UP, 1978) 34–45.

[21] Duvall 16.

[22] Duvall xii.

[23] Quoted by Duvall 8.

[24] Duvall xii–xiii, 17.

[25] Duvall 30.

[26] For Duvall, Joe's slitting Joanna's throat is merely a "justifiable homicide," an act of "self-defense" (23, 24), since Joanna has pulled a trigger on him first. This might be a reasonable inference if Joanna were packing an Uzi. Her gun, however—a "single action, cap-and-ball revolver almost as long and heavier than a small rifle" (*Novels 1930–1935:* 607)—has misfired, and Joe can now easily wrest it from her grasp without fear of being shot. Instead, he resumes and carries out his original murderous intent.

[27] Quoted by Michel Gresset and Patrick Samway, Introduction to *Faulkner and Idealism: Perspectives from Paris* (Oxford: U of Mississippi P, 1983) 8.

[28] There is a telling resemblance between Hawthorne and Faulkner in the erotic domain as well. Though Hawthorne's master concern is passion, he gives us not passion itself but a smirking embarrassment over his prurient relation to it. Nevertheless, his clinical curiosity about the defectiveness of his temperament equipped him formidably to trace the mental gyrations of his most complex creation, Miles Coverdale. In Coverdale, Hawthorne laid bare his own coldness—without, of course, thereby curing it. So, too, Faulkner can see to the bottom of Quentin and Ike in full awareness that their disabilities are, and will remain, part of his psychic makeup.

[29] See "An Introduction to *The Sound and the Fury:* Another Version," reprinted in Brodhead (note 8 above) 25.

[30] Morris, 24. An opposite error is committed by Dirk Kuyk, Jr., in

another new book, *Sutpen's Design: Interpreting Faulkner's* Absalom, Absalom! (Charlottesville: U of Virginia P, 1990). Kuyk's stubbornly literalistic argument condones the brutalities of the "tragic hero" (132) Sutpen, failing to register that Sutpen's incapacity to accommodate the subjectivity of others was already implicit in his original, supposedly noble, "design." For a richer discussion, see Moreland 23–121.

[31] Moreland 132.

[32] Morris 224.

[33] *Novels 1936–1940* 118.

[34] English translations of Bleikasten's first two books appeared as *Faulkner's* As I Lay Dying (Bloomington: U of Indiana P, 1973) and *The Most Splendid Failure: Faulkner's* The Sound and the Fury (Bloomington: U of Indiana P, 1976).

[35] Bleikasten 353.

[36] Thus Bleikasten finds *Sanctuary* illuminated by Freud's equation feces = baby = penis (251–52); he takes seriously Joel Kovel's stale proposal that the white racist is at once "castrating the father" and "identifying with the father by castrating the son" (331); and he frequently bolsters his readings with citations of questionable dogma by Melanie Klein, Sandor Ferenczi, Geza Róheim, and other Freudians and Lacanians of a visionary penchant.

[37] Bleikasten x, xv.

[38] Bleikasten 199.

[39] Bleikasten 356.

[40] Bleikasten 143, 351, 159.

[41] Bleikasten 250–51.

[42] Brooks, *William Faulkner* 71; Duvall 70.

[43] Hugh Kenner, "Faulkner and the Avant-Garde," in Brodhead (note 8 above) 73.

[44] *Lion in the Garden: Interviews with William Faulkner, 1926–1962,* ed. James B. Meriwether and Michael Millgate (U of Nebraska P, 1968) 81.

SEVEN

The Critics Bear It Away

[1] Flannery O'Connor, *Mystery and Manners: Occasional Prose,* ed. Sally and Robert Fitzgerald (New York: Farrar, 1969) 84.

[2] Flannery O'Connor, *The Habit of Being: Letters,* ed. Sally Fitzgerald (New York: Farrar, 1979) 86–87.

[3] For a thorough account of those documents, see Stephen G. Driggers and Robert J. Dunn with Sarah Gordon, *The Manuscripts of Flannery O'Connor at Georgia College* (Athens: U of Georgia P, 1989).

[4] James M. Mellard, "Flannery O'Connor's *Others:* Freud, Lacan, and the Unconscious," *American Literature* 61 (1989): 625–43 (the quotations are from pp. 625, 632).

[5] Mellard 632, 642.

[6] Mellard 635.

[7] Mellard 630.

[8] Brinkmeyer 157.

[9] Brinkmeyer 18, 157.

[10] *Collected Works* 820.

[11] *The Habit of Being* 350.

[12] *The Habit of Being* 125.

[13] *Mystery and Manners* 65.

[14] *The Habit of Being* 74.

[15] *The Habit of Being* 226–27.

[16] *The Habit of Being* 388.

[17] For other Christian readings, not invariably connected to a profession of faith on the critic's part, see Stanley Edgar Hyman, *Flannery O'Connor* (Minneapolis: U of Minnesota P, 1966); Carter W. Martin, *The True Country: Themes in the Fiction of Flannery O'Connor* (Nashville: Vanderbilt UP, 1969); Leon V. Driskell and Joan T. Brittain, *The Eternal Crossroads: The Art of Flannery O'Connor* (Lexington: U of Kentucky P, 1971); David Eggenschwiler, *The Christian Humanism of Flannery O'Connor* (Detroit: Wayne State UP, 1972); Kathleen Feeley, *Flannery O'Connor: Voice of the Peacock* (New Brunswick, N.J.: Rutgers UP, 1972); Preston M. Browning, Jr., *Flannery O'Connor* (Carbondale: Southern Illinois UP, 1974); John R. May, *The Pruning Word: The Parables of Flannery O'Connor* (Notre Dame: U of Notre Dame P, 1976); Harold Fickett and Douglas R. Gilbert, *Flannery O'Connor: Images of Grace* (Grand Rapids, Mich.: Eerdmans, 1986); Marshall Bruce Gentry, *Flannery O'Connor's Religion of the Grotesque* (Oxford: UP of Mississippi, 1986); John F. Desmond, *Risen Sons: Flannery O'Connor's Vision of History* (Athens: U of Georgia P, 1987); and Brian Abel Ragen, *A Wreck on the Road to Damascus: Innocence, Guilt, and Conversion in Flannery O'Connor* (Chicago: Loyola UP, 1989).

[18] Martin, *The True Country* 148.

[19] *Collected Works* 153.

[20] Wood 90.

[21] *Mystery and Manners* 115.

[22] Wood 100.

[23] *The Habit of Being* 201.

[24] See John Hawkes, "Flannery O'Connor's Devil," *Sewanee Review* 70 (1962): 395–402. The article has been reprinted in Robert E. Reiter, ed., *Flannery O'Connor* (St. Louis: Herder, n.d.) 25–37.

[25] See André Bleikasten, "The Heresy of Flannery O'Connor," in *Les Americanistes: New French Criticism on Modern American Fiction*, ed. Ira D. Johnson and Christiane Johnson (Port Washington, N.Y.: Kennikat, 1978) 53–70. Books that join Bleikasten and Hawkes in either rejecting or largely circumventing a doctrinally based criticism include Josephine Hendin, *The World of Flannery O'Connor* (Bloomington: Indiana UP, 1970); Miles Orvell, *Invisible Parade: The Fiction of Flannery O'Connor* (Philadelphia: Temple UP, 1972); Martha Stephens, *The Question of Flannery O'Connor* (Baton Rouge: Louisiana State UP, 1973); Carol Schloss, *O'Connor's Dark Comedies: The Limits of Inference* (Baton Rouge: Louisiana State UP, 1980); and Edward Kessler, *Flannery O'Connor and the Language of Apocalypse* (Princeton: Princeton Up, 1986).

[26] Reiter 28.

[27] *The Habit of Being* 338.

[28] *Collected Works* 830.

[29] Wood 111.

[30] *Conversations with Flannery O'Connor*, ed. Rosemary M. Magee (UP of Mississippi, 1987) 102.

[31] *The Habit of Being* 329.

[32] *The Habit of Being* 537. This is by no means to say that O'Connor actively condoned segregation. Like most Southern writers and intellectuals of her time, she somewhat incoherently combined a tacit white supremacist bent with cautious approval of a gradualist progress toward integration, along some unspecified path that Southerners could be counted on to find within their own "code of manners based on charity" (*Conversations* 104). She was typical in supposing that "the Negro" was already a satisfied as well as a savvy participant in that code and in focusing most of her resentment not on segregation but on Northern busybodies. For an overview of such assumptions in O'Connor's time and of their roots in the previous generation, see Richard H. King, "The South and Cultural Criticism," *American Literary History* 1 (1989): 699–714.

[33] Wood 82.

[34] *Complete Works* 231.

[35] *The Habit of Being* 78.

[36] Wood 116.

[37] *Collected Works* 152.

[38] See especially *Mystery and Manners* 110–13.

[39] *Mystery and Manners* 171.

[40] Asals 130.

[41] Asals 66.

[42] Asals 75.

[43] *The Habit of Being* 100.

[44] The chief record of this struggle between pietistic and ecumenical tendencies is *The Presence of Grace: And Other Book Reviews,* comp. Leo J. Zuber, ed. Carter W. Martin (Athens: U of Georgia P, 1983). There we find O'Connor, writing for regional diocesan papers, arguing for a measure of religious tolerance and relaxed censorship but also displaying a surprising meekness and credulity—as, for example, when she toes the Vatican's shifting line on her cherished Teilhard, or when she takes seriously a theologian's dizzy claim that telepathy and clairvoyance are "gifts which were possessed by man before the Fall and which now appear as rudiments of those powers" (39).

[45] *The Habit of Being* 139.

[46] *Collected Works* 139, 559, 642.

[47] Quoted by Asals 130.

[48] *The Habit of Being* 97, 503.

EIGHT

Mr. Updike's Planet

[1] Joseph Epstein, "John Updike: Promises, Promises," *Commentary* (Jan. 1983): 54–58 (the quotations are from pp. 56, 55).

[2] Gilbert Sorrentino, "Never on Sunday," in *Critical Essays on John Updike,* ed. William R. Macnaughten (Boston: Hall, 1982), 77–79 (the quotation is from p. 78).

[3] John Updike, *Picked-Up Pieces* (New York: Knopf, 1975) 504.

[4] See Bernard Schopen, "Faith, Morality, and the Novels of John Updike," in Macnaughten (note 2 above) 199.

[5] John Updike, *Midpoint: And Other Poems* (New York: Knopf, 1969) 42.

[6] *Midpoint* 33.

[7] *Midpoint* 41.

[8] John Updike, *A Month of Sundays* (New York: Knopf, 1975) 202.

[9] *A Month of Sundays* 192–93.

[10] John Updike, *Assorted Prose* (New York: Knopf, 1974) 274. See also George W. Hunt, *John Updike and the Three Great Secret Things: Sex, Religion, and Art* (Grand Rapids, Mich.: Eerdmans, 1980) 36; and Schopen (note 4 above) 195–96.

[11] *A Month of Sundays* 25.

[12] *A Month of Sundays* 25.

[13] *Picked-Up Pieces* 500.

[14] *A Month of Sundays* 13, 203.

[15] *Midpoint* 40.

[16] Joyce Carol Oates, *"The Coup* by John Updike," in Macnaughten (note 2 above) 80–86 (the quotation is from p. 85).

[17] See, e.g., *Assorted Prose* 182; *Picked-Up Pieces* 91.

[18] John Updike, *Couples* (New York: Knopf, 1968) 439, 443.

[19] *Assorted Prose* 186.

[20] *Picked-Up Pieces* 499.

[21] John Updike, *Bech: A Book* (Greenwich, Conn.: Fawcett Crest, 1970) 158.

[22] *Midpoint* 43.

[23] *A Month of Sundays* 54n.

[24] *A Month of Sundays* 25.

[25] *A Month of Sundays* 25, 70.

[26] *A Month of Sundays* 89, 70.

[27] *Picked-Up Pieces* 13.

[28] *A Conversation with John Updike*, ed. Frank Gado (Schenectady, N.Y.: The Idol, 1971) 11.

[29] *Roger's Version* 22.

[30] See Hunt (note 10 above) 33–34, 64.

[31] *A Month of Sundays* 89–90.

[32] *Roger's Version* 9, 87, 49.

[33] *Roger's Version* 118.

[34] *Roger's Version* 280, 281.

[35] *Roger's Version* 152.

[36] *Roger's Version* 90, 91, 291, 241, 292, 175.

[37] *Roger's Version* 273, 226.

[38] *Roger's Version* 286, 59, 291.

[39] *Picked-Up Pieces* 508.

[40] *Roger's Version* 256.

Index

Adeler, Max, 81
Agrarianism, 118–21, 125
Aiken, Conrad, 115
American Renaissance, as literary period, 24–28, 30–36, 38–44
Anderson, Sherwood, 145
Apriorism, in criticism, 14–15
Aquinas, St. Thomas, 163
Arac, Jonathan, 24, 26–27, 31–33, 36
Arnold, Matthew, 75
Arnold, Ruth, 105
Asals, Frederick, 163–64
Asselineau, Roger, 43–44
Austen, Jane, 74

Baetzhold, Howard G., 62, 65, 85
Baker, Carlos, 90–91, 110–12
Bakhtin, Mikhail, 150
Baldwin, James, 158
Barth, Karl, 169, 173–75, 178, 180, 184
Barthes, Roland, xix
Baym, Nina, 23
Beckett, Samuel, 140
Bell, Millicent, 97
Bennett, William, xiv
Bense, James, 188

Bercovitch, Sacvan, 17–19, 21, 28–30, 33, 41, 44, 189
Berdyayev, Nikolai, 169
Bishop, Elizabeth, 101
Blair, Walter, 68, 193
Blake, William, 155
Bleikasten, André, 138–41, 156, 201
Bloom, Allan, xiv
Brinkmeyer, Robert H., 149–50, 161
Brittain, Joan T., 202
Brodhead, Richard H., 199
Brooks, Cleanth, 44, 119–24, 130, 132, 141, 144
Brown, Charles Brockden, 37
Browning, Preston M., 202
Budd, Louis J., 52, 62
Buell, Lawrence, 189–90

Cable, George Washington, 70
Caldwell, Erskine, 117
Cambridge History of American Literature, 17–18
Canby, Henry Seidel, 22
Canon, American literary, 19–20, 23–25, 27, 31–32, 36–41, 44–47
Carnegie, Andrew, 87

Carter, Everett, 79–82, 84, 194
Cerf, Bennett, 115
Cervantes, Miguel de, 116
Chase, Richard, 21
Cheney, Lynne, xiv
Civil War, American, 26, 34
Clemens, Olivia Susan (Suzy), 65
Clemens, Samuel L. *See* Twain,
    Mark
Cold war, and criticism, 22,
    24–25, 27, 33, 35, 117–20
Coleridge, Samuel T., 41
Columbia Literary History of the
    United States, 189
Conrad, Joseph, 116, 185
Cooper, James Fenimore, 37
Cord, Rachel, 69
Cowley, Malcolm, 93, 95–96,
    114–17
Cox, James M., 86, 195
Crane, Stephen, 64
cummings, e. e., 97
Cummings, Sherwood, 61–72

Darwin, Charles, 57, 64–66, 193
Dauber, Kenneth, 21
Davidson, Donald, 118
Deconstruction, 77–78, 88
Derrida, Jacques, xix, 88, 126
Desmond, John F., 202
DeVoto, Bernard, 68
De Vries, Peter, 153
Dickinson, Emily, 41
Diggins, John Patrick, xix
Dominguín, Luis Miguel, 92
Dos Passos, John, 97, 145
Dreiser, Theodore, 18, 44–45, 64
Driggers, Stephen G., 202
Driskell, Leon V., 202

Dunn, Robert J., 202
Duvall, John N., 125–32, 141, 200

Eastman, Max, 98
Edison, Thomas, 57
Eggenschwiler, David, 202
El Greco, 99
Eliot, T. S., 18, 41, 116, 119, 140
Ellenberger, Henri F., 188
Emerson, Everett, 52
Emerson, Ralph Waldo, 24–26,
    30, 33–34, 39, 44
Empiricism, in criticism, 14–15,
    77, 84–85
Engle, Paul, 144
Epstein, Joseph, 168
Erlich, Gloria C., 188

Faulkner, William, xxi, 18,
    114–42, 145, 163, 200
    Absalom, Absalom!, 115, 121, 125,
        134–37, 200–201
    As I Lay Dying, 125, 137–40
    "Delta Autumn," 134
    "Go Down, Moses" [story],
        123
    Go Down, Moses [novel], 123,
        125, 134–37
    Hamlet, 135–37
    Intruder in the Dust, 115, 137
    Light in August, 121, 125, 131–32,
        140, 200
    Mansion, 141
    "Pantaloon in Black," 123
    Portable Faulkner, 114–17
    Requiem for a Nun, 137
    Sanctuary, 119, 131, 140–41, 201
    Sound and the Fury, 125, 137–38,
        140

Town, 141
Wild Palms, 131
Feeley, Kathleen, 202
Feidelson, Charles, Jr., 21
Feminism, and literary criticism, 38–39, 89, 128–32, 191
Ferenczi, Sandor, 201
Fetterley, Judith, 83–84, 129, 195
Fickett, Harold, 202
Fiedler, Leslie, 21
Fields, James T., 39
Fienberg, Lorne, 195
Fisher, Philip, 45
Fitzgerald, F. Scott, 91, 94, 145
Fitzgerald, Sally, 151
Fitzgerald, Zelda, 98, 111–12
Flaubert, Gustave, 116
Formalism. *See* New Criticism
Foucault, Michel, xix–xx, 126
Freud, Sigmund, 7–9, 13, 147–49. *See also* psychoanalysis

Galton, Francis, 59
Gellhorn, Martha, 92
Gentry, Bruce, 202
Gilbert, Douglas R., 202
Gillman, Susan, 47–61, 72, 192
Gingrich, Arnold, 93
Gordon, Caroline, 119
Gordon, Sarah, 202
Greene, Graham, 155
Gribben, Alan, 62, 196
Griffith, Clark, 83–84, 195

Hartman, Geoffrey, 17
Hawkes, John, 155–56
Hawthorne, Nathaniel, xvii, 3–15, 24, 26, 30–34, 36–42, 44,

116, 133–34, 163, 183–85, 188, 190, 191, 200
Blithedale Romance, 200
"Chiefly About War Matters," 188
House of the Seven Gables, 10
Life of Franklin Pierce, 32, 39
"Minister's Black Veil," 7
"Roger Malvin's Burial," 7
Scarlet Letter, 4, 31–32, 39–40, 42, 183–85, 191
"Young Goodman Brown," 10
Heath Anthology of American Literature, xvii–xviii, 187
Heidegger, Martin, xix
Hemingway, Clarence, 103–5, 107–8
Hemingway, Ernest, xiii, 89–112, 142, 145, 166
"Big Two-Hearted River," 95–97, 109
Death in the Afternoon, 99, 101
Farewell to Arms, 100
For Whom the Bell Tolls, 100
Garden of Eden, 99–101, 102, 198, 199
Islands in the Stream, 100–101
"Last Good Country," 198–99
Moveable Feast, 108
Old Man and the Sea, 108
"Short Happy Life of Francis Macomber," 109–10
"Snows of Kilimanjaro," 110
Sun Also Rises, 94, 110–12
Hemingway, Grace, 103–8
Hemingway, Gregory, 103
Hemingway, Hadley, 101
Hemingway, Jack, 103
Hemingway, Marcelline, 105–6

Hemingway, Mary, 99, 102
Hemingway, Patrick, 99
Hemingway, Pauline, 99, 101
Hemingway, Ursula, 116, 198–99
Hemingway family, and handling
    of literary estate, 92, 198
Hendin, Josephine, 203
Herbert, T. Walter, 188
Hirsch, E. D., Jr., 78–79, 194, 195
Hoffman, Daniel, 123–24
Holmes, Oliver Wendell, 25, 62,
    66
Hotchner, A. E., 99
Howells, William Dean, 64–65,
    73, 196
Hunt, George W., 205
Hyman, Stanley Edgar, 202

Intentionality, as guide to
    interpretation, 36–37, 77–82,
    88, 194–95
Irving, Washington, 24
Irwin, John T., 21, 124–26

James, Henry, 18, 145
Jansenism, and Flannery
    O'Connor, 154, 163
Jehlen, Myra, 28, 30–31, 44, 125
Jenks, Tom, 198
Joyce, James, 98, 142

Kavanagh, J. H., 190
Kazin, Alfred, 112
Kenner, Hugh, 141–42
Kert, Bernice, 91, 104
Kessler, Edward, 203
Ketterer, David, 195
Kierkegaard, Søren, 169, 172
Kimball, Roger, xiv, xvi

King, Richard H., 203
Klein, Melanie, 201
Knapp, Steven, 195
Kovel, Joel, 201
Kristeva, Julia, 126
Kruse, Horst, 193, 195
Kuyk, Dirk, Jr., 200–201

Lacan, Jacques, xxi, 126, 147–48
Lauter, Paul, 187
Lawrence, D. H., 166
Lecky, W.E.H., 62, 65
Left Eclecticism, xiv–xv
Lentricchia, Frank, 47–48
Lester, Cheryl, 199
Leverenz, David, 188
Lewis, R.W.B., 21, 96–97, 197–98
Lewis, Sinclair, 18, 145
Liberalism, xvi–xvii, xxi–xxii, 17,
    21–23, 28–29, 33
Literary History of the United States,
    17–18, 22
Livingston, Paisley, 188–89
Loeb, Harold, 111
Longfellow, Henry Wadsworth,
    24, 39
Lowell, James Russell, 25
Lynn, Kenneth S., 86, 89–112,
    195, 197, 198
Lytle, Andrew, 144

McCarthyism, 28
Macherey, Pierre, 126
Mailer, Norman, 168
Mallarmé, Stéphane, 140
Malory, Thomas, 76
Malraux, André, 115
Manicheism, and Flannery
    O'Connor, 154–55

Marcuse, Herbert, 30
Martin, Carter W., 202, 204
Marx, Leo, 21
Marxism, and literary criticism,
  xx, 48, 115–17, 119, 139
Mathiessen, F. O., xvii, 24–28,
  34, 41, 43, 46
May, John R., 202
Mellard, James M., 147–49,
  161
Melville, Herman, 24–26, 30,
  34–36, 145, 190, 191
  "Benito Cereno," 190
  Moby Dick, 25 26, 35–36, 44,
    191
  Pierre, 35
Meyers, Jeffrey, 91, 95, 102,
  197
Michaels, Walter Benn, 24, 195
Miller, Perry, 21
Milton, John, 76–77, 155
Moreland, Richard C., 126–27,
  132–33, 135–39, 141, 201
Morris, Wesley, and Barbara
  Alverson, 125–27, 132–35,
  137–39, 141
Morrow, Lance, 197

Nationalism, in American
  criticism, 21–27, 119
New Americanists, xvi–xxi,
  17–40, 46–47, 193, 195–96
New Criticism, xv, xvii, 18, 22,
  24, 44, 50, 82–83, 118–20,
  144–46
New Left, xix
Nietzsche, Friedrich, xix
Nissenbaum, Stephen, 190
Norris, Frank, 64

Oates, Joyce Carol, 175
O'Connor, Flannery, xx–xxi,
  143–67, 203
  "Artificial Nigger," 159–60
  Collected Works, 145
  "Enduring Chill," 167
  "Everything That Rises Must
    Converge" [story], 157
  *Everything That Rises Must
    Converge* [collection], 152
  "Good Country People," 145
  "Good Man Is Hard to Find"
    [story], 145, 152, 155, 161–62,
    167
  Good Man Is Hard to Find
    [collection], 151
  "Greenleaf," 152
  "Judgment Day," 157
  "Lame Shall Enter First," 149
  "Revelation," 145, 157, 167
  "View of the Woods," 148–49
  Violent Bear It Away, 145–46,
    152, 155
  Wise Blood, 145–46, 153, 155,
    162, 164 65
O'Donnell, George Marion, 115
Orvell, Miles, 163, 203

Paine, Thomas, 62–64
Parker, Hershel, 4–5, 192
Parrington, Vernon L., 18, 23
Pease, Donald, 24, 26–28, 33–36,
  44, 187, 190
Percy, Walker, 153
Perkins, Maxwell, 98
Pierce, Franklin, 33, 39
Poe, Edgar Allan, 34, 41–42, 116,
  162–63, 191
Poirier, Richard, 21

Poole, Stan, 193
Popular Front, 27
Porter, Carolyn, 125
Porter, Katherine Anne, 115
Poststructuralism, xviii–xx, 14–15,
    36, 128, 193
Pseudoscience, 8–9
Psychoanalysis, 3–15, 52–53, 56,
    64, 87, 105, 118, 126–27, 139,
    147–49, 201

Ragen, Brian Abel, 202
Ransom, John Crowe, 115, 118,
    120
Reconstruction era, and
    American literature, 55, 70,
    118–19
Reising, Russell J., 21
Remarque, Erich Maria, 97
Reynolds, David S., 40–46, 188,
    191
Reynolds, Michael S., 93–94, 197
Richardson, Samuel, 45
Rilke, Rainer Maria, 140
Rimbaud, Arthur, 140
Robinson, Forrest G., 192
Rogers, Rodney O., 194
Róheim, Geza, 201
Ruland, Richard, 187

Salomon, Roger B., 75
Sargent, Mark L., 196
Sartre, Jean-Paul, 115
Schloss, Carol, 203
Schopen, Bernard, 204, 205
Schwartz, Lawrence H., 117, 119
Scott, Walter, 69
Sentimental fiction, 36–39, 44–46
Sewell, David R., 195, 196

Shakespeare, William, 41, 116
Slavery, and American literature,
    26, 58–59, 67–71, 118–19,
    121–24, 134
Slotkin, Richard, 29
Smith, Henry Nash, 29, 68, 73
Social constructionism, 48–49
Social Darwinism, 67, 193
Solomon, Barbara Probst, 198
Sorrentino, Gilbert, 169
Spiller, Robert, 17–18
Stein, Gertrude, 98, 101, 112, 140
Steinbeck, John, 117
Stephens, Martha, 203
Stowe, Harriet Beecher, xvii, 31,
    37–39, 44–46, 190–92
Structuralism, 14
Sullivan, Louis, 25
Sulloway, Frank J., 188
Sundquist, Eric J., 125

Taine, Hippolyte, 62, 66, 69, 194
Tate, Allen, 118–19
Teilhard de Chardin, Pierre, 154,
    163, 204
Thoreau, Henry David, 18, 24,
    30, 33–35, 44
Tompkins, Jane, 4–5, 36–40,
    45–46, 188, 191
Trilling, Lionel, 21, 23–24
Twain, Mark, 18, 20, 47–88, 116,
    145, 175, 192
    Connecticut Yankee, 73–88, 197
    *Huck Finn and Tom Sawyer among
        the Indians*, 72
    Huckleberry Finn, 20, 54, 60–61,
        67–72, 195–96
    Innocents Abroad, 74
    "New Dynasty," 197

*Personal Recollections of Joan of
    Arc,* 54
Pudd'nhead Wilson, 58–59, 61,
    67, 192
Roughing It, 74
Tom Sawyer, 52–53, 60, 68, 71,
    95
What Is Man?, 62, 193
Twysden, Duff, 111

Updike, John, xiii, 153, 168–86
  Bech: A Book, 171, 176
  Centaur, 171, 176
  Coup, 171, 176
  Couples, 169–70, 173, 175
  John Updike Newsletter, 169
  Marry Me, 173, 176
  "Midpoint," 171–72, 174–75
  "Month of Sundays," 172–74,
    176–78, 180–81
  Of the Farm, 176
  Pigeon Feathers, 175
  Poorhouse Fair, 171
  Rabbit Redux, 186
  Rabbit, Run, 173, 176

Roger's Version, 178–86
Witches of Eastwick, 171

Wallace, Henry, 25
Warner, Susan, 37–39, 191
Warren, Robert Penn, 44, 115,
    118, 144
Webster, Charles L., 76
Welty, Eudora, 115
West, Nathanael, 162–63
Whitman, Walt, 18, 24, 27,
    33–34, 42–44
  Franklin Evans, 42
  Leaves of Grass, 27
Williams, James D., 194
Wilson, Edmund, 45–46, 191–92
Wittenberg, Judith Bryant, 129
Wood, Ralph C., 152–54, 156,
    158–61
Wright, Frank Lloyd, 103
Wright, Richard, 117

Young, Philip, 93

Zuber, Leo J., 204

FREDERICK CREWS is professor of English at the University of California at Berkeley, chair of his department, and a member of the American Academy of Arts and Sciences. His ten books include *The Sins of the Fathers: Hawthorne's Psychological Themes, Out of My System,* and *Skeptical Engagements,* as well as the best-selling satire *The Pooh Perplex* and a widely used composition text, *The Random House Handbook.*

ABOUT THE TYPE

This book was set in Baskerville, a typeface designed by John Baskerville, an amateur printer and typefounder, and cut for him by John Handy in 1750. The type became popular again when The Lanston Monotype Corporation of London revived the classic roman face in 1923. The Merganthaler Linotype Company in England and the United States cut a version of Baskerville in 1931, making it one of the most widely used faces today.